Appleton Morgan

Shakespeare in Fact and in Criticism

Appleton Morgan

Shakespeare in Fact and in Criticism

ISBN/EAN: 9783337063870

Printed in Europe, USA, Canada, Australia, Japan

Cover: Foto ©Thomas Meinert / pixelio.de

More available books at **www.hansebooks.com**

SHAKESPEARE

IN FACT AND IN CRITICISM.

BY

APPLETON MORGAN, A. M., LL. B.

PRESIDENT OF THE NEW-YORK SHAKESPEARE SOCIETY; AUTHOR OF VENUS AND
ADONIS, A STUDY IN THE WARWICKSHIRE DIALECT; THE SHAKESPEAREAN
MYTH; SOME SHAKESPEAREAN COMMENTATORS; THE LAW OF LITER-
ATURE; EDITOR OF THE BANKSIDE SHAKESPEARE, ETC.

NEW-YORK:
WILLIAM EVARTS BENJAMIN.
1888.

COPYRIGHT, 1887,
BY APPLETON MORGAN.

THE DE VINNE PRESS, NEW-YORK.

TO

HON. CUSHMAN K. DAVIS,

UNITED STATES SENATOR FROM MINNESOTA,
AN EX-GOVERNOR OF THAT STATE.
WHO,
IN THE MIDST OF PUBLIC DUTIES, HAS TOUCHED, TO ADORN,

THE STUDY OF SHAKESPEARE,

These pages are dedicated,

AS A TOKEN OF RESPECT AND AFFECTIONATE REGARD, BY

THE AUTHOR.

CONTENTS.

PAGE

I. WILLIAM SHAKESPEARE AND HIS ESTHETIC CRITICS.................................. 1

II. MUCH ADO ABOUT SONNETS............... 27

III. WHOSE SONNETS?........................ 44

IV. "SOMETHING TOUCHING THE LORD HAMLET" 90

V. WILLIAM SHAKESPEARE'S LITERARY EXECUTOR—THE FIRST SHAKESPEAREAN REVIVAL 132

VI. LAW AND MEDICINE IN THE PLAYS........ 162

VII. THE GROWTH AND VICISSITUDES OF A SHAKESPEAREAN PLAY........................ 200

VIII. QUEEN ELIZABETH'S SHARE IN THE "MERRY WIVES OF WINDSOR".................... 239

IX. HAVE WE A SHAKESPEARE AMONG US?.... 270

X. THE DONNELLY AND PRIOR CIPHERS, AND THE FURNIVALL VERSE-TESTS............ 283

PREFACE.

These Papers have been indexed in a common table because, if there is anything of value in them, it will not be less valuable when made of easy reference. But principally they are so identified because, although written at differing intervals, there runs through them all a sort of common purpose. That purpose is to protest, as far as one voice can, against what seems to me the cruel and unusual punishment which Shakespeare is just now meeting at the hands of the esthetic critics. These esthetes, divigating their processes from simple demonstration of Shakespeare's beauties, have fallen to counting his lines, his syllables and endings; from this numeration to conceive a certain algebra, and from this algebra to demonstrate the "period" and the chronology of this or that play or poem. Nay, more. They even write his — William Shakespeare's — personal history from the impressions they themselves receive from this treatment of particular passages in the Plays, until there are as many William Shakespeares as there are commentators! My own idea has been that William Shakespeare was a man of like passions with ourselves, whose moods and veins were influenced — just as are ours — by his surroundings, employments, vocations; that his works are for all times that love him, but not (as is shown by the Davenant episode) for those that do not; and that, great as he was and oceanic as was his genius, we can read him all the better because he was, after all, a man.

I admit to having modified — in the course of time and study — a good many of the opinions expressed in these Papers, as well as in my earlier "Shakespearean Myth." But

since I cannot pronounce whether I was right then, or am
right now (without a dogmatism which, so far, I have been
able to avoid), it seems to me best to let them all stand as
they are. All the facts of the Shakespeare case are in, and
all the doubts. The questions arising upon them are, however,
open ones, and, I sincerely believe, always will be. " Those
who have lived as long as myself in the midst of Shakespearean criticism," says the veteran J. O. Halliwell Phillipps, "will be careful not to be too certain of anything."
With such a caution from so revered an authority, younger
students may well wish to keep alertly on their guard against
foreclosing themselves.

Such a caution need not deter the real student of Shakespeare, however, nor hint that he has only a hobby or a
foible before him, and so, presently, only his labor for his
pains. By the study of Shakespeare, should not, I think,
be understood the glorification of one man. In that wonderful renaissance which took place in the Shakespearean age—
that wonderful age of beginnings — almost everything that
we prize, that makes life endurable to-day, was born or was
coming to the throe of birth. Civil liberty, in the revolt of
such men as Raleigh and Essex against the Tudor idea of
government; art, surgery, medicine; the heaven-born doctrine of Equity as a regulator and modulator of the rigors
of the common law (first reduced to a science in the hands of
Lord Bacon): that greatest of truths that a philosophy
which should be of any value to mankind must be born of
knowledge and experience, rather than (as the bewildered
ancients had thought) that all knowledge must be argued out
by hair-splitting dialecticism of words. All these reforms
were beginning to live and move in that wonderful Shakespearean age. It is because some of us believe that of these
reforms and of this renaissance the pages of Shakespeare are
the best and fullest transcript, that we propose still to study
them, not — as the Mussulman studies his Koran — kneeling,
and with bated breath, but standing upright on one's feet;
with the finer glasses that moderns grind, and with the

electric light rather than the lantern and the tallow dip which, in every other field of human research, have been finally relieved from duty. Only let us beware how we subject to esthetic criticism the ocean, or this mighty page of human passion that is vaster than the ocean.

But after all, is it not the truth that Shakespeare — the man — is an ideal to each one of us, and his biography a pasture for poets and for dreamers always, with the personal equation always to the fore? We have no use for dates and documents, muniments and pedigrees. Hamlet and Desdemona, Othello and Macbeth — Love, Rage, Jealousy — every human passion — take their places. Who knows, or who can say, that William Shakespeare was born in the month of April? And what does it matter if he were or were not? "Others abide our question — thou art free!" says Mr. Arnold in his splendid sonnet. But if Shakespeare is free indeed — to reduce him to a splitter of syllables and a counter of "stopped endings" seems to me a thing ungiven, at least

" To the foiled searchings of mortality ! "

Glamorgan, July 13, 1887.

N. B.— Chapter X has been added at the suggestion of my publishers, in deference to certain questions just now of curious interest. And I am very willing to supply it, and happy to put myself on record as of opinion that the Cipher theory of my esteemed friend Mr. Donnelly (while I most thoroughly disbelieve in every word of it, or in any foundation for a morsel of it) is to the full as legitimate an offering to the solution of the Mystery of Shakespeare as what seems to me the rubbish of the esthetic, the inductive and the creative critics.— As to this, I have no modified opinion.

I

William Shakespeare and His Esthetic Critics

QUINCE. It shall be written in eight and six.
BOTTOM. No, make it two more; let it be written in eight and eight.—*Midsummer Night's Dream.*

T is matter of very frequent complaint that our critics and commentators read into Shakespeare much more than they read out of him. But if they find it there, who shall, after all, gainsay them? Why should not poets build better than they know? What else is it that gives what is called immortality to human work? What we have to guard against, I think, is the tendency of esthetic to become creative criticism and so demand from the text of Shakespeare certain propositions as to the man Shakespeare of which the world is yet in reasonable doubt. Loving and ardent study of the glowing text and contribution to its hermeneutics thereby is one thing. But insistence on dogmatical or debatable conclusions therefrom as to

matters of Elizabethan history is altogether another.

In the trial of a question of fact in a court of justice, reliance is had on two sorts of evidence: first, circumstantial, or, as it may be called, narrative or historical evidence; and, second, expert — that is, "self-regarding" or "opinion" evidence. Questions of literary authorship are to be decided in like manner by two sorts of evidence corresponding exactly to these; viz., external evidence (the date, surroundings, and circumstances under which the composition of which the authorship is sought was produced), and, second, internal evidence — that is, the manner and style and text of the composition itself. Now, this internal evidence is itself of two sorts: first, comparative criticism, and, second, textual criticism. The first, as its name implies, is to be conducted by simple comparison, the problem being simply, given a literary work known to be by a certain author, to discover if another work is also by that same author. But this class of evidence is not absolutely reliable. To quote the words of the late accomplished Mr. James Spedding: "In passing upon questions of authorship by means of internal evidence the critic must always be allowed to judge for himself"; that is to say, it is found to be absolutely impossible to remove from the criticism of any one man that personal equation, or "point of view," which arises imperatively from the education, temperament and tendencies of the comparative critic himself. A notable instance of the failure of comparative criticism was in the Ireland Shakespeare-forgery cases, where a whole city full of pundits and critics hesitated as to whether the work of a mere lad was to be accepted as Shakespeare until outside circumstantial evidences came to their aid, and the young forger of the style of the world's greatest poet was surprised in the act of forgery and confessed to the whole. Another well-known case was that of Mr. Collier's alleged discoveries, in 1852, of corrections in the Shakespeare text. No amount of comparative critical acumen (and every Shakespearean critic in England and America worked at them) was able to decide absolutely and finally as to their genuineness. But by and by it occurred to the authorities of the British Museum to go to work with microscope and acids, when they speedily exposed the emendations as of very recent manufacture indeed, scarcely antedating their production by Mr. Collier himself. Thus it appears that, unassisted,— especially at remote dates from the fact,— the chances are very largely against an arrival at the exact truth by unaided comparative criticism. To recur to an example very recently suggested: supposing, in the twenty-second century, a body of comparative critics should be given the official report of the Berlin Conference and the speeches of Lord Beaconsfield, whose tactics in that great parley were singly and alone able to confront an empire in the flush of victory, and to force it to relinquish a prize it had been struggling to possess for centuries, which it had just won by sword and battle; supposing this same body of critics were then presented with a copy of "Lothair," and asked, from internal, comparative evidence only (they having no records of the nineteenth century and no life of Beaconsfield before them), to say definitely whether the same individual who defied and dominated Russia by his statesmanship also wrote the novel — can we doubt what the verdict of these comparative critics would be?

Textual criticism, on the other hand, is capable of being made reliable, but only negatively. It can demonstrate, for example, from the employment of words that were uninvented or unused before certain dates, the age and period earlier than which certain compositions could not have been written, and thus exclude all authors earlier than that age or period. But to pronounce positively as to who was as well as to who could not have been the particular, identical author, it is quite as powerless as any other sort of critical evidence. Hence it follows that — since even documentary, historical and circumstantial evidence is fallible — no one single class of testimony ought to be relied upon; and that in literary questions, exactly as in those submitted for judicial determination, all sorts, classes and kinds of evidence must cumulatively be availed of in order to set out with any hope or chance of reaching the exact truth.

Putting aside any question as to the authorship of the Elizabethan English works so universally credited to William Shakespeare; leaving Baconians, editorialists and pro-Shakespeareans to submit propositions, make postulates and riddle each other's theories and corollaries to their hearts' content by means of all the evidence, historical, circumstantial, textual and comparative: it is proposed in this paper to examine a new candidate for favor which the present century (and the last quarter of it) has developed. This new testimony is called Esthetic Criticism. I do not mean that the invention is of the last quarter of the nineteenth century. It was known before. But earlier it was called merely eulogium, encomium or, perhaps, panegyric. So far as can be discovered, it is only very recently indeed that it has claimed to be actual evidence — actual and undebatable proof as to the actual man Shakespeare, his moods and tenses, his fortunes, follies, hopes and fears.

To begin with, these marvelous works are like a bank of clouds in a brightening sky. Every beholder will for himself happen to see some semblance somewhere in their profile which he may describe in words, but which — since he has no bearing by which to indicate it — he cannot hope to point out to his fellow-gazers. So in the Shakespeare works one will be attracted by a figment of the poet as a whole, another by a detail thereof. As, for example, one will be moved over the picture of dishonored Lucrece sitting lonesome, with full heart, awaiting her husband's return and the moment when her own suicide will be appropriate, while another will wonder at the knowledge of human nature which makes her, in the very depth of her misery, discover herself admiring a picture on the wall. One will see in the "Midsummer Night's Dream" only a beautiful romance, while his co-reader will find in it the touches of a hand used to theatrical business, in that he allows the clowns to play their interlude only until the fun is exhausted, when he makes them omit their epilogue and substitute a dance instead. And so on. Nothing is more natural, therefore, than that each one should, in dealing with the works, write of that which Shakespeare is to him. But when the writer goes further, and insists that the William Shakespeare whose name is associated with these plays was the embodiment of that which he himself finds in the works, and that the whole world shall so consent to understand Shakespeare,— in other words, proposes to write the biography of the dramatist out of his own inner reading of the text of the dramas before him,— this matter of esthetic criticism becomes not only incontinent and inconsistent, but leads at once into all sorts of irregularities and absurdities.

The modern and present exponents of this esthetic criticism, used as a method of writing an author's history from the text of his alleged works, are principally the members of the New Shakespeare Society of London. It would never, of course, have occurred to these gentlemen to write the life of the late Mr. Robertson out of the pages of his comedies "Caste," "School," "Ours" or "Play," or the life of Mr. Boucicault out of "London Assurance," "Arrah-na-Pogue," "The Shaughraun" or "Formosa"; but, all the same, they have given us a beautiful history of William Shakespeare out of his plays alone. Without undertaking to follow the voluminous papers of the New Shakespeare Society, a brief notice of the labors of certain of its school will sufficiently illustrate its methods.

"It is Stratford," cries Mr. Furnivall, "which has given Shakespeare the picture of the sweet country school-girls working at one flower, warbling one song, growing together like a double cherry," etc. "The wail of Constance for the loss of her boy could only have been written by one whose feelings had been lacerated by the loss of a beloved child," cries Mr. Dowden. "Some sacred voice whispers to him [Shakespeare] that the privilege of immortality was annexed to every line he wrote." "I now believe that this strange and difficult play ['Troilus and Cressida'] was written when Shakespeare had ceased to smile genially, and when he must be either ironical or take a deep, passionate, and tragical view of life," etc., etc. Mr. Ward assures us of William Shakespeare's diffident and shrinking nature (proved from a passage in the plays); and we could easily cull volumes of this mental biography from the esthetic works of enthusiasts like the above-named gentlemen. But the above will suffice. It seems hardly necessary to submit that unless that word possess a meaning unknown outside of the New Shakespeare Society, this is hardly "evidence" to an exact mind. Nor, in the present case, admitting it to be "evidence," would it hardly prove an exclusive Stratfordian authorship. For there is certainly the same internal evidence that William Shakespeare was born in Epidamnium or Rome or Troy as that he was born in Stratford. There is certainly much more in the plays about Italy, Rome, and Greece than about England. For one comedy whose scene is Warwickshire there are twelve whose action is outside of England. And certainly no more familiarity is shown with Warwickshire customs than with those of Venice, or Scotland, or the Roman Forum, or the ways of the Cypriotes. And, again, there is precisely the same evidence that Shakespeare had murdered his wife like Othello, and his rival like Macbeth, and had been driven from home by his daughters like Lear, as that he had "buried a beloved child," like Queen Constance, or experienced intimations of immortality, or was of the "diffident and retiring" disposition asserted by Mr. Ward.

No man, as a matter of fact, ever led a jollier life than William Shakespeare. The records, at least, of his jokes and his gallantries survive him, and he died in a frolic. The late Mr. Bardell was knocked on the head with a pint-pot in a cellar. But Sergeant Buzfuz preferred to throw the glamour of pathos over his end by describing it as "gliding imperceptibly from the world and seeking elsewhere that tranquillity which a custom-house can never afford." I am afraid the most that can be said for Mr. Furnivall, Mr. Dowden and Mr. Ward is that they are no whit behind the eloquent sergeant in gush over their hero. But perhaps Mr. Furnivall is striving to elude these entanglements of "internal evidence" when he exclaims: "I wrote the introduction to the 'Venus and Adonis,' and thought I had really persuaded myself that it really was Shakespeare's first work. But on turning to 'Love's Labour's Lost' and the 'Comedy of Errors' after it, the absurdity was too apparent." Or again (forgetting that "Titus Andronicus" was, as a spectacle, much more to the taste of Elizabethan mixed audiences than the bloodless dialectics of Hamlet and Brutus): "'Titus Andronicus' I do not consider. . . . The play declares, as plainly as play can speak, 'I am not Shakespeare's; my repulsive subject, my blood and horrors, are not and never were his.'" And yet, had Mr. Furnivall considered it, he would have found it packed with passages describable only as Shakespearean! The apostrophe to Tamora topping all rivals.

> "As when the golden sun salutes the morn,
> And, having gilt the ocean with his beams,
> Gallops the zodiac in his glistering coach
> And overlooks the highest peering hills:"

(A passage which smacks of Marlowe, indeed, but which it is mere pedantry to assume as his, as if a Shakespeare could not have written it.) Such lines as those wherein Titus lays his dead to rest:

> "Here lurks no treason, here no envy swells,
> Here grow no damned drugs: here are no storms,
> No noise — but silence and eternal sleep!"

Or such true rung verses as —

> "She is a woman, therefore may be wooed;
> She is a woman, therefore may be won!"

Surely these ought not to be below the notice of an esthete! And not only this, but a careful study of "Titus Andronicus" (and it is yet to come) might throw a much-to-be-desired light upon the Shakespearean theater, the stage business and properties, the action and mise en scene employed. The text calls for the following programme:

Act I., Scene 2. Alarbus's limbs are lopped and his entrails feed the sacrificing fire.
Act I., Scene 2. Titus kills Martius, his own son.

Act II., Scene 3. Bassianus is stabbed and killed in the forest. Lavinia, his bride, ravished.
Act II., Scene 4. Martius and Quintus are made to fall into a deep pit containing the body of Bassianus.
Act II., Scene 5. Lavinia's hands cut off and her tongue cut out.
Act III., Scene 1. Titus's hand cut off. Two heads and a hand presented to Titus.
Act IV., Scene 2. Nurse stabbed and killed.
Act IV., Scene 3. Titus gone mad.
Act IV., Scene 4. Clown hanged.
Act V., Scene 2. Chiron's throat cut by Titus. Demetrius's throat cut by Titus. Their bones ground to powder, mixed with their blood, which Lavinia catches in a basin, and a paste made from the compound is cooked into a pie.
Act V., Scene 3. Lavinia killed by her father. Tamora eats the pie made out of her own sons' heads mixed with blood. Lucius kills Saturninus. Aaron is set breast-deep in earth and famished to death.

And this not "to be related by the graphic tongue of some actor," but openly — in parcel at least — performed. Now, what the world would like to know is, How was this sort of thing managed on the Shakespearean boards? We cannot lavish overmuch gratitude upon gentlemen who count syllables and twitter of stopped endings for us. But one who will so substantially contribute to the history of scenic art as to tell us something of this certainly would not miss the gratitude of his countrymen!

But, bad as this is, when our esthete does really consent to "consider" a play, he makes a mess of it. He counts all the "run-on lines," the "stopped" and "unstopped" endings, the "central pauses," and the rest of them — and then tells us exactly in what year this or that comedy or tragedy was written! Doubtless in his first youth young Shakespeare wrote less maturely than in his manhood. Doubtless, habitude and practice brought refinement and celerity. But the remarkable thing about it all is, that—after all the esthetic chronologies are completed—we know no more or less about it than before. Either the esthetes are entirely lost in this numerical fog of their own raising and wander aimlessly about therein, or else, by wonderful good fortune, they find their way back again, and prance triumphantly, with all their colors flying and amid tumultuous cheers, up to the very point from which they started—namely, that they are sure they don't know, and were confident of it all along. And when they do affect a demonstration, the results are marvelous. When a lad, Shakespeare created "Romeo and Juliet," with a maturity of experience and a mastery of passion past the power of all but himself; and, moreover, displayed it in a setting of stage business that today, and for our modern theaters, needs no overhauling. But in his mature manhood he had forgotten passion and stage business alike, produced ragged and uneven affairs like "Pericles," which few except scholars care to read, and which no modern manager could mount on his boards if he would! And then, having chronolized the plays, this amusing person steps up and settles for us these unspeakable sonnets! "About the sonnets" he (Mr. Furnivall) proceeds: "in addition to Nos. 8, 11, 16, 18, 20, and 21, I suppose that 10, 13, and 15 are not his either. About No. 19 I doubt. That 'to sin and never for to saint,' and the whole of the poem, is by some strong man of the Shakespeare breed.[1] * * *

"I cannot admit that the Act ('Edward III.,' Act IV.) is his. . . . Any one who attributes the stilted nonsense in this play to Shakespeare may safely be written down ass."[2] * * *

The difficulties which this method overtakes in its sweep Mr. Furnivall is ready for. Should anybody ask, for instance, how one man should know a thing at one time and be ignorant of it at another, should be eloquent and verbose, deal now in sterling and now in fustian — Oh that is all right, cries Mr. Furnivall; you see Shakespeare wrote his plays in periods and his poems in groups! His second period began with "King John," the first having ended with "Richard II" (p. 40). His third began with "Julius Cæsar" (p. 47). His fourth with "Pericles" (p. 87). The groups are two in number (pp. 45 and 46). In the course of these periods and groups William Shakespeare employs, says Mr. Furnivall, no less than twelve metrical styles, viz., the "light ending," "weak ending," "verse line" (p. 93), "run-on lines" (p. 33), "stopped" and "unstopped" lines (p. 33), "extra syllabic" (p. 97), "central pause" (p. 20), "rhymed lines" (p. 22), "blank verse"(p. 17), "five-measure dialogue" (p. 22), "alternate rhymed verse" (p. 22),— not to mention "six and eight," "eight and seven," etc. (which Mr. Furnivall takes for granted anybody can see), as well as five or six prose styles for the lords, ladies, clowns, beggars, etc.

Or, take the "Merry Wives of Windsor," the only Shakespeare comedy in which, instead of

[1] Introduction to "Leopold Shakespeare," p. 36.
[2] Ibid., p. 101.

France, Spain, Italy or classic lands the scene is laid in England; and which becomes, under the microscope, a local chronicle, packed full of allusions to well-known matters occurring during the twenty-one years between the skeleton quarto of 1602 and the perfected text of 1623. Here we have the names of petty tradesmen, mention of popular song-books and riddle-books, of the discovery of gold in Guinea, the introduction of hackney coaches, of an unpopular parliament, a court ceremonial, of the bear-baitings and other amusements going on at Paris Gardens. These must have been put in by word of mouth as the events themselves occurred. To suppose them carefully memorized, and finally, after the lapse of a generation, inserted in the folio text, is to suppose almost a moral impossibility, certainly a moral absurdity. But see what esthetic criticism tells us of such a play as this, grown by accretion to three times its original bulk as it left the original playwright's pen! Why, we are told that this is a play of William Shakespeare's second period; that he wrote it in 3018 lines, 2703 of which are prose, 227 blank verse, 69 " five measure," 3 " two measure," 3 " three measure," and 3 " six measure"! and much more to the same purport. The author of this system has assured us that his book, which first, so far as I know, laid down his most remarkable rules, is one of the three works extant which "come near to the true treatment and dignity of the subject, and can be put into the hands of students who want to know the mind of Shakespeare."[1] But, exclaims Mr. Halliwell-Phil-

[1] Mr. Furnivall's Introduction to Gervinus's Commentaries, p. xxi. London: Smith, Elder & Co., 1877.

lipps (to whom, after a lifetime of Shakespearean research, this new heraldry must have come with the flavor of a "fad"), could William Shakespeare, when selecting a plot, have given no heed to the wishes of the managers or the inclinations of the public taste? What would Heminges and Condell have said if, on applying to Shakespeare for a comedy, they had been told by the dramatist that he could not comply with their wishes, he being then in his tragic period? That William Shakespeare became one of the richest of Elizabeth's private subjects out of the takings at his playhouses seems, after all, to be the only answer necessary to our esthetic word-counter.

It seems incredible that the New Shakespeare Society should be willing to leave the reasonable doubts and difficulties as to a Shakespearean authorship — which for the last twenty-seven years have been growing more and more emphatic — to mumble and roar about their ears, and solace and coddle themselves with little purrings of mutual confidence; to rest the whole pro-Shakespearean case, that is to say, on mere expressions of personal whim or taste, and to meet all the historical and documentary considerations by simply looking in another direction. But there appears to be no escape from the conclusion that they prefer to do just that; to wit (I quote from my friend Mr. Rolfe's introduction to his "Pericles"):

"In the discussion which followed the reading of Mr. Fleay's paper on 'Pericles' before the New Shakespeare Society, May 8, 1874, Mr. Furnivall remarked: 'I hope the fact I am going to mention will render all further discussion as to the Shakespeare part of the "Pericles" unnecessary.

When I first saw Mr. Tennyson . . . he asked me whether I had ever examined "Pericles." I had to confess that I'd never read it, as some friends whom I considered good judges had told me it was very doubtful whether Shakespeare wrote any of it. Mr. Tennyson answered: "Oh! that won't do. He wrote all the part relating to the birth and recovery of Marina and the recovery of Thaisa. I settled that long ago. Come upstairs and I'll read it to you." Upstairs we went, and there I had the rare treat of hearing the poet read, in his deep voice, with an occasional triumphant "Isn't that Shakespeare?" "What do you think of that?" and a few comments, the genuine part of "Pericles." I need not tell you how I enjoyed the reading, or how quick and sincere my conviction of the genuineness of the part read was. The parts read by Tennyson were almost exactly the same that Mr. Fleay has marked as Shakespeare's; and' Mr. Furnivall adds, 'the independent confirmation of the poet-critic's result by the metrical test-worker's process is most satisfactory and interesting.'"

Now, it must have been a rare privilege indeed to hear the laureate read his favorite passages. That they were the finest passages in the play the testimony of Lord (then Mr.) Tennyson ought to satisfy us; and it is gratifying to know, too, that Mr. Furnivall and Mr. Fleay both agreed with Mr. Tennyson that those passages were "Shakespeare" (that is, what every man means by that phrase — viz., whatever is matchless and sublime in literature). But if evidence, in the ordinary acceptation of the word, of anything, this story about Lord Tennyson is evidence of what anybody reading Mr. Furnivall's and Mr. Fleay's writings can see — viz., that the quantitative-analysis process of the metrical enumerators invariably gives all the great noble and admirable parts — not to the abstraction we call Shakespeare, but to the identical, historical man of that name. In other words, the New Shakespeare Society leave the question just exactly where they find it. After circumambulating their circle they assert that the eloquent passages are Shakespeare's (which is precisely what the world believed before these gentlemen were born), and that if William Shakespeare of Stratford did not write them they can't imagine who did. But while nobody, of course, will disagree with Lord Tennyson that the parts he read are the finest in "Pericles," is the fact of his admiration of certain parts of that play to pass as evidence unimpeachable that the manager of the Globe Theater wrote those parts, and employed outside aid to write all the clowns' and prostitutes' parts, all the badinage and sparkle of wit, all the double-entendre and small-talk of some thirty or forty more, while he, William Shakespeare, only walked in the stately buskin of tragedy himself? I am sure I don't wish to be disrespectful to the New Shakespeare Society, but it seems to me that all their mighty discovery as to stopped and unstopped lines amounts to is that there is no arbitrary rule as to structural forms of tragic and comic poetry, pathos and doggerel — merely this and nothing more! The New Shakespeare Society were certainly not the first discoverers of the fact that the world uses the term Shakespeare as a synonym for what is most sublime and eloquent in literature, and not as the name of any particular rhetorical form.

Again, if there are words in the English language strong enough to assert, and demonstration from internal evidence delicate enough to prove, that many hands and many brains were concerned in composing the works we call Shakespeare, surely Mr. Fleay uses those words and attempts that demonstration in his "Shakespeare Manual," and I read his conclusion to be that of thirty-nine plays not an orthodox Shakespearean ought to accept as canonical the list of thirty-six plays those innocent partners Heminges and Condell supposed to be Shakespeare's; that only twenty are "certainly" or "undoubtedly" Shakespeare's. And of the remaining nineteen any one having patience enough to tabulate the results of Mr. Fleay's demonstration[1] will see that William Shakespeare, à la Fleay, can only retain about two-fifths! So that — whoever William Shakespeare was — it is not (according to the New Shakespeare Society) sacrilegious to show up poor Shakespeare stripped of about half the feathers which Greene declared, three hundred years ago, that William had wrongfully beautified himself with, provided the stripping be done regularly — that is, by means of "stopped" and "unstopped" endings, and so that the name of Francis Bacon is not brought anywhere into the neighborhood of the discussion.

Up to date, then, the external and internal evidence seems to agree in this: that the plays can be separated into text and stage-setting, and that the author of the text, while also author of the poems, was certainly not one and the same individual as the stage editor who sets these plays for his boards. So far, at least, Mr. Furnivall's demonstration of the numerous distinct prose and metrical styles (which he calls "periods") in the

[1] "Shakespeare Manual," pp. 22-56.

plays, and Mr. Fleay's demonstration that between these two there was at least one shrewd enough to know the public taste and turn the knowledge to gold, are not conflicting. The only difference between Mr. Fleay and myself I can draw from the "Shakespeare Manual" is that I am not sure that Mr. Fleay's man of shrewd and ready wit, who made these plays available for revenue, was not the very man we are after,— William Shakespeare by name,— while Mr. Fleay believes him to have been a partner of Shakespeare's whose name is, so far, undiscoverable. I am inclined to so believe, because every record and every tradition as to William Shakespeare shows such to have been his character. Wayward, lovable, clever, brilliant was William Shakespeare, boy and man; and that he became rich as well is matter beyond dispute. Ben Jonson's plays were stuffed even fuller of classicisms than Shakespeare's, but they would not pay for a sea-coal fire. We may be very sure that it was Launce and Trinculo, Barnardine and Boult, the drunken porter in "Macbeth," young Gobbo, and the like, who, by catching the ears of the groundlings, paid Shakespeare's running expenses. Had these plays emptied the theater of the rabble then, we need not be ashamed to believe (because it is the historical fact) they would scarcely have survived to be studied by scholars now.

I have alluded to the Baconian theory because, while I do not accept it, I am not afraid of it; and, moreover, I am not adverse to saying that one of the strongest possible points in its favor is the fact that the esthetes cannot hear of it without dispossession of their mental balance. In his Introduction to the "Leopold Shakespeare" (p. 124), Mr. Furnivall remarks: "The idea of Lord Bacon's having written Shakespeare's plays can be entertained only by folk who know nothing whatever of either writer, or are cracked, or who enjoy the paradox or joke. Poor Miss Delia Bacon, who started the notion, was, no doubt, then mad, as she was afterward proved to be when shut up in an asylum.[1] Lord Palmerston, with his Irish humor, naturally took to the theory, as he would have done to the suggestion that Benjamin Disraeli wrote the Gospel of St. John. If Judge Holmes's book is not meant as a practical joke, like Archbishop Whateley's historic doubts, or proof that Napoleon never lived, then he must be set down as characteristic-blind, as some men are color-blind. I doubt whether any so idiotic suggestion as this authorship of Shakespeare's works by Bacon has ever been made before, or will ever be made again, with regard to either Bacon or Shakespeare. The tomfoolery of it is infinite." In other words, Mr. Furnivall assures us that a man to whom, from the records, not a day's schooling can be assigned, and whom the highest heights of Shakespearean fancy have never credited with more than one or two terms passed in childhood at a provincial grammar-school of the sixteenth century, could write in a score of differ-

[1] To be exact, Miss Bacon never was "shut up in an asylum." She became deranged from her intense excitement and the treatment her book received, undoubtedly. But she died in her own home, surrounded by friends, in Hartford, September 1, 1859.

ent literary styles; while Francis Bacon, foremost classical and contemporary scholar of his time, author of the "Essays" and the "Novum Organum," could only have had one literary style, and therefore could not have anything to do with aught that was not frozen into the sententious mold of his acknowledged works. Granted that the Baconians if not crazy before absorbing their theory, speedily become so by championing it, and are only suffered to run at large by the charity of a long-enduring world, what would our experts in mental pathology say, should these Baconians be heard to assert that Lord Verulam lived in "periods," and that these periods were known to him familiarly as "light ending," "mistaken identity," "weak ending," "central pause," "tragedy," "comedy" and so on! Clearly, the rod and the dark room would come next.

William Shakespeare's genius appears to have been fully as practical as poetical. He elbowed his way from abject poverty to exceptional affluence. He found the play-house a tabooed thing, a vagabond pastime to be enjoyed by stealth. He made it a profession honored by the court and protected by the throne. He captured the populace and brought the city into his theaters. First to occupy the field, he held it alone and amassed a fortune. His successors had no such monopoly. For the next one hundred years in London no manager achieved an income like William Shakespeare's. The plays he mounted were prepared to catch all ears and enchain all tastes. They contain specimens of all known rustic English dialects of the periods they cover, put into the mouths of appropriate speakers. William Shakespeare and his family and neighbors spoke Warwickshire dialect.[1] The condition in life implied by a man's employment of one patois would seem to shut out the probability of his possessing facilities for acquiring a dozen others. No allusions to classical, philosophical or antiquarian lore were necessary to make these plays "draw": were rather inclined, had the allusions been recognized, to injure them. No practical stage-manager would have put them there (they were unnecessary to the *mise en scène* not only, but the audience would have yawned, or perhaps hissed at them); though, if pressed for time or not recognizing them himself, he might have omitted to weed them out. Had William Shakespeare, a practical stage-manager himself, thought them necessary, not being a scholar, he would perhaps have used a work of reference and so inserted them accurately; while a ripe scholar writing the plays might well have tossed in his learned allusions with lofty nonchalance, christened his characters with Greek and Hebrew derivations that only ripe scholars to-day recognize as apposite, and perpetrated the boldest and most astounding anachronisms with airy contempt for the mixed audiences in the pit and the rabble in the gallery. And withal, nothing is clearer in the context than that in every breath he breathed and in every syllable he penned this writer was patrician with the scorn of a Coriolanus for the mob who gave him their suffrages.

[2] See "Venus and Adonis," a study in Warwickshire Dialect. Appleton Morgan. New-York: Press of the New-York Shakespearean Society. 1885.

But such a man, indeed, William Shakespeare was not. Of the two, then, is it not anti-Shakespeareans who best recognize the law of cause and effect, and the improbability of its having been suspended for fifty years to cover the life of the original of the Droeshout portrait? It is fashionable for Shakespearean biographers to cloud over the stubborn facts in their hero's life by complaining that we know so very little about him. As a matter of fact don't we know all about him? Of what other private subject of Elizabeth do we know a hundredth part as much? And yet commentators who load down their editions with historical sources of Shakespeare's plays — accounts of where this overworked man of affairs, pressed with daily care of his investments, leases, rentals, and his two theaters borrowed plots wherever hands could be laid on them — will not allow us to conjecture that, however pressed, he ever condescended to borrow a dialogue or a speech from a scholar who stood at his elbow.[1] But so it is that, while the New Shakespeare Society ransack history for, and crowd their publications with, essays upon the most meager details concerning any individual who can be ever so remotely connected with William Shakespeare,— Greene, Nash, Middleton, Marlowe, Marston, Cyril, Tourneur,— but once mention the name of Francis Bacon, and they touch their foreheads and cry "sacrilege" and "lunacy"!

It is said that William Shakespeare once played before Queen Elizabeth. There is no record of it

[1] It has been conjectured that Holofernes was William Shakespeare's good-humored burlesque of Bacon himself.

in the court minutes, though we cannot find that any of that period have been lost. There is a record, however, that Francis Bacon did. February 8, 1587, certain gentlemen of Gray's Inn, Bacon among them, performed before her Majesty a play called "The Misfortunes of Arthur," which surely no one can read without being impressed with its resemblance to what men call nowadays the "Shakespearean" gait and movement. We are told, however, that it was written by Thomas Hughes, William Fulbecke, Nicholas Trott, Francis Flower, Christopher Yelverton, John Lancaster, and a person rejoicing in the remarkable name of Penroodocke, "and that Francis Bacon devised the dumb-shows" with which its royal representation was accompanied. That Francis Bacon, a tireless and prolific writer — who was to be described as the very acme of the learning and literary expression of his time — should have allowed seven young lawyers, never heard of before or since, to have written the entire play, and contented himself with merely preparing the pantomime, is incredible: certainly hard to believe by anybody who knows anything of the habits of literary men, particularly of the imperious moods of Francis Bacon. In our feverish appetite for a single Shakespearean fact, why not work such circumstantial data as these? I do not allude to them from the smallest desire to coach or nurse the Baconian theory, but simply to show that there is a serious and honest and historical side upon which to attack it, and to record my conviction that an attack upon that side will be regarded with considerably more respect than at the purely sentimental salient now selected. For how much longer will our libraries of Shakespeareana pass completely over everything external and be devoted instead exclusively to esoteric criticism, to transcendental analysis after the German, to mere ad libitum schemework like Mrs. Cowden Clarke's "Girlhood of Shakespeare's Heroines" (a title rather suggesting the Rev. Mr. Cream-cheese's sermon on "The Maidenhood of Lot's Wife"), or to metaphysical questions as to whether Macbeth was incited to murder Duncan by the witches or had conceived the plan before meeting them, or to the microscopical amenities of the New Shakespeare Society?

In justice, however, it should be remembered that all the esthetes are not included in that learned society. There are hundreds of these blind guides outside of it, and scarcely a monthly magazine is able to withstand their ponderous deliverances. And not only now, but to the end of time, will they get into print; will continue to discover William Shakespeare's motives, purposes, and "central ideas" in material which — if he ever handled at all — he tumbled into his plays by the head and shoulders (out of books even then musty) in his haste for an occasion; will go on forever piling their little heaps of dust upon the mighty text, and then sit on those heaps and crow! But I believe the day of the professional commentator is passing, and we may yet be allowed to worship Shakespeare, not on our knees with our spectacles among the typographical errors of the folios, but upright on our feet.

I cannot do better than quote the manly words of Mr. Boucicault: "'Students of Shakespeare!' If this means anything, it presumes that the works of this poet are of such mystic and misty profundity that deep research and kindred inspiration are required to discover his hidden meaning, and these actors are ordained to expound this Bible of the stage. Humbug! Tragedy is a great literary effort designed, not to be read or meditated upon, but to be represented before a mixed audience. Its language, therefore, should be clear and unmistakable as it flows from the mouths of the speakers; its action should be clear and perspicuous. If it is not so, then the poet is at fault. He is not a prophet; he has no reason to be obscure, no reason for misleading or for mystifying the people. If students of Shakespeare who seek to torture the palpable meaning of trivial passages in the text into what are termed 'new readings' at the expense of the poet, to whom they impute obscurity (the very worst fault a dramatist can exhibit)—if such fellows could arouse the sleeping spirit of the grand old man,—recall him, like the ghost in 'Hamlet,' to revisit the glimpses of the moon, and then submit to him their new readings, I can imagine his reply:

"'What on earth does it matter? Either interpretation will serve. I cannot remember which I intended. My dramas were written under the spur of necessity, to meet the crying need of the theater of which I was one of the managers. They will be found to contain errors and blemishes. Let them be so, and do not encourage infatuated worshipers to turn defects into beauties. Nature is full of imperfections, and, if it pleased the Great Author to leave his work so to eternity, why seek to find perfection in every miserable little heap of dust? These trivial details you bring to my notice do not affect the purpose and shape of my play; and if they concern neither the action nor the passion nor the characters, why make so much ado about nothing? I am neither honored nor flattered by blind worship bestowed on my works. If my existence had depended on these text-grubbers, I should have been shelved two centuries ago between Ben Jonson and Massinger, or buried with Beaumont and Fletcher. I owe my existence to the stage, to the actor. No dramatic poet has any existence in the closet!'" Surely here is an injected breath of mountain air in the pent atmosphere of Shakespearean hyperesthesia!

II

Much Ado About Sonnets

WHATEVER the date of its first appearance, it is very evident that when the idea that the Shakespeare sonnets were expressions of hidden and cipher meanings, of unique or interwritten philosophy, mystic or erotic relations between personages contemporary with their composition (were anything, in fact, but some one hundred and fifty-four desultory rhymes in sonnet form), came into English literature, it came to stay. For, often as it has been dismissed and discarded, it is still to the fore; and even now, within this current year of enlightenment, when most other mundane things not responding to the touchstone of nineteenth-century scrutiny have been discarded as rubbish, when even on the stage and in decorative art the romantic, rococo, and purposeless have disappeared — even here are one stout volume and two ponderous essays in as many phlegmatic reviews, which thresh the old floors once more, re-read once more the alleged cryptogram of these everlasting sonnets, and construe it a different way each time.

In following these hermetic essays ordinary criticism is impressed not so much with their ingenuity (for there is no limit to human ingenuity) as with the facility with which not only Shakespeare's sonnets, but any other literary matter not historical, scientific, or didactic, may be so hermetically and allegorically treated. After all, what poem or prose romance exists which cannot be tortured into a set of symbolic types or allegories? Up to date there has not been lavished upon these sonnets anything like the literature, for example, once so popular with what we Americans call "cranks," devoted to that most ominous co-significance between the names Apollyon and Napoleon and the consequent danger to this planet of ours, of which almost any old book-shop will be sure to yield plentiful treatises. The last Napoleon, however, has passed out of sight without leaving so much as a sulphurous aroma in the ether, and it is just among the possibilities that even these tremendous sonnets are not hermetic, allegorical, or even — to what base uses may we come! — biographical at all! The really surprising thing, when one comes to think of it, in Mr. Gerald Massey's immense octavo,[1] is

---

[1] "Shakespeare's Sonnets, never before Interpreted: The Secret Drama of Shakespeare's Sonnets unfolded, with the Characters identified." By Gerald Massey. London: Longmans. 1866.

that he, a poet himself, should have insisted on referring these Shakespeare sonnets to an identified love-affair of the Elizabethan day, when an ideal love-affair would have answered just as well. If Mr. Massey had not been a poet before he became a Shakespearean commentator, we should have perhaps wondered why he selected Southampton as the lover instead of Pembroke (for whose name, by grace of baptism and good nature, "W. H." might perhaps have stood). But, being a poet, why should not any one man —for love-affairs are, after all, pretty much alike, and involve a good many secondary rivalries and friendships—have done as well as any other, or why should we not consider the sonnets as representing the uneven and tortuous course of any ordinary love-affair, when, to a poet, ideals are so much nearer and nicer than actual happenings?

Supposing that it should only be granted for argument's sake that these one hundred and fifty-four sonnets are just one hundred and fifty-four anonymous poems of the Elizabethan era—a catena (to borrow George Eliot's irreverence anent the "Faerie Queene") in which "you see no reason why it should not go on forever, and you accept that conclusion as an arrangement of Providence rather than of the author,"— granted that, what would be first to strike a critical eye? We think it would be — could hardly fail to be — the extreme inequality of the sonnets themselves.

I. Could anything be more marked, more apparent, than this inequality? Here, for example, against the tenderness and pathos of Sonnets xxx. and cvi., in which scarcely a quaint or archaic phrase marks them of their century, we must offset Sonnet lxxxvii., in whose every line occurs an old term of court or musty chancery catchword, making it altogether about as signal an adaptation of old saws and modern instances to complimentary purposes as one can find in the Law Burlesques:

> " Whereas, in sundry boughs and sprays
> Now divers birds allege to sing,
> And certain flowers their heads upraise,
> Hail, as aforesaid, coming spring!"

Is this burlesque any worse than—

> " Farewell! thou art too dear for my possessing,
> And like enough thou know'st thy estimate:
> The charter of thy worth gives thee releasing;
> My bonds in thee are all determinate"?

Or, still more extreme example of this law-letter pedantry, the cxxxiv.:

> " And I myself am mortgaged to thy will,
> Myself I'll forfeit, so that other mine
> Thou wilt restore to be my comfort still.
> .   .   .   .   .   .
> He learned but surety-like to write for me
> Under that bond that him as fast doth bind.
> The statute of thy beauty thou wilt take." . . .

And so on, with "patent," "misprision," "judgment," and the like, employed as a lover's symbols to his mistress. Mr. Casaubon might have written something in this strain had he been a chancery practitioner and attempted a sonnet to Dorothea; or old Tulkinghorn, or Mr. Vholes. But is it not rather hard to imagine merry Will Shakespeare scribbling this sort of thing on the banks of Avon, among the primroses of sunny Stratford, and with the bibulant temptations of Bidford, Pebworth and Marston within easy hailing distance?

Then, again, we have the "though rotten, not forgotten" of the lxxxi. Sonnets cxxxv. and cxxxvi. are plays upon the word "Will," the name recurring once or twice in about every line of them. This is another mood. Whether the name refers to "Will Shakespeare," or to "W. H.," or to a "willy" (which is said to have been the slang for "poet" in those days) is what nobody can find out. But how it has, in any case, anything to do with Lord Southampton's particular love-affairs only Mr. Massey knows.

Is it not a fact to go without cavil that the sonnet form in which most of these are written (for cxlv. appears to be the only one not in that form) is the principal reason for binding them up together? Has any other reason been discovered, or any other relation between them not purely visionary and fanciful? Most of us have smiled, we suppose, to fancy what Shakespeare would say could he rise from his seventeen-foot grave (it was too deep for a well, even if not wide enough for a church-door) and encounter some of the "readings" which have been assigned to him during these last one hundred and fifty years. And as to the rage to find in earlier or contemporary literature the sources whence Shakespeare procured this or that or the other phrase, some hint, perhaps, of William Shakespeare's own treatment of that feature of commentary, could he only come back again, may be gathered from a case quite in point. Recently a Canadian gentleman, a Mr. S. E. Dawson, wrote a little essay upon Lord Tennyson's "Princess." Mr. Dawson sent a copy to the poet and received a reply, a portion of which — as showing how a living poet must feel toward voluntary and dilettante commentary upon his work — is worth reprinting. Says Lord Tennyson:

"I do not object to your finding parallelisms. They must always recur. A Chinese scholar some time ago wrote me that in an unknown, untranslated Chinese poem there were two whole lines of mine almost word for word. Why not? Are not human eyes all over the world looking at the same objects, and must there not, consequently, be coincidences of thought and impressions and expressions? It is scarcely possible for any one to say or write anything, in this late time of the world, to which, in the rest of the literature of the world, a parallel could not somewhere be found. But when you say that this passage or that was suggested by Wordsworth or Shelley or another, I demur; and more, I wholly disagree. *There is, I fear, a prosaic set growing up among us, editors of booklets, book-worms, index-hunters, or men of great memories and no imagination, who* impute themselves *to the poet, and so believe that he, too, has no imagination, but is forever poking his nose between the pages of some old volume to see what he can appropriate.* They will not allow one to say 'ring the bells' without finding that we have taken it from Sir Philp Sidney, or even to use such a simple expression as that the ocean 'roars,' without finding the precise verse in Homer or Horace from which we have plagiarized it (fact!) . . . Here is a little anecdote about suggestion: When I was about twenty or twenty-one I went on a tour to the Pyrenees. Lying among these mountains, before a waterfall that comes down one thousand or twelve hundred feet, I sketched it (according to my custom then) in these words:

"'Slow-dropping veils of thinnest lawn.'

When I printed this, a critic informed me that 'lawn' was the material used in theaters to imitate a waterfall, and graciously added: 'Mr. T. should not go to the boards of a theater, but to Nature herself, for his suggestions.' And I *had* gone to Nature herself."

Is it speaking too harshly — would the commentators have any warrant to themselves complain of the harshness of the characterization? — to apply the sentence we have italicized in the laureate's criticism of his critics to the legions who advertise themselves as Shakespearean cicerones? The trade began about the days of Malone — 1780–1790. Of those ten years Sir James Prior[1] writes vividly: "Editors and commentators appear at every turn in all societies. In the club-house we meet three or four of a morning; in the park see them meditating by the Serpentine or under a tree in Kensington Gardens; no dinner-table is without one or two; in the theater you view them by the dozens. Volume after volume is poured out in note, comment, conjecture, new reading, statement, misstatement, contradiction. Reviews, magazines, and newspapers report these with as little mercy on the reader, and give occasional emendations of their own." And if this was true one hundred years ago, how much truer is it of these days! Mr. White was recently able to show that an incident in "Romeo and Juliet"— which some of our most superæsthetical modern editors had pitched upon as displaying Shakespeare's "deep moral purpose"— was about the only one in the play that hap-

[1] "Life of Edmund Malone." London: Smith, Elder & Co. 1860.

pened to be taken without the slightest alteration or embellishment from the prior story. If this sort of thing is not "imputing one's self to the poet," it would be hard to find a name for it. But the process, which requires considerable ingenuity and periphrasis when applied to the plays, is clear sailing and simplicity itself when worked on the sonnets, which stand alone, sui generis, with no ancestors, antitypes or prototypes; with no sources to reconcile and no references to be consulted. Anybody can do it. There is not a rock in the channel. All we have to do is to forge ahead.

II. In the second place, I think the student of these sonnets would very quickly become satisfied that they are not either autobiographical of their author or biographical of anybody else. The proposition that certain lines in Sonnets cx., cxi., and cxii., such as —

"And made myself a motley to the view,
Gored mine own thoughts — sold cheap what is most
    dear "— [cx.]

. . . .

"That did not better for my life provide
Than public means which public manners breeds.
Thence comes it that my name receives a brand,
And almost thence my nature is subdued
To what it works in, like the dyer's hand "— [cxi.]

. . . .

"Your love and pity doth the impression fill
Which vulgar scandal stamped upon my brow "— [cxii.]

. . . .

"So I, made lame by fortune's dearest spite "— [xxxvii.]

. . . .

"Speak of my lameness, and I straight will halt"—[lxxxix.]

and others, when torn from their context, are autobiographical of William Shakespeare, or make the whole bewildering series autobiographical, cannot, in my judgment, be supported by the facts. Those facts are that William Shakespeare was far too manly a man to be ashamed of his chosen calling; that, if he penned these lines, he penned them long before he had been enough of a public character to have imagined himself as being "branded"— to the extent of some thousands a year — by popularity, or to have been in a position, barring his theatrical connections, for something illustrious in the State. I leave again to Mr. Massey the task of weaving any such autobiographical matter, should it be proved to be so, into Southampton's affairs; or, if already biographical, to Mr. Massey or anybody else choosing to assume it, the labor of bringing them to bear upon the author's career, be he Shakespeare or anybody else. Shakespeare may have been lame. We have no means of knowing whether he was or not, but we must remember that the meaning of words has changed since his day. I doubt if "lame" then, when applied to the writer, meant anything more than any other of a hundred words used in the course of these sonnets in self-disparagement; or, least of all, had any reference to any such physical disability as we understand to be referred to by the word to-day. Similarly, Shakespeare was familiarly known among his comrades of the theater by the sobriquet "gentle," in allusion to his weakness for being considered of "gentle" birth (as shown, among other things, by his extravagance in bribing the officers of the

Heralds' College to issue a grant of arms to his father). I think the word "lame" had, in Elizabeth's day, no more reference to physical deformity or accident than the word "gentle" had to a man's temperament, disposition, or social qualities. And yet, so far as I can discover, no student of the sonnets, however much he may insist that they be read as a whole, but has felt at perfect liberty to isolate lines anywhere and apply them as he pleased. What commentator yet has failed to take from Sonnet lv. the first lines,—

"Not marble, nor the gilded monuments
  Of princes, shall outlive this powerful rhyme,"

or the next,—

"Since, spite of him [Death], I'll live in this poor rhyme"—
[cvii.]

and quote them as evidence that William Shakespeare believed that the sonnets were, either as a whole series, or this or that one in particular was, to make him immortal? Exegi monumentum ære perennius!

I am, I hope, not insensible to the delicious poetry which, in lines or couplets, is scattered here and there among these sonnets, and which in some (like the xviii., l., lx., lxxi., and others) predominates and renders the disappointment at sudden relapses into commonplace all the more dreary. But I feel less and less confident that the best and most satisfactory way to regard the sonnets is the unitary method of Coleridge, Armitage Brown and Massey, and have a surmise amounting to a strong suspicion that we will yet hark back to consider them as fragments merely (as Meres did), whether Shakespeare's or somebody else's.

Mr. Halliwell Phillipps formulates the resultant of an entire lifetime of Shakespearean research when he says: "Those who have lived as long as myself in the midst of Shakespearean criticism will be careful not to be too certain of anything." And, indeed, not only the most wonderful theories but the most astounding of facts pass without comment — seem to be taken as matter of course — if only translated to a Shakespearean vicinity. The Rev. Francis Gastrell,— not a billionaire,— who once lived in New Place, instead of selling out and leaving Stratford town when annoyed by relic-seekers, actually demolished stone by stone that substantial tenement (the first case on record, we believe, of a man willfully demolishing his own real estate in a pique at a handful of rustic neighbors). They dug a grave seventeen feet deep (deeper than most Stratford wells) under the pave of Trinity to receive William Shakespeare's coffin![1] These and a hundred other remarkable tales, that in any other connection would be accounted "yarns," seem to be reasonable and pass without question because pertaining to Shakespeareana! But of them all, surely the most wonderful story is that a village lad, of scant training in a country grammar-school,

[1] The particular absurdity of this story is that the Avon runs close to the walls of Trinity, and at the lowest its surface is scarcely two (or, at the most, three) feet lower than the pavement of the church; so that to dig a hole to that depth strong pumps must have been used inside the edifice itself.

engrossed in London in theatrical pursuits, should re-write into hermetic English verse an entirely original system of Platonic philosophy, as the author of the "New Study"[1] proposes to demonstrate; or exchange hallucinations and premonitions with Dante, as the "Blackwood" paper[2] insists; or compose a nuptial poem to Southampton in cipher, as Mr. Mackay[3] would have us believe!

As to the group of Sonnets lxxviii.-lxxxvi. (from which the existence of a rival poet to Shakespeare is evolved), it seems to me more involution than evolution — as if this "other poet" was conjured into, instead of being conjured out of, the text. Would an average reader — that is, an average of those who read these sonnets at all — notice, in passing to that group, a sudden change in the "you" addressed? that, whereas it has been a "dark beauty," a "lovely boy," a patron, a successful rival in his lady's favor, it all of a sudden becomes a "rival poet"? Why not test it? Would this average reader ever extract, for example, from the lines (lxxxii.):

> "I grant thou wert not married to my Muse,
> And therefore may'st without attaint o'erlook
> The dedicated words which writers use
> Of their fair subject, blessing every book,"

---

[1] "A New Study of Shakespeare: An Inquiry into the Connection of the Plays and Poems with the Origins of the Classic Dramas, and with the Platonic Philosophy through the Mysteries." London: Trübner & Co. 1884.

[2] "New Views of Shakespeare's Sonnets: The 'Other Poet' Identified." "Blackwood's Magazine," June, August, 1884.

[3] "A Tangled Skein Unravelled: The Mystery of Shakespeare's Sonnets." By Charles Mackay. The "Nineteenth Century," August, 1884.

that this poet had "dedicated a book to Shakespeare's patron"; or pick out of other lines in the group such clews as that this poet "had a familiar spirit," was "visited by a ghost," or that Mrs. Fytton, maid of honor to Queen Elizabeth, was the dark lady of Sonnets cxxvii.-clii., because, "in Sonnet cli., where, with respect to her name, the dark lady was spoken of as 'pointed out' for the poet's 'triumphant prize,' there was probably a play on the name Fytton, as equivalent in Elizabethan English to 'fit one,'" and the like? We urge once more, why not test it? For, while commentators might quarrel with the proposition that the less one studies writings as isolated as these sonnets are (of which we cannot find author, subject, date, circumstance, or occasion) the more one knows, it appears to be yet scarcely a figure of speech to so assert in this particular instance. To the myriads of other suggestions as to the study of these sonnets I respectfully add this one. The reverse has led to all sorts of theories. The particular theory advanced in that ponderous paper in "Blackwood's" appears to me no more extravagant than hundreds that have preceded it. If any poet is alluded to in the course of thirty-nine of the sonnets and then abruptly dismissed, it is, to my mind, quite as likely or unlikely to be Dante as to be Chapman or Spenser. (Why not Tennyson or Longfellow?—for we must remember Shakespeare's "prophetic soul.") Perhaps Dante may have written these very sonnets. Somebody must have written them. Perhaps, if these sonnets are a record of Southampton's love-affairs, his lordship himself may be the "poet" meant. The language of compliment is always rather under than over guarded. To be a poet one need not write verses (or perhaps Southampton, like most noblemen of his day, did write verses). Southampton may have had a "Beatrician Shade" to visit him in the night-watches, as well as Dante. Anyhow, most lovers and poets have dreams. And while it is never unsafe to poetically accuse a poet — or a lover — of being visited by familiar ghosts, isn't it very nearly the height of, shall we say craziness, or only zeal, to identify the particular poet or lover or the visiting ghost, from the use of the hyperbole? But, for all that, this very laborious writer of the "Blackwood" paper will have it, not that these sonnets are a record of Southampton's love-life or dedicated to him, but that they are "the song of William Shakespeare's new life"! A right to characterize the "Blackwood" paper can only be earned by laborious perusal. But, having earned that right, we forbear its exercise. Perhaps, however, we may venture the hope that another name is not to be enrolled in our Shakespeareana Lunatica.

If only William Shakespeare could have had a Boswell or a Moritz Busch! We are getting to appreciate those worthies in days when most men are too lazy to write biographies, even of their own ancestors, justifying themselves instead with emptying chests full of old letters upon a shuddering and book-ridden age. But so it is that of the man concerning whom we query most we have neither letters nor Boswells. Libraries of theorems as to the madness — the "subjection," the "lassitude" of his Hamlet; acres of ambling and exasperating minutiæ as to Shakespeare's indebtedness to earlier bards for such wild extravagances as "the roaring sea," the "ringing bells," "the lashing waves," etc., we have in plenty (and it is wonderful how cheaply they can be picked up at the old book-stalls, and how uniformly they are found with uncut leaves). The copyrighted commentator — he of crux and ending, "period" and "group," who stands the comma of distortion eternally between the amities of commentary and common sense — is always on hand with his wheelbarrow-load of dusty and archaic notes. Large attention is paid to the dramatist's political and moral purposes in the plays, and to their chronological order of composition (as if, granted the purpose, the order is of any consequence; or, granted the order, the purpose would suffer), and all these things somehow get themselves into print.

There is more of English that to-day is a dead language than of Greek and Latin put together. There are long rolls of names which the compilers of our literature manuals get into the habit of including, but which are mere echoes; which may have represented readers once, but represent them no more, nor any material for which readers have any use. But among these names that of the man we call Shakespeare does not occur. There is a glamour about that name like the whisper of the spell which bound the Lady of Shalott to an ever-weaving and an ever-growing web. Those to whom it speaks cannot choose but weave and speak in turn, passing ever and always onward the message they themselves have heard. O terque quaterque beati who, reading by sunlight instead of rushlight, can so prolong the legend that, like the wedding guest, the world cannot choose but stop to listen! And yet, blessed as these are, it is not to be forgotten that that way also madness lies. Among the names mentioned in Mr. Wyman's diligent bibliography of one minor branch of Shakespearean controversy (aside from the alleged innocuous lunacy of all the protagonists participant therein) are those of two who, by means of the controversy itself, have been driven mad, besides that of one suicide! It behooves everybody, then, to guard himself vigilantly against excessive and exclusive poring over any material wherein no bank or basis of solidified fact exists upon which to cast a kedge whereby to draw — when all bearings have been lost in foggy and bewildering space — back to moorings. One of the seven wise men of Greece bases his credentials entirely upon his saying, "Let there be too much of nothing." To his sentiment let us add the rider, "even of Shakespearean criticism."

But, heeded or not, of one thing we may be sure. We may open William Shakespeare's grave. We may find the inventory of all the world's goods of which he died possessed — the catalogue of his library, the disposition of his first-best bed. We may even dispose forever of the Bacon-Shakespeare controversy. But neither with any nor with all of these may we lay the question as to what these sonnets mean. That catena will go on forever! As to every other human tangle there is somebody somewhere to be subpœnaed. We can dive to find the submerged Atlantis; trace the successors of the lost tribes; supply the matter of the stolen books of Livy; we can import experts from Siam to testify as to the color of white elephants; but the sonnets will yet and forever remain mere sibylline leaves. As to the thread that will tie these together, neither ghost nor Daniel shall ever rise to depose!

III

Whose Sonnets?

THE process by which the name of Southampton has become associated with these sonnets is not a logical one, nor yet a very ancient one. In fact, it dates only from the moment when to some commentator occurred the happy thought of transposing the initial letters of that nobleman's name. The formula then became —

I. The only other metrical matter supposed to have been written by the supposed author of these sonnets was dedicated to Henry Wriothesly, Earl of Southampton.

II. The initials of "Henry Wriothesly" are "H. W.," which, being transposed, become "W. H."

III. The sonnets are dedicated to "Mr. W. H." *Ergo*, they are a record of Lord Southampton's love-affairs.

This is absolutely the entire case. Except that it has grown with years — having been everywhere welcomed with that love of the unknowable, filmy and mysterious for which the guileless commentator race is remarkable — the above statement covers it completely.

Mr. Wm. D. O'Connor, in his irresistible and piquant little brochure, "Hamlet's Note-Book,"[1] indeed holds that the sonnets were dedicated by T. T. (THOMAS HARIOT) to their author, WALTER RALEIGH, — otherwise the "W. H." wanted. But, while quite as likely as any other solution where solution is only — and from the nature of things can only be — guess-work, Mr. O'Connor's does not seem at all likely to become the popular guess-work. Mr. O'Connor stands alone in his hypothesis; whereas, since Mr. Armitage Brown made the other theory fashionable (especially since Mr. Gerald Massey's tremendous volume [2] "interpreted" them for us so circumstantially), there is no end of exposition for the Southamptonistic view.

But the truth appears to be, not only that Southampton cannot be traced historically into any neighborhood of the sonnets, but only by a forced inference from accidental premises into that of the very poems to which his name became fortuitously attached. In favor of this Southampton-Brown-Massey hypothesis (unless the word has a meaning peculiar and apart when used in a Shakespearean connection) there is no

[1] Boston: Houghton, Mifflin & Co. 1886.
[2] "The Secret Drama of Shakespeare's Sonnets Unfolded, with the Characters Identified," etc., etc. London: Longmans. 1866.

evidence whatever. And we may, I think, go further yet, and assert: first, that it is highly improbable, if not impossible, that William Shakespeare wrote those sonnets; and, second, that if the Massey-Brown translation of them were correct, this improbability or impossibility would be increased to an indefinite extent. Of course, these propositions, at a distance of three hundred years from their substantive, can not be proved like a demonstration in Euclid. But that they can be so nearly established from circumstantial and critical — that is to say, external and internal — evidence as to satisfy most reasonable people, I think may be shown.

In a paper in the "Galaxy Magazine" for January, 1877, the late Richard Grant White pointed out certain passages in "Macbeth," which, in his opinion, William Shakespeare never wrote. Says Mr. White: "The person who wrote these un-Shakespearean passages was probably Middleton. Shakespeare, writing the tragedy in haste for an occasion, received a little help, according to the fashion of the time, from another playwright; and the latter, having imitated the supernatural parts of this play in one of his own, the players or managers afterward introduced from that play songs by him — music and a song, 'Come Away, Come Away,' iii. 5; and music and a song, 'Black Spirits,' etc., iv. 1. This was done to please the inferior part of the audience."

Only those who have attentively followed the course of modern and external or circumstantial Shakespearean study, know how the proofs of Shakespeare's having very often been "in haste for an occasion," and very often "having received a little help" have accumulated. Indeed, the industrious gentlemen of the New Shakespeare Society have unearthed so many different styles and methods in the plays, that, to keep Shakespeare at all, they have been forced to suppose "periods" and "groups" in his workmanship; while Dowden and other esthetic critics, not satisfied with these, have gone so far as to show mental changes in Shakespeare himself; that he wrote certain plays when despondent, others when joyous, others when in deep perplexity with the problem of the future, etc., etc. The real truth is, of course, as Mr. White puts it. Plays are written, always have been and are to-day, under very different conditions from novels, histories, or poems. Managers or playwrights are often pressed for time. There is an audience on the way, and something local or timely has occurred to which a reference will win their applause. Or a change of programme is rendered necessary at the last moment; or news received has been contradicted by later advices. In short, there are a hundred contingencies. And, even when composed at leisure, a play is rarely the entire work of a single workman. One writes the plot; or selects it—as all of Shakespeare's were selected—in some old romance or story-book, or from some historical episode. Another hand may frame the dialogue. Still another supply the speeches, put in the localisms necessary, and introduce relieving parts. Then, at the first reading, suggestions are made and something added or taken away. It is cut or augmented at every rehearsal. Perhaps some actor has tempered the public taste; found just where in his "length" he can bring down the house, and noted it in the margin. Such has been the history of each individual play ever since such things as theaters existed, so that when printed from the actor's copies or "lengths"— as the Shakespeare plays all were — he would be a bold man indeed who should assert — from evidence that a set of plays had been the property of this or that theatrical proprietor — that they were the verbatim monographs of stage-manager or playwright; and he would be a very artless critic who should announce anybody as their author, except under the usual theatrical conditions and stage exigencies, which are apt to be about the same in every age. The fact is, that, not because we know so little but because we know so much of William Shakespeare, his theater and his times, we have long since ceased to imagine him as actually penning all the plays so properly labeled with his honored name. It has come to be pretty widely considered that if, in those busy years of his London enterprises,— into which he embarked penniless, and from which he retired with an annual income of $25,000,— he edited or "set" them all for the stage, it was possibly the utmost he had to do with them. Without accepting that theory, is it quite safe to ignore it? Even were Bacon the playwright Mrs. Pott claims him to have been, the reasons given above would forbid our assigning them entirely to Bacon. As all sources of information seem to have been exhausted, we shall probably be obliged to remain contented with the conclusion of the New Shakespeare Society, that very many hands were employed in them. At any rate, just as one may, if he will, disbelieve in one of Mr. Wiggins's storms without being able to supply another in its place, so one, it seems, is permitted to say that Shakespeare did not, without being obliged to predicate who did, write the always immortal Plays.

But when we come to the sonnets and poems called Shakespeare's, while there still remain the outset doubt and mystery, at least it stands by itself. All minor difficulties have been cleared away. There is nothing composite in the authorship here, and we evidently have only one man to hunt for. It is proposed in this paper to do a little hunting in the neighborhood of the poems and sonnets. If nothing is developed, the mystery is no greater than before. If anything is revealed, it can be largely used in identification of the contributors to the plays: for, whoever wrote these metrical productions had large agency in the drama we call Shakespeare; must, indeed, have been author of almost all the majestic poetry we indicate by the adjective "Shakespearean." The metrical end, I think, is the end to start from in any search for the author of Shakespeare. At present, however, we are going to explore no farther than that end itself.

Let us first glance briefly at the history of the poems and sonnets called Shakespeare's. In 1593 "Venus and Adonis" appears in print with a dedication to Lord Southampton, signed "William Shakespeare." In 1594 appears another poem, "Lucrece," also with a dedication to Lord Southampton, signed by William Shakespeare. In 1598 Francis Meres publishes a work called "Palladis Tamia," probably as fair an example of what literary criticism was in Tudor English days as has come down to us. In this book Meres says that William Shakespeare was accounted for comedy and tragedy as equal at least to Plautus and Seneca, by reason of certain plays, viz., "Two Gentlemen of Verona," "Comedy of Errors," "Love's Labour's Lost," "Love's Labour's Won," "Midsummer Night's Dream," "Merchant of Venice," "Titus Andronicus," "Romeo and Juliet," "Richard II.," "Richard III.," "Henry V.," and "King John." Meres adds, that Shakespeare was further credited with " the sweet wittie soul of Ovid" for "his sugred sonnets among his private friends."

In 1599 a printer named Jaggard (not the same who afterward, with his partner, published the first folio of the Shakespearean plays in 1623) issued a volume of collected verses under the title of "The Passionate Pilgrim." In 1609 appears a volume with the following title-page:

SHAKE-SPEARE'S

SONNETS.

Neuer before Imprinted.

AT LONDON
By G. Eld for T. T. and are
to be fold by John Wright, dwelling
at Christ Church gate
1609

In some copies the imprint substitutes the name William Aspley for the name and residence of John Wright, and in 1640 another—which, doubtless by reason of the Heywood protest to be hereafter noticed, omits the xviii., xix., xliii., lvi., lxxv., lxxvi., xcvi. and cxxvi.—whose title-page reads—

POEMS

VVRITTEN

BY

WIL. SHAKE-SPEARE.

Gent.

Printed at *London* by *Tho. Cotes*, and are to be fold by *Iohn Benfon*, dwelling in St. *Dunftans* Church-yard. 1640.

Now, every one of these five publications, viz., the " Venus and Adonis," " Lucrece," " Passionate Pilgrim," and the " T. T." and Tho. Cotes's " Sonnets," are said, prominently on their title-pages, to be " By William Shakespeare." But the name of an author printed on a title-page in those times was no guarantee of authorship whatever, since members of the Stationers' Company were protected by law in printing what they pleased, and since nothing except what they pleased to print could be issued at all. That there was no copyright in anybody but printers, and no such thing as authors' rights conceived of, and that there was no practice by which an author could prevent wrongful use of his name by injunction—has been demonstrated so often by Elizabethans from Hallam to Grant White, that reference only is here needed to the fact. The monopoly printers were in the habit of selecting a name that would best sell their books, and the most popular books they printed were books of "Songs and Sonnets," such as Slender speaks of when he catches the eye of pretty Anne Page: "I had rather than forty shillings I had my book of songs and sonnets here." To tack Shakespeare's name to their productions was to market them under the most favorable conditions; for William Shakespeare was the most popular caterer to the public amusement in London; his name was in everybody's mouth and, as we shall see farther on, was particularly valuable on title-pages of "Books of Songs and Sonnets," because for eleven years it had been rumored, as reported by Meres, that there were certain sonnets of his in existence in private hands.

I. THE "VENUS AND ADONIS" and "LUCRECE." Reasons for believing that William Shakespeare's name upon these splendid poems does not prove him to have been their author, other than the fact that popular names were always borrowed by printers, are: 1. William Shakespeare's history from his birth in 1564 to their date. 2. His business occupations in London from about 1586 to such date, and 3, his mental and scholastic equipment for writing them.

No. 1. This history the world has by heart. No. 2.

In 1598 William Shakespeare had been in London about twelve years. He had quitted Stratford in or about 1586, in poverty, leaving his wife and children to the care of his father — who was, if possible, poorer still. "Removed prematurely from school," says Mr. Halliwell Phillipps in his "Outlines," "residing with illiterate relatives in a bookless neighborhood — thrown into the midst of occupations adverse to scholastic progress — it is difficult to believe that, when he first left Stratford, he was not all but destitute of polished accomplishments." In those twelve years he has, however, been earning money rapidly. So rapidly, indeed, that in 1589, only three years after his penniless arrival, his father, John Shakespeare, has not only been able to pay his debts and come out of his house without fear of arrest, but to institute the first of the chancery suits against John Lambert for recovery of the Wilmecote estate, which he had been compelled in his poverty to hypothecate. (He brought the second suit against Lambert, respecting the Ashbies estate, in 1598.) In other words, in the years when William Shakespeare is popularly supposed to have been scribbling verses in London, the record is that he was earning money and paying off the family mortgages. That is the record. But, of course, nobody is obliged to look at it unless he chooses. Of course it very rarely happens that the composer of well-known and popular works is willing to pass from life preserving an impenetrable incognito. And yet, as in the case of "Junius," it sometimes does happen. And certainly to whatever lengths speculation may go, — however extravagant the claims of the weaker brains which may be turned by the calm and long-weighed statements of thinkers,— the mystery of the ownership of the Plays during Shakespeare's lifetime—the mystery of the Stationers' registers — is tantalizing. Here are plays constantly pirated, and yet it is impossible to discover that anybody, or any legal representative of anybody named Shakespeare, ever set up any claim to proprietorship in any of these works — works which, beyond any literary production of that age, were (as their repeatedly being subjects of piracy and of registration on the Stationers' books proves them to have been) of the largest market value. And, moreover, nobody ever claimed their authorship, neither William Shakespeare, Francis Bacon, nor anybody else. Besides, not one of the persons called "contemporary witnesses" to William Shakespeare's authorship could answer in a court of justice to-day a reasonable cross-examination as to his facilities for obtaining information on the point on which he was testifying without admitting that he did not have any. (It is to be remembered that the question is not, "Did William Shakespeare's contemporaries believe him to be the author?" etc., but, "Were or were not his contemporaries deceived in so believing?")

These plays were property and sources of revenue to their owners. But nobody by the name of Shakespeare, or of Hall (Shakespeare's executor, named in his will, and who probated that will, with an inventory according to law), or of Heminges or Condell (named in Shakespeare's will, and who after his death claimed to stand as literary executors and next friends to rescue his literary remains from unauthorized and surreptitious editing), ever entered anything, or any assign-

ment, by purchase, gift, probate, or judgment of
a court of law, of anything labeled "Shakespeare"
in the books of the Stationers' Company, which
entry was the only method provided by law in
those days of securing literary property against
piracy and fraud. There were no authors' rights
at that time. The only thing analogous to our
copyright was a printer's right; and entry in the
books of the Stationers' Company secured only
the printer in his right to print (*i. e.*, publish) literary matter for profit.

Heminges and Condell asserted, in 1623, that
all editions of the plays called "Shakespeare," except their own, were "stolen and surreptitious
copies." If the laws of England in those days
are of the slightest consequence in this investigation, it must appear that it was actually these
very men, Heminges and Condell, and not the
other publishers, who were utterers of "stolen
and surreptitious copies." For, whereas all other
printers of Shakespeare's plays observed the laws,
and entered them for copyright, Heminges and
Condell appear never to have heard of any legal
obligations of the sort. Unless they stole them,
it certainly passes man's understanding to conceive how they got hold of them. For, whatever
property could be legally alienated in those days
without a record, literary property certainly
could not be so alienated. The record of alienation could have been made in but one place, and
it was never made there. And yet, where would
the theory of a Shakespearean authorship rest
were it not for these very Stationers' books?—
for entries known to be piratical (according to
modern ideas, although perfectly legitimate then)?

The value of title-page evidence to authorship in those days, when authors had no right, and certain printers every right, to print books, has certainly been demonstrated too many times to need detain us now. If the printers attached William Shakespeare's name for the same reason that they printed at all,—viz., to make money,—they did only what they had precisely the same moral and legal right to do in the one case as in the other; that is to say, they had no moral right, but a perfect legal right, to do either or both.

The question as to what plays, if any, William Shakespeare wrote, was not originated by Miss Bacon in 1856, nor by Mr. W. H. Smith in 1857, but by Messrs. Heminges and Condell in 1623, when they edited, as by William Shakespeare, thirty-six plays, which were not the thirty-six or more plays known as Shakespeare's in his lifetime. This Heminges and Condell canon lasted just forty-one years, not being attacked until 1664, when some persons unknown took the liberty of reconsidering the question and printed a third folio, inclusive of seven plays which Heminges and Condell had either rejected or never heard of. Is it anyway marvelous that such an apparent absence of the least Shakespearean control over these plays and poems in William Shakespeare's vicinity, has led to a search in his neighborhood for others who might have written incognito for the Elizabethan stage?

The truth was, that they used the quartos when they happened to have them; the rest was piecemealed out as well as possible. The impossibility of the actor's copies or transcripts having been always and exclusively in the personal chirography of William Shakespeare himself, is too apparent to need the attention of thinking people. William Shakespeare, a man of large and engrossing affairs, of investments, speculations and ventures, contracts, real estates, rents, and farms, had plenty of men besides actors in his pay. Poet or no poet, he could not have personally been transcriber of all the partial manuscripts or actors' "lengths" put into the hands of each individual stock company, from which the quartos are seen to have been printed. Neither could he nor any other poet have composed thirty-seven, or seven, or any other number of plays, so written "that in his writing (whatever he penned) he never blotted out a line," as Ben Jonson says, or "with scarce a blot in his papers," as Heminges and Condell repeat the hyperbole. Besides, as anybody who takes the trouble to compare quartos with folio will discover, the versions are not the same. Almost all of them are revisions. Speeches, scenes, almost entire acts, are constantly added. The phraseology is altered, enriched, amended with embellishments or more accurate statements as to legal, scientific, or formal matters, a process which requires considerable " blotting." The expression "unblotted manuscript" was merely a figure of speech, employed by Jonson to emphasize one thing, and by the two editors to express quite another, in neither case warranting the twisting, discussion, and literal interpretation it has received from some commentators.

Even in matters Shakespearean that appears to be a reasonable rule which requires evidence to be harmonized, if at all, in accordance with rather than dead against, human experience and the laws of cause and effect. And had only the stage use of such material been sold to the theaters, would it not, then, be a reasonable venture at a solution of the mystery to infer, first, that the unknown authors did not claim them because he had sold them, and because, having no authors' rights, it would have been useless to so claim them; and secondly, that Shakespeare did not claim them because he had never had anything but a right to mount them on his boards (*i. e.*, precisely what we call stage-right to-day), which expired, as to him at least, with the popular taste for the plays as mounted? He would not have entered them in the Stationers' books, because there was no statute providing for or requiring entry of stage-right; nor would his executors or successors have registered them, for the same reason, especially after they had had their day and been forgotten. Of course these plays became known as Shakespeare's. That is by far the simplest feature in the proceeding. If once granted that nobody knew who wrote them, and that everybody knew who brought them out; as between an anonymous author and a responsible mounter, of course they were identified by the responsible name. Whatever commercial value the poems may at any time have had, depended upon the popularity of the name of the author of plays to see which everybody was crowding. Mere poetry, as poetry, was no more of a commercial investment in Elizabeth's day than it is in ours. People are not nowadays in the habit of thinking of Shakespeare as one of the richest private subjects in England, in Elizabeth's reign. But he was.

Was it from poetry he began to send money home to the impoverished household (the ruined father, who had mortgaged his wife's portion; lazy brothers and sisters, helpless wife and babies), began to pay his father's debts, to buy houses and land, a grant of arms, to invest in shares and to farm tithes — kept up, in short, a continual series of investments in London and Stratford? There is the record. But, as we have said, nobody is compelled to open his eyes and look at it unless he desires. And is not this inference rather aided by Shakespeare's Will, as probated according to the English law? It is a careful memorization of his personal effects down to a useful (but not first-hand) article of domestic furniture, which he gives to his wife; though, as far as we are able to understand English probate law of that period, it was hers, had she wanted it, without any Will at all. But this latter Will makes no mention of stage-right in manuscripts which had ceased to be sources of revenue to him, and therefore of no value to his successors. It is simply silly to talk, as the commentators will, of Shakespeare omitting to mention them in his testament because his copyrights in these plays had expired, or because he or his representatives had sold them to the Globe Theater. If they had never been entered for copyright on the Stationers' registers, he or his executors might perhaps have sold them without registering the transaction; but, unfortunately, these plays had been entered on the Stationers' books, and, once so entered, it was impossible to alienate them to the Globe Theater or to any other purchaser except by registry of later date. Whatever else may be obscured in this matter, there is no obscuring the fact that William Shakespeare never had any copyright in the plays. If he had one, it would not have lapsed at the date of his testament. Whatever copyright this entry in the Stationers' books gave, was at common law and perpetual. In the Lenox library, New-York, is preserved in a crystal frame a copy of the great First Folio. Its value is among the thousands, and it is remarkable as being one of the few absolutely perfect copies in existence. But the wonderful thing about this particular copy is that it appears to bear on its title-page the date — not 1623, as it should, but 1622! Of course its history, through all its various owners, down to Mr. Lenox, is well known, and of course there have been theories and theories. But the only explanation hazarded is, that the date was changed to in some way dodge a copyright expired or unexpired; which would be most satisfying, except for the fact that what answered to copyright in those days was perpetual, and therefore could not have expired at all.[1] The idea of a copyright for a term of years was not heard of until the act of Anne, April 10, 1710. If light is wanted as to the laws of literary property in Elizabeth's day, or as to who were owners of whatever literary estate inhered in the Shakespeare plays, why guess at it when law libraries are accessible, and the books of the Stationers'

[1] The microscope shows that the error (that is, if a hoax were not intended) was in a repairing of the title-page; the lower part of the figure 3, which was torn out, having been supplied by a bar —, instead of a hook, ɔ.

Company extant? What escape, then, is there from the conclusion that Heminges and Condell never registered the plays for the simple reason that, having helped themselves to them, they had no legal rights to make a registry of? They were not interfered with, because these plays, having lost for the time their commercial value, the former printers did not esteem them worth a lawsuit. Their printers, Blount and Jaggard, November 8, 1623, did, however, enter the names of sixteen hitherto uncopyrighted plays, and this is all the literary property anybody ever possessed in the great First Folio. If Shakespeare, before his death, had transferred any plays to the Globe Theater, the Stationers' books would show it, and the record of the transfer could not have been affected by the conflagration of that theater. But, except that it shows how the name of Shakespeare could on account of its popularity be placed upon poems as well as plays, to increase their salability, this brief of the legal status does not meet the case in hand. So we must proceed.

No. 3. As to the equipment: There was a grammar-school in Stratford; but the idea of anybody being taught English grammar in an English grammar school — let alone the English language in those days — is utterly inconceivable. There was no such branch, and mighty little of anything in its place, except birchen rods, the church catechism, the Criss Cross Row and a few superfluous Latin declensions out of "Lily's Accidence." Nor did Shakespeare hear the limpid urban English of the poems and sonnets at home or in Stratford streets. For everybody there talked Warwickshire dialect, some idea of which we may draw from the broad specimens contained in the doggerel verses ascribed by Stratford tradition to William Shakespeare himself. And to what sort of a London did young Shakespeare come, on leaving this precious school? "Members of Parliament could not understand each other's rustic patois," says Mr. White. Even the soldiers in Elizabeth's army could not comprehend the word of command unless given by officers of their own county or shire town. London was a huge caravanserie. Only in the court was there uniformity of speech. William Shakespeare was hardly admitted at court yet. But, uncouth rustic that he was, he writes, as the "first heir of his invention," the most elegant, sumptuous, and sensuous verses that English literature possesses to-day. Where, then, did our rustic poet get — not his genius, but his equipment? No Stratford record nor Stratford tradition makes Shakespeare to have attended the Stratford grammar-school. But he may yet have been a faithful student there. Admitting that he was, let us look in on its sessions. Thomas Hunt, the head-master, is hearing little Will Shakespeare his lesson. The recitation is reported by an eyewitness, and is verbatim:

MASTER. Come hither, William; hold up your head. Come, William, how many numbers is in nouns?
WILLIAM. Two.
M. What is fair, William?
W. Pulcher.
M. What is lapis, William?
W. A stone.
M. And what is a stone?
W. A pebble.

M. No, it is lapis. I pray you remember in your prain.
W. Lapis.
M. That is good, William. What is he, William, that does lend articles?
W. Articles are borrowed of the pronoun, and be thus declined: Singulariter nominativo, hic, hæc, hoc.
M. Nominativo hig, hag, hog; pray you, mark: genitivo hujus. Well, what is your accusative case?
W. Accusativo, hinc.
M. I pray you, have your remembrance, child. Accusativo; hung, hang, hog. What is the vocative case, William?
W. Vocativo, O.
M. Remember, William, focative is caret. What is your genitive case plural, William?
W. Genitive case?
M. Ay.
W. Genitive: horum, harum, horum.
M. Show me now, William, some declensions of your pronouns.
W. Forsooth, I have forgot.
M. It is, qui, quæ, quod; if you forget your quis and your quæs and your quods, you must be preeches. [1]

I feel not the slightest hesitation in assuming this scene from the "Merry Wives" to be an episode in Shakespeare's own home life; for the esthetes have assured us that Shakespeare was always writing about himself: that the wail of Constance for her child was Shakespeare's grief for Hamnet; the Duke of Ilyria's advice to husbands to take wives younger than themselves an allusion to Shakespeare's marriage to one his elder, etc., etc. And I accept at once the discovery that, instead of being the greatest of objective poets, he was only a very subjective one after all. But, lest it may still be insisted that Shakespeare some-

[1] "Merry Wives of Windsor," Act iv. Scene i.

times thought of something besides himself and his own experiences, and that this is mere stage travesty and burlesque, let us look a little further. There is no exactly contemporary testimony; but in 1634 the author of the "Compleate Gentleman" says that a country schoolteacher "by no entreaty would teach any scholar further than his [the scholar's] father had learned before him. His reason was that they would otherwise prove saucy rogues and control their fathers." Nay, in 1771, when Shakespeare had been dead a century and a half, John Britton, who had attended a provincial grammar-school in Wilts, says that the pedagogue was wont to teach the "Criss Cross Row," or alphabet, as follows:

TEACHER. Commether, Billy Chubb, an' breng the horrenbook. Ge ma the vester in tha wendow, you Pat Came. Wha! be a sleepid! I'll waken ye! Now, Billy, there's a good bwoy, ston still there, an' min whan I da point na! Criss cross girt a little A B C. That is right, Billy. You'll soon learn criss cross row; you'll soon avergit Bobby Jiffry! You'll soon be a schollard! A's a purty chubby bwoy. Lord love en!

It could not have been much better in William Shakespeare's boyhood days than in 1634 and 1771. Says Mr. Goadby: "It is evident that much schooling was impossible, for the necessary books did not exist. The horn-book for teaching the alphabet would almost exhaust the resources of any common day-school that might exist in the towns and villages. The first English grammar was not published until 1586."[1] Says Mr. Furnivall: "I think you would be safe in conceding that at such a

[1] "England of Shakespeare," p. 101.

school as Stratford, about 1570, there would be taught (1) an A B C book for which a pupil teacher or ABCdarius is sometimes mentioned as having a salary; (2) a catechism in English and Latin, probably Nowell's; (3) the authorized Latin grammar, i. e., Lily's, put out with a proclamation adapted to each king's reign; (4) some easy Latin construing book, such as Erasmus's 'Colloquies,' Corderius's 'Colloquies, or Baptista Mantuanus,' and the familiar 'Cato,' or 'Disticha de Moribus.'"[1] Says Halliwell Phillipps: "Unless the system of instruction [in Stratford grammar-school] differed essentially from that pursued in other establishments of a similar character, his [Shakespeare's] knowledge of Latin was derived from two well-known books of the time — the 'Accidence' and the 'Sententiæ Pueriles,' . . . a little manual containing a large collection of brief sentences collected from a variety of authors, with a distinct selection of moral and religious paragraphs, the latter intended for the use of boys on saints' days. . . . Exclusive of bibles, church services, psalters, etc., there were certainly not more than two or three dozen books, if as many, in the whole town [Stratford-on-Avon]. The copy of the black-letter English history, so often depicted as well thumbed by Shakespeare in his father's parlor, never existed out of the imagination."[2]

But, even had there been books, it seems there were no school-masters in the days when young William went to school who could have taught

[1] "Int. to Leopold Shakespeare," p. 11.
[2] "Outlines of the Life of Shakespeare," 6th edition, i. 52.

him what was necessary. Ascham, who came a little earlier than Shakespeare, said such as were to be had amounted to nothing, and "for the most so behave themselves that their very name is hateful to the scholar, who trembleth at their coming, rejoiceth at their absence, and looketh him returned as a deadly enemy."[1] Milton says their teaching was "mere babblement and notions."[2]

"Whereas they make one scholar, they mar ten," says Peacham, who describes one country specimen as whipping his boys on a cold winter morning "for no other purpose than to get himself into a heat."[3] In fact the birch-rod seems to have been, from the days of Ascham, at least to the days when Sergeant Ballantyne and Anthony Trollope went to school, the principal agent of youthful instruction and instructors in England. Peter Mason, a pupil of Nicholas Udal, master of Eton, says he used to receive fifty-three lashes in the course of one Latin exercise. Sergeant Ballantyne (whose schooling must have been somewhere *circa* 1810–1820) said that his teachers were cold-blooded, unsympathetic tyrants, who "flogged continuously" and taught nothing in particular.[4] And Anthony Trollope's and Charles Reade's experiences, as related in their memoirs, are directly to the same effect. The conclusion being that a maximum of caning and a minimum of parrot-work on desultory Latin paradigms, which, whether wrong or right, were of no

---

[1] Works, Bennet's edition, p. 212.
[2] Works, Symond's edition. London: Bentley, 1806. Vol. iii. p. 348.
[3] "Goadby's England of Shakespeare," p. 100.
[4] "Some Experiences of a Barrister's Life," p. 6.

consequence whatever to anybody, was the village idea of a boy's education in England for long centuries easily inclusive of the years within which William Shakespeare lived and died. The great scholars of those centuries either educated themselves, or by learned parents were guided to the sources of human intelligence and experience. At any rate, they drew nothing out of the country grammar-schools. The forcing systems of Mr. Wopsle's great-aunt, or of that other eminent educator Mr. Wackford Squeers, senior, seem to have been — so far as the English branches are concerned — improvements on the methods of rural pedagogues in the sixteenth century. We are not advised whether or no the boys were taught to cipher, but if they were, probably it exhausted their scientific course. Beyond the horn-book very little reading and writing could have been contemplated in a land where, from a time when the memory of man runneth not to the contrary to the eighth year of George the Fourth, immunity from the penalty of felonies was granted to any one who could make profert of those accomplishments.[1]

But self-training requires, if not leisure, at least a sufficient lapse of time; and in the case of William Shakespeare we can find neither, between his graduation — if so it be — at the temple of learning in Stratford-on-Avon and the authorship of the two great poems, the one hundred and fifty-four sonnets and the plays assigned to him by Francis Meres in 1598. I do not allude to the dedications of these poems to Henry Wriothesley,

[1] Benefit of clergy was only abolished in England by Act 8, Geo. IV. ch. 28.

Lord Southampton, which were signed "William Shakespeare," because whoever wrote the poems could have written the dedications, and because dedications were not always signed by the authors of the books dedicated, as will appear presently when we come to look at the dedicatory inscriptions under which the sonnets were first printed. Whoever wrote the poems, it was quite natural that, being printed in 1593 and 1594, they should have been dedicated to Southampton. Indeed, it would have been matter of surprise if they had not been so dedicated. Southampton was the standing patron of all the poets and dramatists of those days. Chapman calls him, in his "Iliad," "The choice of all our country's noblest spirits." Nash says, "Incomprehensible is the height of his spirit, both in heroical resolution and matters of conceit." "Who lives on England's stage and knows him not?" asks Beaumont. Gervinus says that all the poets and writers of that day "vied with each other in dedicating their works to him."[1]

But, in discussing these questions, one must never lose sight of the fact that there can be no manner of doubt but that the "Venus and Adonis" was everywhere credited to Shakespeare, and, being the most popular work of its day, that the accuracy of its assignment to him would naturally have been discussed. And that the authorship was discussed — and very publicly, too — proof has but just come to light. In one of Thomas Hearn's volumes of miscellanea in the Bodleian library (forming a part of Dr. Rawlinson's collec-

[1] "Shakespeare Commentaries," p. 446.

tion, and numbered Rawlinson D. 398), Mr. Macray, a Fellow of the Royal Society of Antiquaries, was fortunate enough to recently find two manuscript plays, "The Pilgrimage to Parnassus," and the First Part of the well-known "Return from Parnassus," the two evidently forming, with the long extant Second Part, a trilogy dating from 1597-1601.[1] In this long-lost First Part of the "Return," one Gullio — a sort of Armado for verbal conceits — makes a speech, which is actually constructed out of perverted passages from Shakespeare's "Venus and Adonis" and "Romeo and Juliet." His fellow, Ingenioso, detects the plagiarisms, and points them out in asides to the audience. "We shall have nothing," he remarks after one misquotation, "but pure Shakespeare, and shreds of poetric that he hath gathered at the theaters." A second cento from Shakespeare calls forth from Ingenioso the exclamation: "Marke, 'Romeo and Juliet!' O monstrous theft!" and he greets with "Sweete Mr. Shakespeare!" a third (and this time correctly) quoted extract from the "Venus and Adonis." Gullio then desires that Ingenioso compose for him poetical love-letters "in two or three divers vayns, in Chaucer's, Gower's, and Spenser's and Mr. Shakespeare's," adding:

"Marry, I thinke I shall entertaine those verses which run like these [from 'Venus and Adonis']:

[1] "The Pilgrimage to Parnassus, with the Two Parts of the Return from Parnassus." Three Comedies performed in St. John's College, Cambridge, A. D. MDXCVII.-MDCI. Edited from MSS. by the Rev. W. D. Macray, F. S. A. (Oxford : Clarendon Press.)

'Even as the sunn with purple coloured face
Had tane his laste leave of the weeping morne, &c.'
O sweet Mr. Shakspere! I'le have his picture in my study at the courte."

Later on, Ingenioso presents the love-poems to his master. Three stanzas in imitation of Chaucer are rejected as "dull, harshe, and spiritless." Those imitating Spenser, beginning:

" A gentle pen rides prickinge on the plaine,
This paper plaine, to resalute my love,"

are rejected, and the parodist is directed to proceed in "Mr. Shakspear's veyne." A stanza modeled on the "Venus and Adonis" or the "Lucrece" follows, and draws this comment from Gullio:

"Noe more! I am one that can judge accordinge to the proverbe, *bovem ex unguibus.* Ey marry, Sir, these have some life in them! Let this duncified worlde esteeme of Spenser and Chaucer, I'le worshipp sweet Mr. Shakspere and to honoure him will lay his 'Venus and Adonis' under my pillowe, as wee reade of one (I doe not well remember his name, but I am sure he was a kinge) slept with Homer under his bed's heade."

These fragments being genuine, it is impossible to deny that they show a popular disposition to echo a judgment in favor of the Shakespeare over the Chaucer or Spenser performances. (I say echo, because the theater of those days was no place to give voice to expressions that would be or that were unpopular. Audiences burst upon the stage and tossed the actors in blankets, or worse, upon very slight provocations. For long years the presumption was always against a poor player, who must be very careful what he allowed to pass his lips.) Of the long familiar allusions to Shakespeare in what this discovery proves to be the Second Part of the "Return," Mullinger remarks that they seem "to convey the notion that Shakespeare was the favorite of the rude, half-educated strolling players, as distinguished from the refined geniuses of the university." And, adds Mr. Macray, "those in the second play — which all come from the mouth of Gullio, the arrant braggart, the empty pretender to knowledge and the avowed libertine, and from his page — tend to show that, while the 'Venus and Adonis' was the best known of the already published writings, this, in the esteem of Cambridge scholars, made Shakespeare to be regarded as specially the favorite of the class which that character represents. Certainly, the popularity assigned to him is not of a sort to be desired; but the popularity itself is indisputable." Whether, in view of the rigid limitations put upon actors just noticed, these remarks of Mr. Mullinger and Mr. Macray are justified, I am inclined to doubt. Possibly the audiences of those days were not as apt to distinguish between objective and subjective — between what the actors spoke in character and what they uttered to attract popular approval — as these reflections might imply. My further reason for differing with Mr. Macray would be the fact that the scholar in the newly discovered Play does not speak disparagingly of Shakespeare, — although he speaks always in the character of a scholar, — and that he compels the ignorant esteem for his poet by quoting his salaciousness merely. To prove his hypothesis, Mr. Macray should show —

it seems to me — that by citing bad verses of Shakespeare's he made even the ignorant to despise him.

II. "THE PASSIONATE PILGRIM." — It is not remarkable, perhaps, that we find no copyright entries on the Stationers' books in the name of Jonson, Marlowe, or other of the contemporary poets and dramatists, for these were continually in straitened circumstances. But William Shakespeare, being an exceedingly wealthy and independent gentleman (if besides, one of the largest owners of literary property of his time), it is remarkable that the only legal method of securing literary matter, and putting it in shape to alienate, was never taken by him, or in his name. We have seen how that silence of his Will as to any literary property whatever is explained by the commentators with utter indifference to the English law which would have vested in his executor, Dr. Hall, any literary property accruing to him at Shakespeare's demise; and how even more necessary in that case would have been a registration by Dr. Hall as executor of these literary rights in order to alien them to purchasers. But facts themselves are more welcome than even conclusions of fact. The state of affairs under which title-pages meant everything or nothing, according to the printer's whim, is not only deducible from the situation but is capitally illustrated by the circumstances under which the next "Book of Songs and Sonnets"— purporting to be by William Shakespeare — saw the light. "The Passionate Pilgrim" was a collection of amorous rhymes, by various known and unknown authors, in lyric, ballad, and sonnet form. Among known authors, it contained fragments of verse by Heywood, Marlowe, Barnefield, and Griffin, and snatches, too, of songs from the Shakespeare Plays. Neither Marlowe, Barnefield, nor Griffin, nor their representatives, appear to have raised any protest at the fraud. And certainly Shakespeare, whose verses they were not, raised none. He was alive, actively concerned in his London affairs, and could not have been ignorant of the publication. Moreover, he was rich and important, and what he could not have done by law he might have done by influence — procure removal of his name. What he did not see fit to do, Dr. Heywood, an author of some repute, but not of as much social account as Shakespeare, did. He publicly printed his protest, and compelled Jaggard to take the name "William Shakespeare" from the title-page. It has been restored, however. The contents, moreover, have been largely augmented by a further poem or threnos, "The Phœnix and the Turtle" (found in a book — "Love's Martyr; or, Rosalind's Complaint," said to be by one Robert Chester, printed in 1561 — reprinted by the New Shakespeare Society in 1878), and another called "A Lover's Complaint" (which was printed with the sonnets in 1609). But they all — of diverse and sundry authorship, and, as Swinburne says, cognate only by reason of the porcine quality of prurience — go in together, and nobody doubts to-day that William Shakespeare wrote the whole ollapodrida known as "The Passionate Pilgrim," and every word, line, and parcel thereof. "No explanation of this proceeding" (at the time of the first edition) "on Shakespeare's part is known to exist," says Mr. Richard Grant White, referring to Heywood's detection of the cheat. When we remember that not only this publication, but fifteen plays which even commentators admit that William Shakespeare did not write (but which they coyly print as "doubtful," now and then), no less than the poems and sonnets we are now considering, traveled under Shakespeare's name during his lifetime, we may be pretty sure that Mr. White knows of "no explanation," because none exists or ever did exist anywhere, or at any time.

Nor was this a solitary instance of Shakespeare's tacit consent to covinous use of his name. Says Mr. Halliwell Phillipps: "A far more remarkable operation in the same kind of knavery was perpetrated in the latter part of the following year by the publisher of the 'First Part of the Life of Sir John Oldcastle,' 1600, a play mostly concerned with the romantic adventures of Lord Cobham. Although this drama is known not only to have been composed by other dramatists, but also to have belonged to a theatrical company with which Shakespeare had then no manner of connection, it was unblushingly announced as his work by the publisher, Thomas Pavier, a shifty bookseller, residing at the grotesque sign of the 'Cat and Parrot,' near the Royal Exchange."[1]

[1] "Outlines," sixth edition, i. 164. In a postscript to his "Garden of Cyrus," Sir Thomas Browne complains that his name was being used to float books that he never wrote. See Bohn's edition of Browne's Works, vol. ii. p. 564.

This time there was no concealment of motive. The first edition did not sell. But when Shakespeare's name was attached the second had a wide and considerable circulation. But Mr. Phillipps, while indignant at Pavier, has no word of censure for the silent beneficiary of the fraud.

III. THE SONNETS.—That William Shakespeare took no part in the publication of these in 1609 is apparent from their dedication. Whether he refrained by reason of no interest in the material, or because quite as indifferent in their case as in the case of the fraudulent plays or poems, is, of course, matter for anybody's conjecture. This dedication has been so tortured and twisted and worried by commentators desiring to connect them with Lord Southampton as dedicatee and William Shakespeare as dedicator, that the only safety is to print it as it originally stood:

TO · THE · ONLIE · BEGETTER · OF ·
THESE· · INSVING · SONNETS ·
M! W. H. ALL · HAPINESSE ·
AND · THAT · ETERNETIE ·
PROMISED ·
BY ·
OVR · EVER-LIVING · POET ·
WISHETH ·
THE · WELL-WISHING ·
ADVENTVRER IN ·
SETTING ·
FORTH.

T. T.

Now, without wasting as many words as commentators have written volumes to prove the identity of "Mr. W. H.," it is quite apparent that — whoever he was — he was not Henry Wriothesley, Earl Southampton, who never was "Mr. W. H.," and never could have been, in the nature of things. And to anybody with a mind not already made up, it is equally impossible to conceive that these initials stand for William Herbert, Earl of Pembroke. Principally, of course, because, when simple Mr. William Herbert, the future earl was not in any historical or geographical vicinity to anybody who wrote sonnets or dedicated other people's sonnets to patrons. Nor was the boy at school as yet anybody's patron. But — exiling William Himself, William Hewes, William Hall, William Hart, and all the other Williams — this dedication, for a composition written in the turgid and tiresome prose of the day — albeit there is nothing therein to suggest a pen that ever wrote a line incorporated in a Shakespearean play — is singularly intelligible. Any publication in those times was properly styled "a venture," and the person launching a venture is naturally an "adventurer." "In setting forth," then, the adventurer, "T. T.," that is, the well-known printer, Mr. Thomas Thorpe, wishes some friend of his ("W. H.") all happiness and a long life. He is issuing a book of poetry, and expresses himself somewhat poetically. He describes the long life bespoken for his friend as "that eternity promised by our ever-living poet." And he alludes to Mr. W. H. as "the only begetter of these sonnets." All poets are by courtesy immortal, *i. e.*, "ever-living," and every poet promises eternity to somebody. But what is a "begetter"? — clearly one who gets or procures. "I have some cousin-germans at court," says Dekker in "Satriomastix," "shall beget you the reversion of the master of the king's revels." The procurer of these sonnets, then, feels himself at liberty to dedicate them to whom he will. Precisely, perhaps, as William Shakespeare dedicated the "Venus and Adonis" and the "Lucrece" to Southampton, as their "begetter"— seeing that the probabilities are something against his having been their author — so T. T. dedicates to his friend, Mr. W. H. Had W. H. been a noble lord, humble printer as T. T. was, the dedication by other than the noble lord's proper title would have been an insult rather than a compliment, and would have been just as insulting coming from William Shakespeare as coming from T. T. But, however read, it proves that the dedicator of a book needed not in those days to be its author.

But perhaps the sonnets printed as above were not the same as those which Meres says Shakespeare circulated among Shakespeare's private friends. In 1840 Mr. Hallam added a note to his mention of the sonnets to the effect that he had come to doubt whether these were the sonnets mentioned by Meres.[1] Mr. Hallam does not state his reasons. But they were probably something as follows: The sonnets are no sonnets, but a continuous poem. If Shakespeare wrote this poem, how could he have passed the separate stanzas around among his private friends as "sonnets"?

[1] "Literature of Europe," vol. iii. p. 300.

And how could he have consented to see them,
eleven years afterward, printed as one hundred
and fifty-four isolated "sonnets"? A precisely
parallel case would be to suppose that Lord Tennyson would silently suffer the Trübners or the
Longmans or any Victorian publishing house to
take his "May Queen" or "Princess," and, numbering the verses consecutively, print them as
"Rhymes" or Quatrains, or Madrigals, or what
not, "by Alfred Tennyson"! But, says Mr. Massey, this poem is not the poem of William Shakespeare's, but of Earl Southampton's, private
love-life! If so, why was it written by William
Shakespeare? And if William Shakespeare was
only hired by Southampton to write it, why was
it not circulated among Southampton's rather
than among Shakespeare's private friends? In
other words, among noblemen rather than actors,
among the court rather than the coulisse? Their
friends were not the same by any manner of
means. In the perspective of ages events are
foreshortened, and gaps of years and castes disappear. It is not strange, then, that we come to
forget, in the incessant coupling of the names of
Southampton and Shakespeare, the great social
gulf between the noble earl and the Stratford boy
who ran the Globe Theater. Admitting that the
earl patronized all the actors and poets of his day,
and among them Shakespeare, we must not draw
from that an incredible proposition that the rigid
social rules of Tudor days were relaxed; or, if
practically relaxed within the precincts of the
theater, that they were so interchangeably relaxed
in courtly circles that the peer and the peasant

were inseparable everywhere. One may be a very valuable patron without becoming alter ego of the patronized. And even if Southampton had been the Rothschild of his time, and able to make Shakespeare a present of £1000 (which equaled at least $25,000 to-day; Mr. White puts it at $30,000, and Mr. Halliwell Phillipps as high as $60,000), instead of the poor peer he was, even that would not make them yoke-fellows. But if Southampton knew Shakespeare, or Shakespeare Southampton, let it be demonstrated autobiographically or biographically, from some source other than the material called " biographies" of William Shakespeare. Let us find it in some of Southampton's papers, or in the archives of some of his family, descendants, contemporaries, or acquaintances. If Damon and Pythias are friends, let Damon have an opportunity, as well as Pythias, of testifying to their comity. Microscopical search for three hundred years has failed to unearth a trace of it. But, all the same, no account of William Shakespeare is ever printed of which a description of the Southampton - Shakespeare friendship is not a feature. The $25,000 story is fast disappearing from Shakespearean biography. The Southampton friendship must be bolstered up historically, or else follow it.

But, admitting that these sonnets were the same as mentioned by Meres, his list of Shakespearean works must either stand or fall in its integrity. Obviously we cannot, at this date, sort his testimony into what we wish and what we do not wish to believe. It will be remembered, that at the same time that Meres mentions the "Sugred

Sonnets" (and in the same connection), he also enumerates certain dramatic works as by William Shakespeare. But it is startling to discover that, while accepting the Meres mention as proof of the authorship of these sonnets, all commentators, living and dead, incontinently reject the Meres list of plays. There is no such play as "Love's Labour Won," and John Manningham, of the Middle Temple, says that the Shakespeare play founded on Plautus's "Menæchmi" was called "Twelfth Night," in 1602. Mr. Fleay finds in the "Romeo and Juliet" traces of Peele and Daniel. He agrees with Ritson that there are grave doubts as to Shakespeare's hand in the "Comedy of Errors." Upton, Hanmer, and most modern commentators doubt if the "Two Gentlemen of Verona" could possibly be written by the author of "Hamlet," even allowing for "periods" and "groups" and eras of "stopped" and "unstopped" endings, "run-on" lines, and all other marvelous triangulations of the text. "Titus Andronicus" is everywhere scouted as none of Shakespeare's. So long ago as 1687 Ravenscroft claimed information that William Shakespeare only "touched it up." But modern commentators disbelieve even this agency. "'Titus Andronicus' I do not consider," says Furnivall. "The play declares, as plainly as play can speak, 'I am not Shakespeare's; my repulsive subject; my blood and horrors are not and never were his.'" From Theobald down to White, Hudson, and Dowden, Shakespeareans are unanimous in relegating this play to the shades, and in insisting that Meres must have been a most unreliable chronicler whatever his status as a critic, in mentioning it as Shakespeare's. And, of course, from their unanimous verdict there can be no appeal. Meres's excuse may be that he was deceived by the theatrical conditions. For Shakespeare's claim to these plays is solid enough on proprietary grounds. But no such loophole of excuse or pis aller obtains as to these "sonnets among his private friends," Shakespeare's name on a title-page being not only no proof of, but — since his detection in "The Passionate Pilgrim" affair — actually a presumption against, his authorship. (A further evidence of this is that the 1640 or Cotes edition of the "Poems written by Wil. Shakespeare, gent," was a bunching of one hundred and forty-seven of these sonnets, scraps of the Heywood nugæ; "Lover's Complaint," sundry translations from Ovid; and other rhymes which have entirely disappeared from modern editions.) And there was no stage-right in non-theatrical verse which William Shakespeare could have purchased.

That the one hundred and fifty-four sonnets actually form a connected poem was unknown until about 1836, when Mr. Charles Armitage Brown (who shares with Coleridge the honor of having been their first reader) discovered their connection. Until then, while there were dozens of editions, the editors do not seem to have considered it necessary to read before editing — any more than Meres had thought it necessary to read before reviewing — them. (George Steevens declared that nothing but an act of parliament would make him read them, and he lived and died deprived of some of the most exquisite poetry in the language in consequence.) Nothing is more evident, therefore, than that these unread Sonnets were kept alive in their Elizabethan days, as thereafter, simply by the popularity of Shakespeare's name — much as the mere rumor of that name attached to a bit of anonymous doggerel has kept his bones alike from inspection of the curious and the canonization of worshipers.

Now, William Shakespeare, loved and loving gentleman as he was, is understood to have been very shrewd in money matters. None knew the meaning of poverty better than he. Had he not been so, and rightly so, his father would never have stirred outside the door; the Lambert mortgages would have remained unpaid; nor would the Quineys have swarmed around for their kinsman's crumbs, and nudged each other to look up good things where he could place the wealth they saw him hoarding. Is it not, therefore, impossible to suppose him ignorant of or indifferent to the cash value of his own name? Is it not quite as impossible, again, to believe that, if printed at his own instance, he allowed his publisher to dedicate a book to one of his (the publisher's) friends; that if dedicated to either of his own patrons, Pembroke or Southampton, he (Shakespeare) was unable to write his own dedication; or, writing it, asked his publisher to sign it? If the escape from these difficulties is not by way of assumption that Shakespeare sold the use of his name to the printers of anonymous poetry precisely as he appears to have sold it to the printers of anonymous plays, then those difficulties are hopeless indeed! The plays, on the ground of stage-right or of copyright, might be Shakespeare's, even if not composed by him. But the Sonnets, if his, he must either have written or not written. He could not have done both.

To recapitulate. Either these "Sonnets" are those mentioned as circulating among Shakespeare's private friends prior to 1598, or they are not. If they are, they are as doubtfully his as is the rest of the list of literary matter given by Meres, so far as we know. If they are not, then they have no claim to be called Shakespeare's except from the fact that his name was put on the title-pages of three books of verses among which verses they appeared, at one time only four of them, at another more of them, and at another less; and the value of title-page evidence as to the authorship of Tudor literature we are able to very adequately estimate. In the one case Meres, not reading the literary matter he eulogizes as "sugred," supposed it to consist of "Sonnets"; and so to the support of the Shakespearean authorship has only hearsay testimony to offer. But, inadmissible as this sort of evidence is anyway, what becomes of it when Mr. Massey and Mr. Brown dispose of what little probability of the Shakespearean authorship is left over from Meres, by testifying that Shakespeare's Sonnets have nothing to do with Shakespeare, but are a record of Southampton's private amours! And, in either case, even a Shakespeare must base his claim to literary matter on something stronger than a legend on a title-page.

Nobody can refuse to William Shakespeare personal love, admiration, and gratitude. But what he never claimed let us not supply to him. The tendency to enlarge the attributes of those we worship is as laudable as is the effort of a good judge — according to Littleton — to amplify his jurisdiction. But the tendency may be produced, not only to absurdity, but to disastrous moral ruin. The boy Ireland was disgraced by making what was only legitimate literary parody over into a hateful lie. And what sadder sight has this generation seen than John Payne Collier, a scholar who for fifty years enriched English archæology and letters, dying in almost unnoticed obscurity, shipwrecked by a temptation to discover what was undiscoverable?

A late writer on the legalisms of Shakespeare takes for his legend Hamlet's question, "Why should not this be the skull of a lawyer?" It seems by no means sure that there is any skull at all in that grave under the chancel in Stratford Church. There is no name on the slab that covers it. The mural tablet says distinctly that the remains of William Shakespeare lie "within this monument"; and the grave of Mrs. Shakespeare and her husband are not pointed out as one and the same, though we are told that she did earnestly desire to be laid in the same grave with the body of her departed liege. It seems the world is never to know what is in that grave. For the Shakespeareans are still scared from opening it to see, by a witch's curse three hundred years old (albeit it is only against "moving," and says nothing about looking at certain bones); and, if anybody but a Shakespearean attempts to touch things, the Stratford beadle proposes to pitch him into the Avon forthwith.

Surely no man lived who more reverenced Shakespeare and all that sounded of him than the lamented Dr. Ingleby. Himself a life trustee of the tomb at Stratford, he urgently demanded that the tomb be opened and its contents reverently perpetuated, instead of being allowed to suffer entire disappearance and obliteration by the processes of time. He prepared a careful volume to show that other poets — lesser men — had been so honored by loving countrymen, who even after death continued them in grateful worship. Why should not we honor William Shakespeare by opening his grave and enlisting all the resources of science to preserve whatever mortal is still to be found therein — where every passing day leaves less and less to venerate? How much longer is this pious and patriotic duty to be delayed? While we are making our speeches about Shakespeare, organizing societies and pageants, and writing books about him, we permit his actual bones to rot ignobly, because — because some cobbler, by an oversight of his betters, managed to scratch a witch's palindrome upon the stone that was to cover them! It is ridiculous. How, seriously, can nineteenth-century England suppose her neglect of her so great son justified by a piece of anonymous doggerel? It is some time since Englishmen wore dried bats' eyes for charms and shivered over incantations. Besides, it is always a coup d'esprit to outwit a wizard's curse. Dr. Ingleby and Lord Roland Gower have both shown how easy it would be to dodge this one by merely changing the gender or number of the "frend" who was to "move" the bones. Even, therefore, if it had ever been proposed to "move" the bones from the custody of Trinity, or from Stratford (which it certainly never has been), that rubbish has survived its jurisdiction.

But there is another view to be considered, and one which, as a proposition of law, I believe to be unassailable. There nowhere exists a right to demand that succeeding generations shall respect any one man's place of sepulture. As against one's contemporaries and the vicinage, indeed, a dead man's representatives may resist encroachment upon the earth where his ashes lie. But as against posterity — never; otherwise civilization must find itself brought to a limit, for all earth is a graveyard, nor can we tread except upon what has once been human mold. To be sure, the exact conditions have not yet arrived here, since Shakespeare's grave is still under a consecrated roof. But some day even Stratford's Trinity will crumble, and what was once Shakespeare be desecrated. Even, therefore, at the risk of its being called desecration, is it not better for this generation — to whom Shakespeare is so much and means so much — to disturb that tomb, rather than that another generation (who may know and love less, or not at all) should trouble it?

It seems to me a peerless and paramount duty, rather than a privilege or a license, to open, repair, and restore the Shakespearean sepulcher. Probably not even a Stratford vestryman — certainly no one of the national trustees of the birthplace — will claim that after two hundred and seventy years of utter neglect no repairs or restorations are needed. Perhaps the Stratford vestryman is chary of restoring the tomb, from experience of sundry of his own methods of "restoring" the noble pile of Trinity (which remind something of Timur Beg's method of restoring the East, or of Herod's restoration of infants), and, if so, he should be thanked for keeping hands off. But the world has a share in that tomb under the roof of Trinity, and could doubtless find archæologists at once tender and expert for the task!

But, supposing the mortal remains of William Shakespeare to lie in that grave, who and what was he when living? It is demonstrated that he was no attorney's clerk, as Lord Campbell believed, but a ripe, learned, and profound lawyer; so saturated with precedents that at once in his sublimest and sweetest flights he colors everything with legal dyes, sounding every depth and shoal of poetry in only the juridicial key. And, moreover, he was a constitutional aristocrat, who believed in the established order of things, and wasted not a word of all his splendid eulogy upon any human right not in his day already guaranteed by charters or by thrones. But while the rolls at Westminster and the Inns of Court contain no allusion to William Shakespeare the barrister, the records of the British stage show that, just at the time the text makes him out the lawyer, he is managing two great theaters in London. Other documents exhibit him as a large speculator in real estate, enjoying an income of $25,000 per annum, at about the date when Messrs. Massey and Brown believe him to have been a poet scribbling sonnets to Lord Southampton, sonnets which, on perusal, turn out to be not sonnets, but together a sort of rhymed diary of Southampton's own private love affairs (at least they coincide with those affairs by a little squeezing, according to Massey, Brown, and others). Add to all these that William Shakespeare was at once a butcher's apprentice and a student of the Stratford grammar-school; that the curriculum at that grammar-school consisted entirely of a venerable birch-rod, Lily's Latin paradigms, the "Criss-Cross Row," and the Church catechism; that the graduate of this grammar-school (for if, as the Baconians allege, he did not attend that temple of learning, it is an eternal verity that he went to no other educational institution) wrote the "Venus and Adonis" as the very first "heir of his invention," etc., etc.; and no wonder our brains reel when we try to ask ourselves, Who was this immortal, anyhow, and who wrote the divine page called his? Was this the William Shakespeare who in silence repeatedly allowed his own name to be credited with the works of other men, and who encouraged the attributing of whatever was splendid or successful in literature to himself? A man who in these days could permit himself to become beneficiary of so fraudulent a transaction as was the "Passionate Pilgrim" affair of 1609, could not have long survived the moral effect of his act. Was the Tudor sense more callous?

But, whatever the name, and whoever the author — plays, poems, sonnets, we have them all! — all bound in one mighty book, that age cannot wither nor custom stale; perennial in our hearts and households forever. If a word is better than the truth; if the name "William Shakespeare" is of more value than historical identification of the magnificent and matchless literature which the world worships as Shakespearean; if — as pipes a bard of recent gush —

> " Though modern science claims, 'tis very plain,
> Memories are written in the folded brain;
> We feel them in our hearts — and feeling knows
> Profounder wisdom than our science shows —
> The spiritual, fanciful ideal—" [1]

then by all means let traditionists hug the name! But be the substance ours — the Book!

[1] William Leighton. "Shakespeareana," vol. i. p. 1.

IV

"Something Touching The Lord Hamlet"

THE acting conceptions of Hamlet have been almost as numerous as the tragedians who have personated him. Burbage, the great Hamlet of Shakespeare's own day, is said to have required from the dramatist's hand the queen's description of the prince as "fat and scant of breath." Betterton, of course, omitted it, being (as indeed were Garrick, Kean, and as is Edwin Booth) small of stature and of meager build. Betterton also omitted the passage commencing

"Angels and ministers of grace, defend us,"

while Garrick discarded the entire graveyard scene of the fifth act, and took such other liberties as became a true inheritor of the traditions of Dryden and Davenant, who worked over the great text quite at pleasure, turning Macbeth's witches into a ballet, giving Miranda a brother, and making Shylock a low comedian with a red nose, or Portia a soubrette, with imitations of leading local barristers, as happened to hit the ribald tone of their day.

But while the actor may not be asked to overlook exigencies of taste and audience, or managers to maintain a purity of context at the expense of empty houses and bankruptcy, editors, commentators, and critics cannot be permitted an equal license of interpretation. These may, indeed, put their multitudinous knowledge into foot-notes; but between the foot-notes and the text a broad line is to be drawn, below which is their prerogative, but above which they can only read like the rest of us.

And yet when Ophelia exclaims, " Oh! what a noble mind is here o'erthrown," she appears to have given the keynote to about two centuries of commentary. Doubtless to that gentle lady so did appear the princely lover, who chided her in brusque speech, and with rough denials dismissed her from his presence. But I cannot help thinking that the exegesis which credits Hamlet the Dane (as we have him in the First Folio) with madness, indecision, a disjointed and palsied will, or other insignia of a mind diseased, is drawn not so much from a desire to corroborate Ophelia as from a certain finical overstudy of the crude "Hamblett" of Belleforest, or that earlier Saga of a rude and formative literature, the "Amleth" of Saxo Grammaticus; if, indeed, it be anything else than a supercilious and redundant sapiency and show of profundity in the commentator himself. That our average Shakespearean commentator is given to overmuch "letting of empty buckets into empty wells" is very familiar criticism. There are many commentaries to write and very little to write about, and the temptation to archæological minutiæ on the one hand, or esthetic rhapsody on the other, is perhaps too strong for resistance. But a ruthless sweeping away of both alike will, I think, reveal the Hamlet that Shakespeare himself wanted; and this Hamlet, I think, will turn out a very different sort of person from the one the commentators manufacture for us.

Prince Hamlet — as we have him in the First Folio — seems to me a manly, punctilious, and rational gentleman, with a legally balanced mind, conservative in method and tendency, with a lawyer's caution and respect for the conventional and established order of things; above all, suspicious of intuitions, surmise, and guess-work. Far from being infirm of purpose, like that whilom Macbeth who let "I dare not" wait upon "I would" — who dared not to think, much less to look upon, what his own hands had wrought — here was, it seems to me, a man whose deliberate and solemn judgment, once committed to an act, was suffered neither to relax nor hurry its due issue and performance. Surely that was an impatient and impertinent ghost who came a second time from his prison-house to complain of the "almost blunted purpose" of such a man as this! He had taken a prince's word, this ghost, that while memory held its sway his message should be remembered, and should have rested in the assurance. For the prince had weighed long and considered deeply before giving his word or putting any reliance upon or believing in ghosts at all. He is rather disposed, on the whole, to jeer at the very idea of such things as unpent spirits, released from their confine, revisiting the glimpses of this moon; albeit in the days of Shakespeare all kinds of specters, supernatural and disembodied shapes, were conceded a constant interposition in sublunary matters: nay, men were put to death upon their testimony for many years after Shakespeare's own funeral.

The story of "Hamlet" is not a record of usurpation, murder, blood, and death like "Macbeth," nor of domestic tragedy like "Othello," nor of madness like "Lear." Rather is it the history of purposes adhered to and of the end which compassed them. The man who, living consecrated to a purpose, accomplishes that purpose before he dies, is not ordinarily held to be a failure, infirm of resolution, weak and listless of that purpose. To every self-regarding, trustful, determined, and just man must come, at some time, deliberation as to method; as to consequences—hesitancies, interruptions of time and circumstances. Did not Prince Hamlet, perhaps, eat and sleep between the ghostly interview and the catastrophe of his revenge, during the visit of the players, their rehearsals and performance, the accidental killing of Polonius, the interval in which news of that accident could have reached Laertes in France, and his recall, the embassy to England, the escape, the return, the funeral of Ophelia? Was there no more interval to these than the waits and betweens of the play at our theaters?

Had the dramatist whose completed work is before us in the First Folio desired to portray a madman named Hamlet, he had plenty of models at hand. The Belleforest "Hamblett" would rend his clothes, "wallow in the mire, run through the streets with fouled face, like a man distraught, not speaking one word but such as seemed to proceed from madness and mere frenzy; all his actions and gestures being no other than the right countenance of a man wholly deprived of all reason and understanding; in such sort that he seemed fit for nothing but to make sport to the pages and ruffling courtiers that attended in the courts of his step-father." But is it not the patent fact that Shakespeare followed no such model; that he deliberately rejected the childish Saga and the almost equally crude "Hamblett" tale, and created a new Hamlet with attributes of his own, whose story bore only the most attenuated resemblance to these? And if Shakespeare deliberately discarded all the former Amleths and Hambletts, why should we restore them? What have they to do with Hamlet the Dane, in inky cloak, who did not rant nor grovel, but cherished only

"That within which passeth show"?

To me this somber and stately prince bears no likeness to predecessors who were very mountebanks in silly apings of a mind diseased. Is it not the very paradox of esthetic criticism to leave the perfect work of a master, and go back to the childhood of a re-utilized tale for an inconsequent and irresponsible lunatic "who fails to act in any definite line of consistent purpose; neglects what he deems a sacred duty; wastes himself in trifling occupations; descends to the ignoble part of a court-jester; breaks the heart of a lady he dearly loves; uselessly and recklessly kills her father, with no sign of sorrow or remorse for the deed; insults a brother's legitimate grief at her grave, and finally goes stumbling to the catastrophe of his death the most complete failure, in the direction of the avowed purpose of his life, ever recorded"? [1] The esthete who thus declaims, might, perhaps, have labored under provincial disadvantage. Old Dr. Johnson, to be sure, once delivered himself of a valuable note to the effect that "the pretended madness of Hamlet causes much mirth"; but surely, not since the old doctor's day has a metropolitan English stage so interpreted the masterpiece of a master.

To begin with, it is to be remembered that our Hamlet is an Englishman, and the Denmark in which he moved — an English court, ruled by an absolute monarch of the Tudor cast, one Claudius, a very passable Henry VIII., not quite so far along in uxoriousness at his taking-off, perhaps, but well in for it. No amount of scenic or critical realism will enable us to confess a further obligation in Shakespeare to Denmark than for a very limited stock of allusion and nomenclature. There certainly is neither habitude, cast of thought, method, or custom that can be called Danish or that suggests itself as characteristic of Denmark's warlike, simple, sturdy and unphilosophic inhab-

[1] "The Subjection of Hamlet," p. 16. William Leighton. Philadelphia: Lippincott & Co., 1882.

itants of any dynasty or date, in the salient points and characters of the play.

The characteristic of the particular tragedian who enacts Hamlet — the blonde wig, the Danish court-dress, the mantle of fur; the portraits hung on the chamber-wall, or worn "in little" on the actor's breast; the Tudor scenery which Garrick used, or the barbaric court with its rude arches and columns hung in arras; its figures draped in habit of old Scandinavia — all these, while alike creditable to the study and conception of this or that actor (and valuable as relieving the spectator from a too monotonous usuetude), are still redundant, if we are to ask who, after all, Hamlet, in the mind's eye of his creator, Shakespeare, was.

Hamlet, to the true critic, "in spite of all temptations to belong to other nations," must ever be and remain an Englishman. From the Prince's philosophy of life and duty, the courtier phrases of Polonius and Osric, to the burlesque dialect and dialectics of the grave-diggers, every speech and sense put into the mouth of the dramatis personæ is purely English — English thought, methods, habits of reasoning, analogies, and expression are everywhere before us. There was nothing incestuous in the marriage of Claudius to his brother's widow, by Danish laws, traditions, or customs. The technical denial of consecrated sepulture to suicides, the polishing of young gallants at the French court, the employment of strolling players — every act, law, tenure, or custom on which the action of the play is anywhere suspended — is English, and English only.

Add to all these that the succession from Claudius is stated in such unmistakable terms of English law that nothing but sheer good-nature can admit a flavor of Denmark into it.

> ". . . Our valiant Hamlet
> Did slay this Fortinbras, who by a sealed compact,
> Well ratified by law and heraldry,
> Did forfeit, with his life, all those his lands
> Which he stood seized of, to the conqueror;
> Against the which, a moiety competent
> Was gaged by our king; which had returned
> To the inheritance of Fortinbras
> Had *he* been vanquisher, as, by the same covenant,
> His fell to Hamlet." — (I. i. 87.)

Had the wager between the two kings been a legal one in England (and by importing the legend Shakespeare so assumed it), then the above is an exact statement of the result, by Anglo-Saxon tenure, in equity. Technical terms of the lawyers' craft are "packed into this passage so closely as to form the greater part of its composition," says Mr. Davis. Others have shown that not only was the argument of the grave-digger a legitimate travesty on the old case of Hales *vs.* Petit, but that in the entire graveyard scene clowns, priests, court and all travel closely within the customs sanctioned by English canon law of the period. And Horatio, at the last (as if conscious that a Platonic suicide were out of place in Denmark), explains that he is "more an antique Roman than a Dane."

What we are contemplating, then, is not a Danish but an English Hamlet — a Hamlet as he left the hands of Shakespeare, his creator; a Hamlet dispossessed of the personal equation of his particular interpreter, or the dust-heap of this or that particular annotator; the Hamlet, in short, of the play as we have it finally in the First Folio, not as it might have been or ought to have been according to this or that more or less adult alienist or protagonist. The oldest son of his father, he should have been king on his father's decease. But while at Heidelberg, his uncle has cut, not only the purse of the Empire, but, by marrying the queen, "the rule"; and — Hamlet not consenting — has usurped the throne, not only as king-consort but king in fact. Therefore Prince Hamlet is simply (for us, who cannot go behind the facts) an English prince in waiting — the crown-prince — in his minority entitled to princely maintenance, but only so long as he remains a cipher in the state. In this sense only can the King say to him, "Be as ourselves in Denmark." The crown-prince who should trifle with state affairs would have become, in Tudor usage, on the instant, a crown prisoner instead.

This Prince Hamlet is restive. His first speech is a sotto voce bitterly expressive of this very status. Left alone a moment later, a friend, a late arrival from a German university, tells of a ghostly visitor, and brings witnesses to his story of the apparition — which, however, Hamlet declines, even upon the testimony of these three, his sworn friend among them, to believe. But his curiosity is aroused, and he proposes to see for himself. Just here the industrious gentlemen who find "trilogies" and "groups" among the Canon Plays might well pause to point us to the fact that this ghost of Hamlet's father is the only ghost in all Shakespeare which allows itself to be visible to outsiders, to spectators who are merely third persons to its business or message. Cæsar and Banquo, and Henry and Clarence and the young princes sent their shades only to the party who had unkindly assisted in their mortal taking-off. Even if not an intentional proof, certainly it is an afforded proof of the conservatism and manliness of Prince Hamlet that to convince him something even more than "the sensible and true avouch" of his own senses is dispatched. A disbeliever in ghosts is to be made over into a believer, and the mettle to be worked upon requires nothing less than cumulative presumptive evidence. This stage passed, however, Hamlet consents to see the Ghost alone. But even afterward, although profoundly impressed with the interview, he will not yet admit to his friends that he believes. He makes light of the whole affair, and, to assure them how faintly the eerie rencontre has touched his reason, puns and quibbles and jokes about it with careless, even heartless, badinage. We had supposed that it was only your true German mind, with its strata of "under-soul" and "over-soul," which can see in this badinage, even if it be a little forced, the gambols of a maddened mind. But it seems there are others who forget that it is only with things familiar that we joke and trifle. Had Hamlet been afraid of that ghost, those of us who are willing to allow Shakespeare somewhat to say of his own creations will not be indisposed to admit — in the teeth even of the vast German introspection — that Shakespeare's text might, perhaps, have so made it appear.

But whether Hamlet be or no, Hamlet's friends are afraid of it; and so, like the prince that he is, he puts himself courteously into a frame of tolerance with their mood. In heroic vein he swears them on his sword to secrecy; and then, when ready for the whisper, puts them by with platitudes; in short, acts as any gentleman would who finely, but firmly and irrevocably, wrests it out of any one's power to trifle with what he will, nevertheless, in private deeply ponder over. Firmly, but yet playfully, so as not to wound the feelings of those to whose kindness he is, and may hereafter wish to become, indebted for his evidence, he refuses to share his secret; and when, from reflection, causation, and rational assessment of cumulative proof, he finds the ghost's statements walking all-fours with his own intuitive perceptions, even then this legal-minded, this exact young prince will press to no conclusion—will neither upon supernatural testimony nor intuition base an overt act. He will, for the present, do nothing more than doubt; and, lawyer-like, he still gives the benefit of the doubt to the de facto King. Even the vision which three other sane men have seen may yet be the chimera of his own melancholy:

> "The spirit that I have seen
> May be the devil; . . . yea, and perhaps
> Out of my weakness and my melancholy,
> As he is very potent with such spirits,
> Abuses me to damn me."

And then he adds,—again the lawyer and acute and accomplished weigher of evidence,—

> "I'll have grounds
> More relative than this!"

Wherein lies the "madness," so far, at least, in the mental processes of Hamlet, Prince of Denmark?

There is a play, out of the Italian, made upon the murder of one Gonzago. Here are strolling players, who have a power, nevertheless, of recitation, of which Hamlet himself has felt the force. Hamlet has heard that one's conscience may be — may, has been — reached by such players as these. He conceives a plan of using this very play about the Gonzago murder to test the story he has heard, if so be it may deduce "matter more relative." He revises the dumb-show of the act of murder to suit the one portrayed by the Ghost, interpolates a speech or two of his own, and gives minute direction to the actor intrusted with them how to render his lines, beyond all peradventure effectively. And in the result, and not till then, will the prince recognize the "sensible and true avouch" not only of those senses to which the apparition has appeared, but of a whole court. Then, and not till then, will this "madman," this crazed Hamlet, "take the Ghost's word for a thousand pounds."

And now ensues a scene which for two centuries or so the chorus of commentators has declared to be a breaking-forth of Prince Hamlet's dementia. But what says the play? Shall not this pensive, this calm and self-repressing Hamlet at least allow himself a burst of exultation at the complete success of his long-maturing schemes? That he does not declaim in rotund periods, that he does not call on the avenging gods, is purely characteristic of the balanced and self-correcting brain. Why, he says, in relaxing vein to his friend, if my fortunes should some day turn against me, don't you think I could get a living with a strolling company of players myself? Yes, indeed, I think you might at least claim in time half a share in the profits of the troupe, says Horatio. To which Hamlet replies, still in complaisant mood, Nothing less than a whole share for me; and recites in the popular vein a verse, wanting the final rhyme, which Horatio suggests could have been completed in perfect appropriateness to the occasion:

"For thou dost know, O Damon dear,
    This realm dismantled was
Of Jove himself; and now reigns here
    A very—'Claudius!'"[1]

only for "Claudius" Hamlet says "pajock" (that is, "peacock," or anything that is mere pretense and show without substance). The playfulness of two friends unbending may hardly pass as madness with minds not maddish themselves.

The parry of harsh words with poor Lady Ophelia, leading up to the abrupt dismissal, affords another recitement for the "madman" view. Per-

---

[1] This reading is suggested to me by Mr. Davis, and seems to me far more likely than the usual run of conjectural emendation. Horatio says to Hamlet, "You might have rhymed." And "Claudius" is certainly as good a rhyme to "dismantled was," as Hamlet's earlier

"It came to pass
As most like it was,"

or his later:

"For if the king likes not the comedy,
Why then, belike, he likes it not, perdy."

Besides, the text shows that a "Claudius" is exactly what Hamlet is telling Horatio, that "dismantled Denmark" now possesses in the place of "Jove himself."

haps all lovers' vows and dicers' oaths are madness. But here are lovers' vows reconsidered; and reconsideration is not quite the regulation act of a madman. In the leisure of a prince, no doubt, Hamlet has had love-passages with the sweet lady. But Ophelia, though not possessing the powers for mischief possessed by Cordelia (spoiled and petted daughter of a doting sire, who, because she would not say she loved him better than anything else, precipitated all the misery and terror of that terrible tragedy upon a fond old head), and injuring nobody but herself, would never have made a wife for Hamlet. To be sure, attention is turned from the poor girl's weaknesses by the domination of the tragedy in which she figures, and by her final sacrifice to its inexorable situation. But nothing can conceal the want of character, of faith, of love for Hamlet even (that hero with whom all other women who have ever lived are in love), which marks her every pose. Who can forget, for example, that Samson and Delilah scene in which the girl becomes a spy's accomplice and draws her lover into speech for the benefit of old Polonius behind the arras?—a plot arranged with perfection of circumstantiality beforehand by Ophelia and Polonius together in full hearing of the orchestra. But, apart from the easy complaisance that would make her Polonius's willing tool, we know that it was only the exceeding commonplace which was Ophelia's characteristic. Witness Hamlet's attempts to open a conversation with this wallflower. She cannot even talk about the weather:

HAMLET. Lady, shall I lie in your lap?
OPHELIA. No, my lord.
HAMLET. I mean, shall I lie my head in your lap?

OPHELIA. Ay, my lord.
HAMLET. Do you think I meant country matters?
OPHELIA. I think nothing, my lord.

And she doubtless told the truth. Disconcerted with his failure, Hamlet makes a rather coarser speech than even the license of the age allowed. But the gentle complaisance of the commonplace is not interrupted thereby.

OPHELIA. What is, my lord?
HAMLET. Nothing.
OPHELIA. You are merry, my lord.
HAMLET. Who, I?
OPHELIA. Ay, my lord!

Which would discourage even a Hamlet. The prince makes one more attempt, however; but, except that Ophelia overlooks his entendre, and corrects him as to the date of the late king's death:—"Nay, 'tis twice two months, my lord," and asks of the first player who appears:

"What means this, my lord?" and "Will he tell us what this show meant?"—Ophelia has nothing to offer in the way of entertainment. As lovers' interviews go, the dainty banter between Rosalind and Orlando, or (brief as it is, and only Shakespeare could have afforded to make it so brief) the flirtation of Bianca and Lucentio, or even the rather metallic badinage of Beatrice and Benedick, are certainly prettier reading. Clearly, Ophelia is not a lover's heaven, intellectually, for Hamlet. The death of her father, not the loss of Hamlet's love, drives the poor girl mad. In her madness we see her revealing no depths of emotion, but rather mixing nursery tales (such as that the owl was a baker's daughter) with passing songs, thus betraying the very inmost of her, and leading Laertes, in recognition of her vacant mind, to mumble sadly, "thoughts and remembrance fitted" (*i. e.*, mingled all in one). The deep pathos of the history need not indeed be blinked to see that here was no bride for Hamlet, however he may have amused himself with the girl. But what matters poor Ophelia to the now gruesome story of the play? Now that the Ghost's story has become a truth to the deep-thinking man, now that he sees how henceforth his is a life committed to great purposes, there must be no more sports with Amaryllis in the shade, nor with the tangles of Nerea's hair; no more of marriages. There must be harsh words sooner or later, and abrupt speeches. They may as well come now as further on. A murderous and usurping king is to be done for, a dear father murdered to be avenged. After that, Ophelia again, perhaps. But, until the times have been set right and the cursed spite of duty performed, it is needs must to wipe away all trivial, fond records. They, with all saws of books, all forms, all pressures past, all dilettante matter in idle courtier life or at Wittenberg by youth and observation copied, must be expunged from the book and volume of a brain hereafter to be filled alone by that dear father's commandment, brought by that father's own perturbed spirit to mortality again. Indeed, we have found no madness yet. Perhaps it were better for Prince Hamlet if we had. Even in this inter-scene it is not hard to recognize the tender reluctance of the gentleman who is obliged, in harsh half-dialogue and half-soliloquy, to tell the lady that she must release for ever all thought of the man who perhaps loved her once. It might, we even think, have been kindlier done by taking the Lady Ophelia herself into a prince's confidence. The woman who loved a Hamlet might have acquiesced in his honor and the noblesse oblige of it. At least, a woman like Macbeth's lady would have acquiesced. But perhaps Ophelia was not a Lady Macbeth.

So far we go with the text. Hamlet so decides, and we are reading, not composing, his story — reading it, not from Saxo Grammaticus or Belleforest, or the esthetic commentators, but from Shakespeare. Hamlet assumes aberration, perhaps to soften his cruelty, perhaps in cold blood; but, anyhow, Ophelia is to be sacrificed, and sacrificed she is.

Thereafter, the Ghost's word once taken, we see Hamlet sword in hand. Twice he strikes at the King, who has, in the face of the court, confessed the murder of his predecessor (confessed it certainly as plainly as Macbeth at the banquet revealed the taking-off of Banquo). The first time, Hamlet drops his point because King Claudius is at his prayers, and the prince will not run the risk of having England (that is his Denmark) take its priest's cue and canonize a sovereign slain, like Becket, at the altar; the second time, so luck will have it, kills Polonius instead. Conscience-stricken as he is, Claudius yet proposes to make things endurable for himself. He has this troublesome prince announced as mad to the court (to whom explanations of the killing of Polonius and of that scene at the play are in order), and proclaims that the throne, in tenderest solicitude, will arrange that he be sent abroad for change of scene and treatment. Outside it is bulletined to the populace that Prince Hamlet is dispatched on embassy to England to exact a long-delayed installment of tribute-money. But such items leak through the sieve of courts, and the very grave-diggers have the truth of it. Had Hamlet been the madman the commentators make him and Ophelia thought him, he had, perhaps, never penetrated the subterfuge. But he had been on his guard against plots to get him out of the way. Even when the King had called him "cousin" and "son," and invited him to "be as ourselves in Denmark," Hamlet had been swift to interpret the purposes for which Rozencrantz and Guildenstern were imported, and had mentioned to those insinuating gentlemen that he was not quite yet bereft of reason; nay, nor a pipe to be played upon. He sees it to his advantage to accompany and outwit the spies, and he does it with rare effectiveness. But our commentator is not disconcerted with this ruse contre ruse, and is ready with his hermeneutics; cites many learned works in mental pathology, and shows how normal to a mind diseased is a certain penetrating shrewdness. Hamlet having been pronounced stark mad to begin with, all the res gestæ is to be bent to that end, and bent it accordingly is.

But one scene more is to intervene ere the purpose of a prince is made a fact accomplished — the scene at poor Ophelia's grave. To read madness into the intense pathos and philosophy of that monologue over Yorick's skull and the mortality that turns Cæsars into clay, puts even our commentators to their reading. But they do it somehow. It is a tribute to the vast penetration of the people, to the great common consent of mankind, that this scene will subdue and dominate and hold the breath of vast audiences, and that not an individual will miss the modulated lesson of it all. How many of these vast audiences read, or think of reading, a volume of our commentators in order to comprehend that exquisite height of dramatic intensity? Doubtless not one. And yet our commentator will write, and the old bookstalls will teem with the books so written, and the copies are always choice finds because "uncut."

That could hardly be a chronicle of a human life which recorded that its subject never lost his patience or his temper. It must be confessed that a very few moments after this high strain, Prince Hamlet is human — is sane enough to entirely lose his. He has been through much. And to a man so deeply conscious of the perspective of events, so keenly cutting below the surface and into the motives and hearts of men, so contemptuous of mere words and noise and phrases, to see Laertes, tricked out in the fopperies of France — playing maudlin mourner (however sincerely), where he, Hamlet, had suppressed everything — it was hardly to be borne without a little touch of nature. But he is not long beside himself. In not one single item of action, under no touch of mental agony or doubt, does Hamlet cease to be a gentleman. He apologizes to Horatio for his moment of temper:

"But I am very sorry, good Horatio,
That to Laertes I forgot myself . . .
. . . But, sure, the bravery of his grief did put me
Into a towering passion."

And, not satisfied with this, begs pardon of Laertes most humbly:

"Give me your pardon, sir; I've done you wrong."

For surely a brother has a right to mourn in whatsoever vein he pleases at his sister's grave! He knows when he rants that a hostile court are taking notes to pin lunacy once more upon him, and he rants when it serves his purpose that the court should so annotate him. He contents himself:

"I loved you ever; but 'tis no matter;
Let Hercules himself do what he may,
The cat will mew, the dog will have his day!"

The excitement of return; of the meditation on mortality, on Yorick's skull and on Cæsar turned to clay; of the funeral in consecrated ground and the sudden confronting of the court, are subdued into only just this little measure. After all, the cat will mew, the dog will have his day — and so, enough.

With unerring perception, once more a calm and determined man, Hamlet falls in with the King's second subterfuge of the wager, and instantly recognizes the perfect and fitting opportunity — for all these days, months, and years awaited — sent by Fate at last. At last he will have a weapon in his hand in full view of the court and in the presence of the King — a King not at prayers, but on his throne. He will make short work of him now. The matter is out of scheming, and the prince has only to bide the hour. The weight of the disjointed times off his mind, he has leisure and mood for trifling. He can fool Osric to the top of his bent, or he may for the first time talk of himself to his only friend: "Thou wouldst not think how ill's all here about my heart; but it is no matter." But—when Horatio would undertake to put off the sword-play,— "Not a whit. . . . If it be now, 'tis not to come; if it be not to come, it will be now; if it be not now, yet it will come; the readiness is all." The readiness of long years, the readiness that never has relaxed through all the interruption of events — the readiness is all; and here it is!

There is surely very little of the "court jester" in the closing scene, when the dying Hamlet, although he has accomplished his never-relented-from purpose, and has no wish to live, yet—as his blood ebbs—remembers that this accomplished purpose may be set down to a moment's impulse, and the long, silent struggle for opportunity, the once more accorded lesson of revenge, be never known by those whose judgment he could yet wish kind to the last prince of a lapsed dynasty! Perhaps Hamlet foresaw — let us admit the fancy for a moment — the long line of commentators who to-day, as for the last one hundred years, are interrupting the reader of Prince Hamlet's story at every word by superimposed numeral or asterisk or other zodiacal sign, to ask him if he is quite sure he understands what he is reading, and wouldn't rather please stop and see what a nice little wheelbarrow-load of archaic and dusty débris they have just trundled up and emptied at this, that, and the other point; who are bending, perhaps, all their little sapiency to prove the incapacity, the shiftlessness, the puling imbecility, vacillation, and all the rest of it, of Hamlet the Dane — perhaps Prince Hamlet saw all this in his mind's eye when he said to Horatio:

> "O good Horatio! what a wounded name,
> Things standing thus unknown, shall live behind me!
> If thou didst ever hold me in thy heart,"

(for Horatio was himself proposing to drink the cup and follow his friend)

> "Absent thee from felicity awhile,
> And in this harsh world draw thy breath in pain,
> To tell my story."

— Endure the buffetings of life to say a word for me; show why I broke Ophelia's heart, by mischance killed her harmless old father, why I took the Ghost's word for a thousand pounds; put down the poisoned cup, and tarry here to report me and my cause aright — nothing extenuate, but tell them the story of harsh fate, and of my duty all, all done! "If thou didst ever hold me in thy heart," do this for Hamlet! "The rest is Silence!"

We confess that unless, indeed, Hamlet is a mystery for each man to read himself into — unless every man is to make of Hamlet what he himself under the circumstances would have been, and unless it is of no sort of consequence what Shakespeare drew him to be — we cannot read any blunted purposes into the soul of this English prince. Under what standard of comparison does he merit the interpretation? He did what he set out to do. Even a Corsican vendetta is satisfied if the man allotted to kill his man kills him finally. I never heard of any time limit in the matter. And the text equally disposes of the Karl Werder theory that Hamlet failed to kill the King because searching for a popular pretext. It was himself, not Denmark, that he had waited to satisfy. Surrounded by Claudius, the conscience-eaten; Polonius, the parasite; Osric, the flunky; Laertes — true cub of Polonius, coming from dissipation in Paris to remouth his father's platitudes and do the cat's-paw for a murderous and cowardly King — surely not by confronting him with these does Prince Hamlet appear "cruel, evasive, dilatory, infirm of purpose, a court jester"! Surely not out of this precious directory shall we select Hamlet as the madman! In Macbeth, indeed, we had the man who would "proceed no further in this business"; in Brutus one whose "whole mind," spurred amid his rhetorical patriotism to a single overt act,

"is suffering the nature of an insurrection";

but not in the Hamlet of Shakespeare can we find one of these paradoxes.

And yet what little necessity for any analysis at all to find a madman, when we consider that Horatio is at Hamlet's side? Surely to no one but a Shakespearean commentator is it necessary to suggest that Horatio was no keeper of lunatics, nor quite the person to figure throughout the play as the friend, confidant and alter ego of a madman. The esthetic critic who can conceive of Horatio clear-minded, strong-headed, acute, practical, who checks his friend with a

"'twere to consider too curiously to consider so,"

and who, when all is over, could sum up the whole piteous story of his lifelong and now lifeless friend:

"Give order that these bodies
High on a stage be placed to the view;
And let me speak to the yet unknowing world
How these things came about: so shall you hear
Of carnal, bloody, and unnatural acts,
Of accidental judgments, casual slaughters,
Of deaths put on by cunning, and forc'd cause,
And, in this upshot, purposes mistook
Fall'n on the inventors' heads";

continuing — during the entire period covered by the Shakespearean chronicle — the follower of a man who had better have been in a madhouse — is, perhaps, best as he is: an esthetic critic! To such a one Hamlet the Dane may have been a candidate for Bedlam. But King Fortinbras knew better. And we leave Hamlet the Dane forever with the noble eulogium of a just man tenacious of his purpose:

"Bear Hamlet, like a soldier, to the stage;
For he was likely, had he been put on,
To have prov'd most royally: and, for his passage,
The soldiers' music and the rites of war
Speak loudly for him."

So far we have gone with Shakespeare. The reader who desires to settle the question for himself may now, if his patience will sustain him in the tedious task, read here the "Amleth" itself, and perceive, not only by how extremely attenuated a cord can we infer an indebtedness in Shakespeare to the childish Saga, of which he could have only seen the Belleforest adaptation, but how despotic and dramatic his treatment of the trifle he borrowed even from that.

8

AMLETH.

In the reign of King Rörick, Gervendel was governor and commander in Jutland. At his death the king appointed his two sons, Hardvendel and Fenge, in their father's place, to defend and govern Jutland in common. Hardvendel took to the sea and made a great name for himself as a Viking. When he had spent three years in this manner, it happened that King Koller of Norway went in search of him to try his luck, whether he would be able to overcome so mighty and renowned a lord. Having searched for him a long time, they happened both to run up with their ships under an island in the high seas. They landed, each on his side, to wander about and enjoy the beauties of the place, when they met unawares in the wood. Hardvendel addressed the king and said: "As you have challenged me, and we shall have to fight it out before we separate from this island, it would seem to me most advisable, if so it pleases you, that we take up the combat alone between ourselves, to show what we are able to do, each without the help of any one else."

King Koller was struck with the young man's clever and manly words, and replied: "As you leave it to me to choose between a standing battle or a single combat, I shall prefer what you propose. If we two fight it out together without any further noise, the others will better judge of our valor, and we shall finish this quarrel the sooner. But as we are uncertain how this fight will end, we will agree on two points before we begin. The first, that the one who gains the victory will provide for the proper and honorable interment of the other in the presence of both our armies; though we may differ in mind and purpose, we are united in the interest of human nature. It would be inhuman to let our anger so get the better of us that it should last after the death of the other. Our anger and jealousy shall fall to the ground when one of us falls, and great honor will be attributed to him who honors his dead enemy. Another point we must not forget: It often happens that a knight is so hardly wounded that, though he remains alive, he would prefer a thousand times to die. In death all grief and pain is forgotten, but, if alive, he suffers daily from the injury done to his body and his limbs; we will therefore agree to pay ten pounds of gold as compensation to the one who is crippled in such a manner."

After having pledged themselves to these conditions, they at once began the combat without waiting, though they met for the first time; neither could the enjoyment they had had from the beauties of the scenery turn their hasty minds and manly courage. Hardvendel forgot, in his eagerness, to hold his shield before him. He seized his sword in both hands and struck repeatedly so hard on Koller's shield that it fell from him in splinters. With the same stroke he cut off one of his legs. As this wound proved fatal, he was interred, as agreed upon, with great ceremony. After this, Hardvendel pursued and killed Sela, Koller's sister, also a very able Viking and warrior.

Having spent three years on the seas, Hardvendel returned home and made himself so agreeable to King Rörick, by presenting him with the best part of his booty, that he obtained the hand of Geruthe, the king's daughter. By her he had a son called Amleth. His brother Fenge became envious of his good fortune, and watched for an opportunity to take his life. Not content with having killed his own brother, Fenge took to himself his wife, Geruthe. Fenge was not only a tyrant, but cunning and false, and endeavored to hide his wickedness behind the mantle of piety and virtue. He pleaded that he had killed his brother to protect the pious and noble lady Geruthe against her hard and impious husband, at whose hands she had suffered much ill treatment without any fault of hers. These lies succeeded, and would so even nowadays with many princes and lords, who honor at their courts calumniators and flatterers.

When Amleth, Hardvendel's son, became aware of this, he feared for his own life; and, to save it, he pretended to be out of his mind. He rolled himself in the mud, and smeared his face and his body therewith. Sometimes he sat in the ashes at the fire-place and brushed the coals to and fro. Sometimes he bent pieces of wood, made them hot in the fire, and shaped them into hooks. When asked what he meant them for, he answered, "I make spears to avenge my father's death." Some thought his answer silly; but such pieces of work, which he preserved carefully, helped him later on, as will be seen, to fullfil his purpose. Others, who thought more of his doings, suspected that he was not so mad as he appeared, but that he concealed his wisdom behind silly and treacherous pretense. In consequence, they formed a scheme to test him in secrecy with a beautiful woman, in order to discover whether he would allow himself to fall in love with her. For it is in accordance with human nature to be unable to dissimulate when in love and to resist love's cravings when alone with the beloved object. A large forest was chosen for the purpose. Amongst those who accompanied him on his way thither was one who had been brought up with him. He thought of their old associations, and gave Amleth a secret hint to be on his guard, as he knew it would cost him his life if he gave the slightest indication of a sane mind, especially if he touched the woman who was to meet him in the forest. Amleth thought as much himself, and, as they brought him a horse, he mounted it the wrong way, turning his back to the horse's neck and his face to its tail, to which he fixed the harness, as if he did not know any better. As they proceeded through the wood they met a wolf. Amleth asked what it was. They said, "It is a filly." Amleth replied. "Fenge has too few such fillies in his stables." In jesting thus he insinuated that wolves and wild beasts might take his stepfather's life and revenge his father's death. He always contrived to put his words in such a manner that he could not be caught in what he said, though he never told a direct falsehood. When passing along the sea-shore, his followers pointed to the white sand, and asked him what he thought of such beautiful fine flour. He answered, "It has been ground by wind-mills from the white froth of the wavy sea." Having proceeded far into the forest they left him, that he might feel without restraint toward the young lady whom they had arranged to meet him unawares. But his former playfellow gave him a warning. He caught a wasp, stuck it upon a straw, and let it fly toward Amleth. When he saw this he knew at once that a snare had been set for him. He went further on into a thicket with the young lady, where no one could see them. She had been brought up from childhood with Amleth, and he besought her, on account of their friendship, to return his love but not to betray him, and she did so.

On his return home he was questioned in jest whether he had won the heart of the young lady. He answered, "Yes," and on their questioning him, added, "we sat on a couch made of the roof of a house, a horseshoe and the comb of a cock." They all laughed at this answer, but he had taken parts of all these with him, when he went into the forest, in order that he might always be able to speak the truth. They also questioned the young woman; but she denied his assertions, and they all believed her, as no one had seen what had taken place. His friend also told how he had warned him by the signal he had sent. Amleth answered that, in fact, he had seen something flying before him with a straw in its tail. They all laughed at this, but his comrade was pleased at this cautious answer. As they had failed in snaring Amleth this time, one of Fenge's friends advised him to try in another way to discover Amleth's dissimulation. Fenge was to pretend to leave home on important business, and meanwhile lock Amleth up alone with his mother. The counselor offered to hide himself in the place to listen to their secret conversation, convinced that, if Amleth was the least sane, he would not conceal his plans from his mother. But Amleth was on his guard. He began, as usual, to run about the house, threw out his arms as if they had been wings, and crowed like a cock. Finding a heap of straw in which the spy was hidden, he jumped about upon it until he felt something beneath his feet. He then got a sword and thrust it through the concealed man. He afterward dragged him out, killed him, and cut his body into small pieces. He boiled the parts in water, and threw them into the pig-sty to be devoured by the pigs. After having done this, he turned to his mother, who shed tears over his madness, and said to her: "You wicked woman, who take into your arms the one who murdered your dear husband, and who love the man who made your son fatherless. Only brute animals live in such a manner together. You have shown that such is your nature, having forgotten so soon your first husband. It is not without reason that I pretend to be mad, because the man who did not spare his own brother will not have pity on others of his blood and kin. It is indeed not madness to defend one's own life by feigning madness. My father's death weighs on my heart day and night. Might I only find the opportunity to avenge him! But such designs cannot be executed at once. It requires great cunning to overcome so hard and cruel a tyrant. Do not bemoan my madness, but your own shame and dishonor." With these hard words he turned his mother's heart from sin to virtue, from her unnatural love toward her former faith in his own father.

When Fenge returned home and asked about his spy, Amleth said that he had seen him fall into the pig-sty where he had been devoured by the hogs. Though this answer was true, it was received with derision. Fenge would now have murdered Amleth, but he feared his grandfather, King Rörick, and his mother's anger. He therefore sent him with letters to the King of England, not caring if he threw disgrace on his good friend in order to escape suspicion himself. When Amleth was ready to start, he told his mother when a year and a day had elapsed to say she had tidings of his death. She was then to have the hall hung with black cloth, sewn together as if for his funeral. Amleth promised that that same day he would return to her. He then took his departure with two of his stepfather's men, who had letters engraved on staves, as was the custom in those days, in which the King of England was requested to take Amleth's life. One night, on the passage, while his companions were asleep, Amleth found the letters about them, and, having read the message, he effaced the words and altered their meaning so as to tell the king not only to kill his two companions, but also to wed Amleth to his daughter. On their arrival the men delivered the letters, not knowing that they were betraying themselves. The king, concealing his intentions, received them all in a friendly manner. But Amleth would not eat or drink what was offered him. They all wondered that the young foreigner should despise the royal, costly dishes as if they were food for servants. The king secretly ordered one of his men to hide by night in

Amleth's chamber and listen to his talk with his
companions. These asked him why he had not
partaken of the food and drink as if they had
contained poison. Amleth answered them, saying: "The bread tasted of blood, the beer of iron,
and the meat of dead men's corpses." But not
only did he criticise the dinner, but the host himself. He said that the king had the eyes of a
thrall, and that the queen behaved in three things
like a maid-servant. When these words were related to the king next day, he said: "Either this
man is very clever, or he is more insane than anyone else." He sent for his steward, and asked
whether a battle had ever been fought on the
fields where the corn for the bread was grown.
The steward answered that the corn was grown
on account of its fertility in which dead men's
bones were still to be found: a battle had been
fought there in former days. When the king
heard this he perceived the truth in Amleth's
words, and asked, "Whence came the pork?"
The steward confessed that the pigs had escaped
and eaten of the corpse of a dead robber. The
beer was then examined, and in digging by the
well whence the water had been taken, a great
number of rusty swords were found at the bottom. Perceiving that Amleth was right about all
this, the king sent for his mother before him, secretly, and asked who was his father. His mother
at first answered that she knew of no other man
but his father, the king; but on being threatened
with torture, she confessed that a servant and
thrall was his father. Later on the king asked
Amleth himself why he found fault with his queen

who behaved so kindly and friendly toward him. But Amleth answered that in three things her manners were those of a common and vulgar servant. For example, she covered her head with a mantle when walking; she turned her robes up to her belt; and, lastly, she swallowed what she picked out of her teeth after the meals.

The king told him that her mother had been a captive and in thralldom, in order to explain that she had such manners from habit rather than from blood and birth.

The king praised Amleth's cleverness, and gave him his daughter in marriage. The day after the wedding, he had his two comrades hanged, according to the wish expressed in Fenge's letters. But Amleth feigned to be offended, and the king, to conciliate him, gave him a large sum of gold. This he melted into two hollow staves, which afterward he brought back with him to Denmark.

After having spent about a year in England, Amleth asked leave to go home, and carried nothing with him but the aforesaid two staves. On arriving in Jutland, he took off his smart clothes and covered himself with rags. He reached his father's house, where he found everybody in great glee. He entered the hall where they held his funeral. They wondered at his return, and reproached one another for mourning the one who stood alive amongst them. When they asked him what had become of his comrades, he drew forth the two sticks and said: "See! here they are both." Amleth then busied himself with pouring out drink for the guests, so as to make them the more merry and drunk. But to be able to walk about with more ease, he tucked up his garment with his belt. The guests could not endure to see him now and then draw his sword, and try the edge on his nails. They, therefore, hammered a nail right through the scabbard and the blade. He went on pouring out drink till they all became very drunk, lying down to sleep where they sat. When he had so far succeeded, he let all the cloth, with which the walls were hung, fall down, covering them entirely therewith, and fastening it together with the hooks he had made in former days, so that not one of the drunken guests could move or make his escape. He then set fire to the house above them, till it was all in flames. Then he hastened to the dormitory, to which Fenge had been carried by his servants, took his sword from beside the couch, and hung his own in its place. He then woke him, saying: "Fenge, thy good men are burning into ashes, and here is Amleth with his hooks to avenge his father's death."

Fenge jumped to his legs, and while he tried to draw the sword at his bedside, Amleth killed him.

Having killed his stepfather, Amleth hid himself till he had learned what the common people would say about his deed, when they found the hall burned down to the ground, and only a few bones spread in the ashes, without any sign how it had happened. Some mourned over Fenge's death, whose body was found pierced by a sword. Others rejoiced in their hearts that the perpetrator had safely escaped.

The public excitement having subsided, Amleth made his appearance, and called together to a meeting all those whom he knew to be truly devoted to his father, and spoke thus to them:

"I trust, my good Danish lords, that you will not feel at all offended at the punishment inflicted upon Fenge and his Court when you remember the murder committed on King Hardvendel, you who were sincerely attached to my lord and father. Do not look upon this body as being that of an honest king, but as the remains of a cruel murderer. Remember your own great grief when you saw your true lord and king lying shamefully murdered without reason by his own brother. Your eyes moistened with woe and pity over the mutilated body of Hardvendel, so mutilated that hardly one limb hung on to the other. And who could doubt that this tyrant committed the murder but in order to deprive our country of its liberties? His traitor hand made at one stroke my father a corpse and you his thralls. Would any one of you be disposed to praise Fenge's cruelty more than Hardvendel's goodness? Remember how virtuous was Hardvendel, his impartiality in dealing between man and man, how graciously he received one and all. Now that this tyrant has met with his fate, you will acknowledge that the country has suffered no injury, but has greatly benefited. Who will mind that 'falseness has cut its own master's throat'? I acknowledge having given this man his death. I acknowledge having revenged my father and my country. I have done alone what you, one and all, ought to have done, and not with one hand, but with both your hands. Let it be reckoned in my favor that I have performed this manly deed without any man's advice or assistance. Not that I doubt that, if I had called upon you, you would readily have given me your assistance for the love you bore to my father, and which I am assured did not die with him. I thought it right that these traitors should be punished, but that you should not be concerned in it, and I deemed it unnecessary to call on you to help me in what I was able to perform alone. The others were burnt into ashes, but Fenge's corpse I spared for your hands, that you might burn it, and satisfy your just wrath upon it. Here, here, take courage; gather fuel, light the fire to burn that infamous corpse, the instrument of all evil; scatter his poisonous ashes to the winds, and let these limbs find no grave. No place in our fatherland shall be said to preserve his remains, neither water nor earth. Such must be the funeral of a tyrant and a murderer who did not spare his own kin and blood.

"And what shall I say of the misery and grief which I have suffered these many years? You know it all better than I can tell you. My stepfather aimed at my life. I lived in sighs and tears, in fear for my existence. You felt angry that I seemed in my insanity unable to avenge my father. But in this I perceived that you kept your faith, and that you had not forgotten my father's death. Have pity on my poor bereaved mother, once your queen. Rejoice that the double shame and dishonor have been removed from her, which she suffered when she was forced to marry her husband's brother and murderer.

"I hid my talents under the cloak of insanity. But whether I be worthy now to acquire the realm is for you to decide. I am the next by birth, by right, and by desert. To me you owe your liberation from evil and the good that has befallen you."

With such words the young lord moved every man's heart with pity. Their emotion having subsided, they unanimously elected him their king, having great confidence in him, and admiring his having been able so long to deceive everybody, as well as his having so bravely fulfilled his task.

After having arranged everything in Denmark, according to his own designs, he fitted out three costly vessels and sailed to England to confer with his consort's father. He took along with him many fine young warriors, richly equipped, in order to appear now in splendor, where he formerly arrived in an unseemly manner. He had his shield engraved and painted with all the manly deeds performed by him since his childhood, as a proof of his valor and strength. It represented his father's death and his uncle's unlawful marriage; how Amleth made his hooks; how he rode along the sea-shore into the forest and concealed his love; how the spy was killed, sodden, and thrown to the pigs; further, how he performed his journey to England and returned home. There hung his comrades on the gallows, while he sat at his wedding-feast with the king's daughter. Here you saw how he poured out drink for Fenge's guests, and afterward fell upon them, killed and burned them. The shields of his men and servants were all gilt, that his suite might appear the more stately.

The King of England received them well, and as they sat down at the banquet given in their honor, he inquired how fared Fenge. He only then learned from Amleth that he, about whose health he inquired with interest, was dead. And when he heard that Amleth had been his bane, he felt great inward grief, because he and Fenge had sworn a mutual engagement to avenge each other's death. He was much moved by conflicting thoughts; on the one side, his love for his daughter and son-in-law; on the other hand, his faith to his friend, and the strong oath by which he was bound to him. At last the sworn faith got the upper hand, and he decided to avenge the death of his friend. But in order not to act against the laws of hospitality, or to have an open feud with his own son-in-law, he invited Amleth, his own queen having recently died, to take upon himself the mission to proceed to Scotland, and to persist till the queen of that country consented to become his wife. He made this request to Amleth in order that the latter might lose his life through foreign hands; because he knew well that this Scotch queen loved maiden life, and not only refused all suitors, but that all those who ventured to propose to her found their punishment and death.

Amleth prepared at once for the journey, and proceeded to Scotland accompanied by his own men as well as by a number of English. Having passed the border country and finding a pleasant green meadow country alongside a brook, he thought he would enjoy some rest; he placed his sentinels and lay down to sleep. The queen, being informed of the arrival of these foreign guests, sent out ten of her men to gather information. One of these men succeeded in getting through the line of Amleth's guards, and withdrew with great skill and care his shield from under his head, with the letters of which he was the bearer, and carried them off so secretly that he was seen by no one. The queen, on seeing the shield, knew at once who was its owner, and having read the letters and learned that the King of England desired to marry her, she altered the words of the letters so as to imply that the king had demanded her hand not for himself but for Amleth, preferring a young husband to an old one. She also inserted in the letters many of Amleth's deeds corresponding with the shield, and used thus the same stratagem as Amleth had used toward his comrades.

When Amleth woke, he became aware of what had happened, but laid himself down again as if he were asleep, waiting to see what would occur. Soon after, the queen's spy returned, and deposited what he had formerly taken away. But Amleth seized the messenger and put him in chains. He then woke his followers and proceeded to the queen, to whom he delivered the king's sealed letters. The queen, whose name was Hermentrude, read the letters, and praised Amleth for his manly deeds; how he had avenged his father's death, delivered his mother from her shame, and recovered the sway from the man who aimed at his life. He having risen to royal glory, she thought him worthy of sharing with her the crown and scepter she had a right to dispose of, an offer many before had canvassed for, but paying for such presumption with their lives. She begged him to turn now his mind toward her, and to look more for birth and position than for beauty. Having said this, she embraced Amleth, who, moved by her loving words, took her in his arms and pledged his word to her. They then sent word to their friends and the lords of Scotland, and, the wedding having taken place, they proceeded to England with their men, who followed secretly with a hidden design.

On arriving in England, Amleth was met by his wife, the king's daughter, who had learnt what had happened, and who came hastening toward him saying, that, though she had good reason to complain, her love was greater than her anger. She begged him not to turn his heart away from her, for the sake of their son, and warned him against the schemes of her father, who was offended because Amleth had won the lady whom he had wished to marry.

While they were thus conversing, the king himself arrived and met Amleth with sweet words and a false heart, inviting him to be his guest. Amleth saw the fraud, but in order not to show fear or apprehension, he took with him only two hundred horsemen, and put on his armor under his clothes. On arriving at the king's residence, under the porch the king thrust his sword at Amleth, and would have run it through him had not his armor protected him. Amleth was slightly wounded, and returned at once to his men. He sent the Scotch spy to the king to explain to him how all had happened, so as to show his own innocence in the matter. But the king followed at his heels and slew many of his men. Amleth was in consequence in great danger the following day, and was obliged to raise up his men's dead bodies with sticks and stones and tie them on to their horses, that his army might look stronger than it was in reality. The dead men ranged in battle order were nearly as many as the live ones. This was a wonderful warfare, but Amleth succeeded notwithstanding. The English were seized with terror, and were overcome by the dead, whom, when alive, they had themselves defeated. The king fled, and was slain by the Danes, who followed hard upon him. After this victory, Amleth won much booty in England, and then left with his two consorts for Denmark.

In the meantime King Rörick had died, and was succeeded by Viglet, his son. He tormented Amleth's mother, saying that her son had by false pretenses assumed the government of Jutland, which to bestow belonged only to Denmark's king, residing at the castle of Leyre, the capital. Amleth kept his counsel, and, sending presents taken out of English booty, he showed King Viglet all due honor and service, till he found an opportunity to revenge himself. He then sent him an open challenge, and defeated him. In this same war he also defeated Fialler, the commander in Sconen, who fled to a place called "Undensacre," but which place nowadays is quite unknown.

Viglet collected his forces anew from Seeland and Sconen, and challenged Amleth to fight. Amleth foresaw his own ultimate defeat, but preferred to die with honor rather than to live with shame. He was only anxious about Hermentrude's fate, and desirous to secure for her a good husband before he separated from her. But Hermentrude said she would follow her lord and master in the war, and she was not a true woman who feared to die with her husband. This promise Hermentrude did not keep. Amleth having been slain in Jutland by Viglet, she willingly betrothed herself to him.

Such was Amleth's end. Had he been as fortunate as he was clever and brave, he would have come up to Hercules's renown, and gained a name among the greatest warriors. The field in Jutland where he was buried is still called after him: "Amleth's Heath."

Shakespeare never saw the original of the story he was to be credited with immortalizing. I am informed and believe that the above translation was made by the Compte de Falbe, from a manuscript, loaded with much marginalia in the chirography of the twelfth century, which is now in the Royal Museum at Copenhagen, and which is supposed to be contemporary with the one used by Federsen. But its perusal ought to dispose, at once and forever, of any idea that Shakespeare — in his tragedy — intended setting a picture of Danish life and manners before his audiences. Undoubtedly Hamlet notified his friends that he, perhaps, might see fit at times "to put an antic disposition on;" doubtless Amleth counterfeited what he supposed to be the orthodox insignia of madness. But, however willing the Danes may be to present their Amleth to Englishmen, I fail to see why Englishmen should be anxious in return to make Denmark a free gift of their Hamlet.

V

William Shakespeare's Literary Executor — The First Shakespearean Revival

N the year 1680, Mr. John Aubrey — in the first morsel of Shakespearean criticism on the record — said that William Shakespeare's "comedies will remain wit as long as the English tongue is understood — for that he handles mores hominum : now our present writers reflect much upon particular persons and coxcombites that twenty years hence they will not be understood." But there was to come a time, and that not so greatly distant, when the very quality which Aubrey noted was to work the decadence of his poet; — a time when Englishmen — who had passed through the lashed and tossed days of tempest, revolution and plague which ended with the restoration of the second Charles — sought relief from the passions of humanity in artificiality and bagatelle, in trifles and infinities that should stir not too deeply their overtaxed and

overstrained souls, but should bring instead a respite from the mores hominum, until haply peace should come to stay a little. Little as Shakespeare had contributed to the climax (for he was always and everywhere the apostle of order — of the rule and of the throne as opposed to riot, or even an attempt at popular liberty) —he came very near to perishing in it. And there is very small doubt that his memory and works would have suffered seriously had it not been for a gentleman who claimed an other than sentimental interest in perpetuating him.

Whether connected with William Shakespeare by any natural tie or not, certainly Sir William Davenant was the nearest approach to a literary executor that William Shakespeare ever had. And that it was he, and he alone, who carried William Shakespeare through a cycle which cared nothing for him, but (as Pepys's and Evelyn's diaries sufficiently evince) preferred artificial Frenchiness and libertinism, ought to be remembered. After Davenant's death, Dryden wrote a preface to his own and Davenant's version of " The Tempest," in which he says: " Sir William Davenant did me the honor to join me with him in the alteration of this work. It was originally Shakespeare's, a poet for whom he had a particularly high veneration, and whom he first taught me to admire." And we shall see there is plenty of other proof of Sir William's sturdy, and — as it had to be in that age — stubborn loyalty to the great poet of all time — of every time, it seems, except that one.

Young William Davenant, after some preliminary schooling, entered Lincoln College in 1621.

But he scribbled poetry instead of studying, and soon left without taking any degree. He attracted the attention of the gay Duchess of Richmond, and for a while became her page, from which service he entered the household of Sir Fulke Greville, Lord Brooke, who had been a friend of Sir Philip Sidney, and was himself something of a poet. When Lord Brooke died, in 1628, Davenant was left unprovided for, and began to earn his livelihood by his pen alone. His bent was for dramatic poetry, probably the most remunerative sort of verse, at that time, as now. At any rate, he produced a lot of plays, all of which were successful. Among the first were "Gondibert," "The Just Italian," and "The Cruel Brother." In 1637, Ben Jonson, the then poet-laureate, died. Davenant was appointed in his stead, with a salary of £100, but the "butt of sack" was, for some reason, withheld. Davenant now became one of that brilliant throng who, in the days of Charles I., the Parliament and Charles II., surrounded the varying fortunes of the royal family. His associates and literary contemporaries were Waller, Carew, Sir John Suckling, Dryden, and Abraham Cowley. Thomas Hobbes the philosopher, Lords Somerset, Clarendon, and Jermyn were his intimates. When Waller, Hobbes, and Suckling fled to France, in the troubled last days of Charles I., Davenant followed in the train of the wandering Queen Henrietta Maria. A dramatic poet, he was especially hated by the play-hating Puritans. In 1641 he was charged in Parliament with having taken part in a conspiracy to raise an army; was imprisoned, liberated on bail, forfeited it, and succeeded in

reaching the shores of France, from whence he
published an ineffectual memorial pamphlet addressed "To the Hon. the Knights, Citizens, and
Burgesses of the House of Commons assembled in
Parliament." Commissioned by the queen, he returned to England with supplies for the royal
army; saw active service at the siege of Gloucester
in 1643, as Lieutenant-General of Artillery, and
there received the honor of knighthood at the
royal hand.

He again returned to France, resumed his place
in the court of Queen Henrietta Maria, and while
there became a Catholic. After Charles's execution he headed a colonizing expedition to Virginia, with the queen's sanction, but his ship was
captured, and he was thrown into prison at Cowes,
becoming for the second time a parliamentary
prisoner. From here he wrote, in imminent prospect of decapitation: "But 'tis high time to strike
sail, and cast anchor — though I have run but
half my course — when, at the helm, I am threatened with death, who, though he can visit us but
once, seems troublesome." He was released, however, and pardoned, owing to Milton's interposition (a favor he was able to reciprocate after the
Restoration, when Cromwell's secretary, Milton,
in turn, was threatened). After his release from
the Tower he bade a long farewell to politics,— in
whose service he had endured almost everything
except actual decapitation,— and resumed his calling as a dramatist. He opened and managed,
until his death, in 1668, the Duke of York's
Theater, in Portugal street, London. He was
honored in death by burial in Westminster

Abbey, under the inscription on his grave, "O rare Sir William Davenant." Such was Sir William Davenant's history—the history of a man of letters of those reckless and fitful days of anarchy and social upheaval; no higher, perhaps, but certainly no less illustrious than that of any of his compeers. We come now to the peculiar and memorable service he rendered not only England, but the transatlantic world—every world, indeed, which reads to-day its Shakespeare.

In 1623 had appeared the first collected edition of Shakespeare plays — dedicated, not to Shakespeare's supposed patron, Southampton, but to the Earls of Pembroke and Montgomery (whose names then appeared for the first and last time in a Shakespearean connection), and printed at the charges of W. Jaggard, Ed. Blount, I. Smithweeke, and W. Aspley. Evidently the plays had been in a decadence, since the editors, John Heminges and Henry Condell, apologize for this unexpected dedication on the ground that the above-named noblemen "had been pleased to speak approvingly" of the plays, and to show them (the plays) "some little favor." It is difficult, in these days of newspapers and magazines, to imagine England without a periodical, with no such person as a book reviewer or literary critic; or that a volume, so priceless to-day as is this First Folio, could have attracted by its appearance no public attention whatever. Here came from the press for the first time what purported to be a complete collection of the works of a man, who, a few years before, had been not only a popular manager in the metropolis, but the known producer of magnificent transcripts of contemporary and antique manners, whose fame had brought him imitators, and whose name upon a title-page had circulated even the trashiest and stagiest material, so eager had people been to purchase something claiming to hail from this great man. But, except the ingenious conjecture of the Baconians, that Bacon and his poverty may have had something to do with it, we can find no reason for the collection, and no chronicle of its reception by the English public. Shakespeare was dead, deader than he has ever been since, and from contemporary records we can find no hint or warrant for conjecture whether the volume issued by Heminges and Condell was a success or a failure; whether it sold or was still-born. The edition might have been, however, a very large one. The specialists who devote themselves to tracing these volumes record them as having appeared in divers widely separated localities, which, in those days of tardy and difficult locomotion, bespeaks a considerable circulation. But, as we have said, only speculation and surmise is at hand to aid in our investigation.

But, if there was little sale for the great dramatist's works in 1623, and if the volume had been little considered and noticed, there was a particular reason for it. Puritanism was just making itself felt over England. The Shakespeare plays indulge in only very few and very covert digs at Puritanism, possibly because Puritans were not at their first sufficiently numerous to make travesty of them popularly appreciated; but largely, no doubt, because the queen did not discourage them; and Shakespeare was too devoutly careful of his theatrical licenses to poke fun where he was not perfectly sure of his ground. He had made one grave mistake when he gave the name of the Protestant martyr, Oldcastle, to his chiefest comic character — had been forced to write an abject apology (where it stands to-day) into the very text of his piece, and was by no means anxious to reinvoke the experience. In 1614, however, when Shakespeare had satisfied himself in worldly possessions and retired to Stratford (to operate his farms as placidly as if there had never been such things as plays and play-houses, and to forget entirely the work and works from which his affluence sprang), the peculiarities of the new sect had become prominent enough to warrant Ben Jonson in launching at them his "Bartholomew Fair." But — in spite of ridicule or cold steel, satire or villainous saltpeter — Puritanism was the coming power, and, until its culmination in Cromwell, nothing could repress its strides.

The immense renaissance of intellectual activity which the Elizabethan reign had witnessed — which had produced Shakespeare himself, and made an English drama out of the once puerile and extravagant miracle-plays, mysteries and moralities — had not passed without awakening a love of and craving for written lore in the popular masses. And it came to pass that there was to satisfy this craving only one book of anything like general circulation, and that book happened to be the Bible, of which the King James version of 1611 had just superseded its predecessors, and become accessible to everyone. The classics, the translations, English poets and dramatists — the euphuistical and turgid novels and essays which we now open as curiosities — then circulated only among noblemen and the higher classes near the throne. But the Bible speedily became the one literary resource of the masses. As reading was still a fine art, crowds flocked to churches and private houses to hear it read. Good readers were in demand, and fair salaries paid for their services. The weird and massive grandeur of that King James version took hold upon every heart. It happens that we of this generation, who have within a year or two witnessed the excitement with which the revised version of the New Testament was received,— how it was peddled in cars and on the street corners, and discussed as news from mouth to mouth,— can imagine something of the tremor with which the King James vulgate was received. But we must multiply the excitement more than ten thousand-fold. We must fancy at the date this King James version appeared there was practically no other book for millions of the people, no newspapers, no serials, no interchange of printed opinions. We have witnessed, too, how reluctant our contemporaries of this generation have been to surrender the diction of the old version — seen how jealously even those who regard the Bible as a purely literary performance cling to its sonorous and stately gait, its grand periods, its sweet promises and awful denunciations, and so can imagine how, read aloud, that version affected a people who heard and read no other printed words.

People began to remember what they heard read out of the Bible. As we nowadays quote in conversation from a hundred or a thousand books,— from the latest novel or the morning's newspaper,— so did people then quote in common talk among themselves from the only book they possessed. From a mere interest the Bible began to exercise a power. We must also remember every one then believed in a personal God, angry and very powerful; and in a personal devil, crafty, and very powerful in his way, too. Every one believed, further, that whatever men did under the influence of the latter would be punished pitilessly by the former power. The devil was, to be sure, yet to be identified by John Milton; but, under the influence of the Bible, men began to see him everywhere, and to suspect his sooty influence in everything that partook of relaxation, amusement, or personal comfort. This was the rise and opportunity of the Puritan. It was not long before he shut up the theaters to the masses by his denunciations. Poetry, the classics,—almost any book except the Bible,—were doomed and damned; the bear-pits were preached against; bear-baiting being denounced, not, as Macaulay said, because it gave pain to the bear, but because it gave pleasure to the spectator; the May-poles were allowed to rot, and there was no more dancing around them on the village green. The devil was asserted to personally attend every dance, and to find his readiest victims in those who wore colors or gay clothing, a ribbon or a ring. Every lurid or thunderous passage in the King James version was launched at amusement of any sort, and—the people being furnished with chapter and verse to verify the terrible quotations they were assured meant themselves — the effect was revolutionary. The whole country put on a sour face, and moved about with elongated visage and funereal tread. The Puritan was everywhere. He lived to see his error; lived to see the most terrible reaction that blood and war ever brought to a suffering and well-meaning people. The exiling of amusements in themselves innocent, innocuous or indifferent, turned every man into a purist, and the result was not well. With the plays, the memory and the text of William Shakespeare went into exile and abeyance. The work he had done was superseded — to be replaced, as we shall soon see — by something ten thousand times worse than the worst he had ever countenanced.

When the theaters were denounced, and actors, playwrights, and plays openly asserted to be the earthly agents of this personal devil, but one result could be looked for. The drama became viler than it had ever dreamed of being. From the license which even in Shakespeare, purest of all his age, often shocks us, the stage became prurient and the play unspeakable. Just as to-day, a Maine law or a prohibitory statute has no other operation except to increase demand and deteriorate the quality of supply, so the suppression of tolerable substituted only the rotten and the deadly. Then, as now, to denounce a thing unduly made it tenfold more vicious, and drove men to secretly encourage what before they only endured. Plays were, at their best, only tolerated in Shakespeare's time. Female parts were taken by boys, and ladies only ventured in the audience in disguise. This was all changed now. The defiance of the stage to the Puritan was a license of filth and indecency that makes the laxest among us shudder. This was the first harm that Puritanism did to England. It converted its secular literature into a cess-pool. Shakespeare, bad as it sometimes is, became far too pure for the English stage. But now the stage, whatever it was, only lived in a corner, and was soon entirely suppressed. Another edition of the Folio was printed in 1632, and there are many who believe John Milton to have been its editor. But this supposition, based on the verses by Milton prefixed to that Folio,— just as Jonson's had been prefixed to its predecessor,— finds little aid or comfort in contemporary records. At that date the long struggle between King and Parliament, Cavalier and Puritan, was brewing and breaking; rebellion was already accomplished in the hearts of conspirators to fester there for the supreme act. Charles was ruling, or trying to rule, without any parliament, and John Milton, who was to be the pamphleteer of his party, and the gad-fly of royalty through the reign of terror now hastening to its approach, had but just quitted Christ College and begun to prepare himself for public life by the seclusion, during which he produced "L'Allegro" and "Il Penseroso," after Italian models, and the masques of "Arcades" and "Comus," and the elegy of "Lycidas," in the Greek vein. To these succeeded a little foreign travel, after which, as the world knows, he lived twenty years in midst of broil and battle, with a pen in constant service — sending out that tremendous list of diatribe and exhortation which it requires a bibliography to record or recall. But Milton was an honest man, and could hardly, one would think, have made one of the counts in his indictment of Charles the fact that that sovereign read in his closet the Shakespeare to whose memory he himself wrote the sonnet, "What needs my Shakespeare for his honored bones," etc.

We have, as to Charles First's admiration for Shakespeare, to be sure, only an item to the effect that Caliban was his favorite character ("most did they admire the new language almost with which he is endowed for the purpose of expressing his fiendish and yet carnal thoughts of his master"). But, whatever Milton's appreciation of Shakespeare, he probably was careful not to expatiate upon it in the period which followed. Under the restored monarch, fresh from Gallic pastures, the theater awoke, and fired a parting volley at its late suppressors in a license which surpassed all past efforts — which it taxes language to express — a license which finally became so extravagant that repels even the professional reader to-day with its bestiality. In those days, almost all literature was commonplace, except the drama, and that was carrion. Shakespeare was too pure and clean for the days of Charles II. He had to be done over by such men as Dryden, Ravenscroft and Tait to suit the ladies and gentlemen of whose doings Pepys and Evelyn kept diaries. But it is interesting to see how Davenant at once managed to keep the works of his master, Shakespeare, alive in the swim and to avoid financial martyrdom in the process.

The great plays, we have seen, were dead — deader than they have ever been since. We happen to be able to realize precisely the difficulties experienced by Sir William in his crusade against the prurient and vitiated taste of the day, and the appetite and license which came back again with the restored king. John Evelyn, born in 1620, a courtier who had followed the royal fortunes, and at the Restoration had become a favorite at court, — one of "the mob of gentlemen who writ with ease,"— kept a diary of these days. This Evelyn diary gives, among other things which interested the diarist, very full lists of the plays the court witnessed; and bristles with evidence that, even for Davenant's sake, Charles II. could hardly be prevailed upon to sit out Shakespeare. "The old plays," says Evelyn (apropos of Hamlet, which he saw February 28, 1666), "begin to disgust this refined age, since his majesty is so long abroad." A much more methodical diarist than Evelyn was Mr. Samuel Pepys, and his record is to the same effect as Evelyn's, exhibiting, if anything, even more emphatically, how utterly the Shakespearean plays were caviare to the general, and out of taste in the period of which he wrote.

"Sept. 29th, 1662 — To the King's Theatre, where we saw Mid-summer Night's Dream, which I had never seen before, nor ever shall again; for it is the most insipid, ridiculous play that I ever saw in my life.

"Jan. 1, 1663-4 — Saw the so much cried up play of Hen. VIII., which, though I went with great resolution to like it, is so simple a thing, made up of a great many patches, that besides the processions in it, there is nothing in it good or well done.

"Aug. 15, 1667 — To the Duke's House, where a new play; the house full; so we went to the King's, and there saw the Merry Wives of Windsor, which did not please me at all, in no part of it.

"Nov. 1, 1667 — To the King's House, and there saw a silly play and an old one: The Taming of the Shrew.

"1663-4 — Jan. 5th. I saw the Indian Queen acted, a tragedy well written, so beautiful with rich scenes, as the like had never been seen here, or haply except rarely on a mercenary theatre."

And he notes also that, August 1, 1666, he saw "Othello," "which, having lately read The Adventures of Five Hours, it seems a mean thing"; though he liked Davenant's "Macbeth," with its music and dancing. And, when spending some money in books, Evelyn makes a note that he looked over Shakespeare, but finally chose "Hudibras, the book now in greatest fashion for drollery."

The result was that Sir William, finding that his patrons would not come and see Shakespeare as he was, to save himself from bankruptcy bethought him of adding to their representation the charm of music and dancing, in the French mode, and of putting certain of the speeches into verse and setting them to scores. In other words, Davenant first introduced what we call Opera into England, if he did not actually invent opera itself. Nine of the Shakespeare plays were thus kept in commission by Davenant, either represented in "runs" or alternately with others. In those days of vicious tastes, such a course would hardly have been persisted in by a man seeking to repair a fortune depleted by the long civil disturbances, had he not cherished a strong personal regard for the memory of the great dramatist, or inherited a taste for something better than the very weak and slim pabulum then monopolizing the stage, like the "Indian Queen," or "The Adventures of Five Hours," which Mr. Diarist Pepys found so delightful.

Plays were rendered, even at this date, with very little aid from movable or "practicable" scenery. A sign announced the name of the new play, and served as programmes or bills of the play do now. Another sign — frequently replaced — denoted the scene. There were a few scenic trees, rocks, a broad traverse to conceal the balcony in the rear of the stage, and a trap-door appears to have been invented as early as the days of Dekker, perhaps by Dekker himself. The incessant changes of scene called for by the original stage directions of the Shakespeare plays themselves indicate very clearly this poverty of scenic contrivances. Their representation would have been almost impossible had a stage to be cleared and refurnished at each. But what the Shakespearean stage lost by its uninvented accoutrements, we of this age have gained. The rich pictorial diction, the noble descriptive passages over which we gloat to-day, were necessary then to carry to the spectator's eye what, in these times, would be expressed by the scene-painter in rough distemper. Take, for instance, "Shakespeare's cliff," in "King Lear." Here the scenic effect being entirely wanting, the idea of vast headlong distance was necessary to be conveyed in words, by describing how

"The crows and choughs, that wing the midway air,
Show scarce so gross as beetles: half-way down
Hangs one that gathers samphire,— dreadful trade!
Methinks he seems no bigger than his head.
The fishermen that walk upon the beach
Appear like mice; and yond' tall anchoring bark
Diminish'd to her cock;" etc.

All this nowadays would be expressed with carpentry and canvas, and our libraries would be losers to just that extent. Nor was Shakespeare himself without a deep sense of the scenic imperfections of his day. The chorus in "Henry V." constantly says to the audience, "Play with your fancies, and in them behold," etc.; "Suppose that you have seen," etc.; "O do but think you stand upon the rivage and behold," etc.; "Or may we cram, within this wooden O, the very casques that did affright the air at Agincourt?" etc.

Davenant, however, determined to secure both; that is, he retained the word-painting, and called in both "carpentry and French." Up to his time a divided curtain, attached to rings running on a rod, was pulled apart when the show began. He substituted the drop curtain we now possess, widened the stage from the cramped box strewn with rushes (or, on rare occasions, with tapestry carpets) to the broad proscenium of the present style. He changed the hour of performance (always by daylight in Shakespeare's time) to evening. It seems beyond dispute that about all we have of "practicable scenery," and the contrivances which add so much to the modern stage, began abruptly with Davenant's determination to rescue the Shakespeare plays from limbo, and put

them on a plane to at least compete with the
prurient and palsied trash the appetite of his day
preferred to them. The claim is a bold one, but
is, I think, fully warranted by the record; and is of
note, since therefrom it appears that to the influence
of William Shakespeare and his memory we owe
not only all that is best in the text of the English
drama, but what is best in its stage setting as well.

In the course of his endeavor, Davenant associated with himself one of the most interesting
minor characters in English history of that period
— Inigo Jones. Inigo Jones was born in London
in 1572, eight years later than William Shakespeare. We know nothing of his career until, at a
date not certain, Pembroke, attracted by his genius,
sent him to France, Germany, and, above all,
Italy, then, as now, the home of graphic art.
While in Venice, he was attracted by the works of
Palladio, and on his return introduced his style,
which seems to have completely dominated him,
into England. We have, however, no record of
his life until about 1605, when James I. employed
him to devise scenery for the masques of Ben
Jonson. It will always remain one of the stumbling-blocks of Shakespearean study that great
Shakespeare, the alleged favorite of two courts,
wrote none of these masques; whereas Ben Jonson, his lesser light, was always employed at them.
(It is claimed, indeed, that the " Midsummer
Night's Dream" is a masque devised for courtly
representation, although the court records of
Elizabeth and James give no color to the claim.)

But certainly it is only a lesser marvel than the
non-acquaintance of Shakespeare and Bacon, this

inability to trace any coincidence of career between the former, the leading stage-manager, and Inigo Jones, the leading scenic artist and designer of costumes of those days. So great was Jones's repute, such the extreme confidence placed in him, that, in preparing the bodily part of Jonson's "Masque of Blackness," Jones was allowed by the Government £10,000 (present value of money) for his disbursement, with no account to be made thereof. In the same year he was summoned to Oxford to superintend three spectacles, and in the next year he worked at the splendid "Masque of Hymen," planned to celebrate the marriage of Essex and Frances Howard. On this occasion one of the Jones contrivances was a globe, large enough to hold all the masquers, arranged in tableaux, and to turn on its axis in a horizontal plane without any machinery of support visible to the audience. Jones and Jonson long continued in a sort of Gilbert-Sullivan partnership, but finally quarreled. Townshend, Carew, Shirley, and Heywood afterward became, for short periods, Jones's coadjutors, though we know nothing of their joint product. But, in 1634, a masque, "The Temple of Love," was presented by the queen and her ladies at Whitehall, written by Davenant and contrived by Jones. Five or six other masques had followed this (indeed, it is said that Davenant owed his first favor at court to his services as libretto writer to Jones). So these two were by no means unacquainted, when, in his series of Shakespearean revivals, Davenant secured, as employé rather than as coadjutor, the services of the veteran artist, and Betterton was dispatched to

Paris to study the details of arrangement of the French stage. The result was an impressive "opening run," and Sir William would certainly have been warranted had he advertised (as our own managers do) that "positively no expense whatever had been spared to make this Shakespearean revival a complete success."

The opening piece chosen for this first "Shakespearean Revival" on record was "The Tempest," as re-written by Dryden and Davenant. Two innovations — the placing of the orchestra band between performers and audience, and the giving of the female parts to women — signaled the occasion. The latter novelty was stormed and hissed at, the manager was cursed and the actresses insulted. But, as the interest of the play progressed, the audience first deferred their indignation, then acquiesced, and finally forgot all about it. The next day there were a few mutterings, but they blew over, and so the change grew into a success, and audiences soon came to wonder that they had ever been contented with anything else.

The play, as Shakespeare left it, was reënforced with the character of Hippolyto, who had never seen a woman (to offset Miranda, who had never seen a man), and Miranda was given a sister, Dorinda. To this succeeded altered versions of "Julius Cæsar"; a burlesque on "Antony and Cleopatra" entitled "All for Love"; and "A Law Against Lovers," in which Dryden and Davenant welded up together "Measure for Measure" and "Much Ado About Nothing." In this latter, Shakespeare's Claudio is the sinner; Angelo (out of "Measure for Measure") is made a brother of Benedick, and Beatrice his ward. The situation turns on Benedict's and Beatrice's love, but mutual objection to matrimony, and Angelo's determination that they shall come together in lawful wedlock or not at all. The comic parts are supplied by the rebellion of the nursery-maids, wet-nurses, and milk-women against a law which will depopulate the country. The scene is laid in Turin; Benedick, Beatrice, and Viola (who is made Beatrice's sister) come on with songs and dances, and the Disguised Duke is the universal friend who makes everything turn out right in the end. A brief allusion to one other of Davenant's successes in this rehabilitating of Shakespeare must suffice for our purpose. There is, as everybody remembers, a famous scene in "Robert le Diable," where the graves in the Campo Santo at Pisa open, the dead arising slowly in their cerements, when, all at once, these cerements fall away, and the whole scene transforms into a brilliant ballet. Something of this sort appears to have been introduced by Davenant into "Macbeth." He made the witches to appear in larger groups than the original three, and used them in precisely this way — making their ghostly machinery vanish, their witch-rags drop off, whereat they became coryphées, and the stage a brilliant fairy-piece. Even the finical Pepys had to admit that he liked this sort of thing vastly. And it is worth noting that to this same era we seem to be indebted for the idea of modern burlesque. At least I can find no earlier trace of the tragedy travesty, where all the characters, after being foully murdered, come forward for the song and dance, than the play in which Nell Gwynn was killed, and a soldier coming in to take off her body, she jumped up with—

"Hold! are you mad, you damned, confounded dog! I am to rise and speak the Epilogue!"

In 1679, John Dryden by himself remodeled "Troilus and Cressida." He called it "Truth Found Too Late." In his preface (dedicated to the Earl of Sutherland) he says he found the style of Shakespeare "so pestered with figurative expressions that it is as affected as it is obscure; the author seems to have begun it with some fire; the characters of Pandarus and Troilus are promising enough, but, as if he grew weary of his task, after an entrance or two he lets 'em fall, and the latter part of the tragedy is nothing but a confusion of drums and trumpets, excursions and alarms. The chief persons who give name to the tragedy are left alive. Cressida is left alive and is not punished." "I have undertaken to remove that heap of rubbish. . . . . I new modeled those characters which were begun and left unfinished, . . . made, with no small trouble, an order and connection of the scenes, and . . . . so ordered them that there is a coherence of 'em with one another, ... a due proportion of time allowed for every motion, ... have refined the language," etc. Mr. Dryden's process of "refining the language" was to make this "Troilus and Cressida," or "Truth Found Too Late," one of the smuttiest plays ever read. Every suggestive situation in the original he enlarged upon and elaborated. He made the action of the play to consist, not of the pathetic story of a brave warrior palsied in the midst of crashing arms by the falseness of a heartless harlot, but of the actual commerce of the two, as watched through a keyhole by Pandarus, and described by him, as Chorus, to the audience. But Davenant, in spite of his own excesses, will be found to have touched the text more tenderly, adapting it only just as little as necessary to the salacious taste of the time, and with much more honor and decency always. He had the heart for better things, at least. If he were not custodian of the works of the man he claimed as a parent, then they had no custodian, and — son of Shakespeare as he claimed to be, poet as he was, laureate as he became — in an age of which he was neither the worst nor the worthiest, he deserves grateful remembrance forever for being the first to bring back from oblivion, to the English stage they have never surrendered since, the dramatic works that once held the stage of William Shakespeare.

The literary fashion set by Dryden and his day long controlled England, and many years were to elapse before the poet of all time regained his birthright. John Dennis, a critic of a rather later day, declares that Shakespeare "knew nothing of the ancients, set all propriety at defiance, . . . was neither master of time enough to consider, correct, or polish what he had written; . . . . his lines are utterly void of celestial fire," and his verses "harsh and unmusical." Dennis was, however, persuaded to be so good natured to this erratic and friendless Shakespeare as to work over the "Merry Wives of Windsor," and to touch up "Coriolanus," which latter he brought out in 1720, under the title "The

Invader of His Country; or, The Fatal Resentment." (The play, however, did not prosper, which he attributes to the fact that it was played on a Wednesday!)

Pope, in his "The Narrative of Dr. Robert Norris concerning the Strange and Deplorable Frenzy of John Dennis," relates how the aforesaid Dennis, being in company with Lintot, the bookseller, and Shakespeare being mentioned as of a contrary opinion to Mr. Dennis, the latter "swore the said Shakespeare was a rascal, with other defamatory expressions which gave Mr. Lintot a very ill opinion of the said Shakespeare." Lord Shaftesbury complains at about the same date, of Shakespeare's "rude and unpolished style and antiquated phrase and wit." Thomas Rymer knows exactly how "Othello"—which he calls "a bloody farce: the tragedy of the pocket handkerchief"—ought to have been done. To begin with, he is angry "that the hero should be a black-a-moor, and that the army should be insulted by his being a soldier." Of Desdemona, he says: "There is nothing in her which is not below any country kitchen-maid; no woman bred out of a pig-stye could talk so meanly." Speaking of expression, he writes that "in the neighing of a horse or in the growling of a mastiff there is a meaning, there is a lively expression, and, I may say, more humanity than in the tragical flights of Shakespeare." He is indignant that the catastrophe of the play should turn on a handkerchief. He would have liked it to have been folded neatly on the bridal couch, and, when Othello was killing Desdemona, "the fairy napkin might have started up to disarm his fury and stop his ungracious mouth. Then might she, in a trance of fear, have lain for dead; then might he, believing her dead, and touched with remorse, have honestly cut his own throat, by the good leave and with the applause of all the spectators, who might thereupon have gone home with a quiet mind, and admiring the beauty of Providence freely and truly represented in the theatre. Then for the unraveling of the plot, as they call it, never was old deputy recorder in a country town, with his spectacles on, summing up the evidence, at such a puzzle, so blundered and bedoltified as is our poet to have a good riddance and get the catastrophe off his hands. What can remain with the audience to carry home with them? How can it work but to delude our senses, disorder our thoughts, scare our imaginations, corrupt our appetite, and fill our head with vanity, confusion, tintamarre and jingle-jangle, beyond what all the parish clerks in London could ever pretend to?" He then hopes the audience will go to the play as they go to church, namely, "sit still, look on one another, make no reflection, nor mind the play more than they would a sermon." With regard to "Julius Cæsar," he is displeased that Shakespeare should have meddled with the Romans. He might be "familiar with Othello and Iago as his own natural acquaintances, but Cæsar and Brutus were above his conversation." To put them "in gulls' coats and make them Jack-puddens," is more than public decency should tolerate — in Mr. Rymer's eyes. Of the well-known scene between Brutus and Cassius, this critic remarks: "They are put there to play the bully and the buffoon, to show their activity of face and muscles. They are to play for a prize, a trial of skill and hugging and swaggering like two drunken Hectors for a two-penny reckoning." (This extract is from Rymer's book, which he entitled "A Short View of Tragedy, with Some Reflections of Shakespeare and Other Practitioners for the Stage.")

To return to John Dryden: In or about 1700 he published in his "Defence of the Epilogue" a postscript to his tragedy, "The Conquest of Grendala," in which he says: "Let any man who understands English read diligently the works of Shakespeare and Fletcher, and I dare undertake that he will find in every page either some solecism of speech or some notorious flaw in sense." Dryden denounces "the lameness of their plots," made up of some ridiculous, incoherent story, either grounded on impossibilities, or at least so meanly written that the comedy neither causes your mirth nor the serious part your concernment. . . . . . He writes, in many places, below the dullest writers of our own or any precedent age." Of the audiences who could tolerate such matter, he says: "They knew no better, and therefore were satisfied with what they bought. Those who call theirs the 'Golden Age of Poetry,' have only this reason for it: that they were content with acorns before they knew the use of bread." Later on, on the continent, Voltaire was, from a critical point of view, very severe with Shakespeare. He declared "Hamlet" "the work of a drunken savage," and that Shakespeare knew not how to make his kings "completely royal." From a rare pamphlet, "Essay Upon the Civil

Wars of France, extracted from Curious MS., and also Upon the Epick Poetry of the European Nations from Homer down to Milton, by Arouet de Voltaire," we extract a few further Voltairian comments: "Shakespeare has a genius full of force and fecundity, of nature and sublimity, but without the least spark of good taste, and without the least knowledge of the rules. . . . The merit of this author has ruined the English drama. There are such beautiful scenes, there are passages so grand and terrible in these monstrous farces which they call tragedies that his pieces have always been played with success. Time, which alone gives reputation to men, renders at length their faults respectable." "These pieces are monsters in tragedy. There are some plays, the action of which lasts several years, the hero baptized in the first act, dies of old age in the fifth. You see upon the stage wizards, buffoons, grave-diggers digging a grave. In a word, imagine what you can of most monstrous and most absurd: you will find it in Shakespeare." But in reading these comments we must remember that in France these were the days when classic models prevailed so imperatively that a piece not regarding the terrible unities of place, time, and event, was hissed off the stage even by the clackers. French plays of the period were stupendous speeches delivered en grande tenue, awful in the reading nowadays, hardly imaginable as anything but awful then. Voltaire believed Shakespeare to have been a barbarian because he had thought no more of these precious Unities (if, indeed, he had ever heard of them) than does a baby playing with buttercups think of the structural rules of botany;

but did not, like Dryden, criticise them because they were not nasty enough, or kindly indicate how they could be made nastier. It is at least an interesting question whether — had these plays really been the subjective arithmetic, the formal trigonometry the esthete of our day asserts them to be, and had Shakespeare himself been the purely artificial person with a knack at syllable-counting they make him out — the classicists, from Dennis to Voltaire, would not have gone into ecstasies over them.

The history of Shakespearean criticism is largely a history of extremes. Shakespeare could hardly have fared worse than at this period. But when the tide was at its full it began to ebb very rapidly indeed. David Garrick seems to have been the instrument of the reaction. The antipode was touched, perhaps, in the days of Malone, of which we have already quoted Prior: "Editors and commentators appear at every turn and in all societies. In the club-house we meet three or four of a morning. In the park we see them meditating by the Serpentine, or under a tree in Kensington Gardens. No dinner-table is without one or two. In the theater we find them by the dozens."[1] Here was a revenge indeed brought in by the whirligig of time, for the dramatist whom Denham thought nothing compared with Cowley, and whom Phillipps (the nephew of Milton)[2] pronounced "the laughter of the critics!"

In a room of the Garrick Club there stands a memorial at once of Shakespeare and of Davenant, precious beyond estimation. It is the bust

[1] Ante, p. 35.   [2] Theatrum Poetarum.

known as "the Devonshire Shakespeare." It seems that, in 1737, sixty-nine years after Davenant's death, his structure on Portugal street, known as the Duke's Theater, ceased to be used as a play-house, and was altered into the china warehouse occupied by Spode and Copeland (whence the "Copeland," well known of China collectors). In 1845 this old warehouse was in its turn torn down, to make room for enlargement of the Museum of the London College of Surgeons. In the course of demolishment,—which rendered the ground-plan of the old theater plainly visible,—a terra-cotta bust fell from some concealed niche. Put together, the fragments made a passable bust of Ben Jonson, and fitted a bracket on one side of an old door-frame. Search for a corresponding bracket, on the other side, led to one being found, not only, but, standing securely upon it, a bust of William Shakespeare. In the course of its subsequent history, this bust was purchased by the Duke of Devonshire for three hundred guineas, and by him presented to the Garrick Club. For ourselves, at least, we believe it to be a representation of Shakespeare. Nor can we imagine that Sir William would have displayed in his theater an inadequate or poor likeness. At any rate, if genuine at all, it is the most valuable portraiture we possess; showing Shakespeare after middle-age maturity, and possessing a circumstantial authenticity which the death-mask can only be conceded by many grains of allowance. The face is that of a man who might have been a very unpleasant creditor, and certainly looked more like a capitalist than a poet: just such a stern, kindly man of affairs as we have come to believe Shakespeare was; a man with too high a sense of justice to let his neighbors defraud him, even in the matter of payment for "malt delivered"; who went into the plays for the same reason that he went into the Stratford tithes — because he saw a profit in them; and who, to his last moments, showed, as a man, the manly elements which determined and enabled him, by hard personal work, to relieve the rigorous penury of his family, restore them to affluence, institute legal proceedings to recover the maternal estates surrendered in duress of poverty, buy his father a grant of arms, and make solid investments in metropolitan properties. There certainly is no richer trait in William Shakespeare's private character than the firmness of purpose which, even in stress of poverty, held him to his determination to spend his last days in affluence in the home of his youth, and his final accomplishment of it in the teeth of envy, jealousy, and even courtly disfavor. It is the justum ac tenacem propositi virum which is delineated in every groove and furrow in the face of that Devonshire bust.

Davenant, of course, had both enemies and traducers in plenty. Richard Flecknoe lampooned him, in 1668, in a pamphlet, "Sir William Davenant's Voyage to the Other World" (of which pamphlet, however, nothing at all is remembered to-day). But, by his contemporaries who knew him best, Davenant seems to have been held in constant esteem, admiration and affection. The "Biographica Dramatica" says that "honor, courage, gratitude, integrity, and vivacity were the prominent features of his mind," and Dryden cannot estimate too highly his literary excellence. "I found him," says Dryden, "of so quick a fancy that nothing was proposed to him on which he could not quickly produce a thought extremely pleasant and surprising — and those first thoughts of his, contrary to the old Latin proverb, were not always the least happy; and as his fancy was quick, so likewise were the products of it remote and new. He borrowed not of any other, and his imaginations were such as could not easily enter into any other man. His corrections are sober and judicious, and he corrected his own writings much more severely than those of another man, bestowing twice the labor and pains in polishing which he used in invention." In these days we do not estimate men according to their ability to "produce a thought extremely pleasant or surprising," or as their fancies are "remote and new." But the quotation serves to show that Davenant was abreast of the culture, and passed muster in the opinion, of the best of his contemporaries. Nor should we, ordinarily, demand more than this. We must remember that the centuries, so far, have hardly developed more than one man who "was not for an age, but for all time." And after all, say what we will about Davenant, we must not lose sight of the fact that he was the godson, even if not the son, of an immortal Shakespeare.

VI

Law and Medicine in the Plays

"The first thing we do, let's kill all the lawyers."
II. King Henry VI., iv. ii.—78.

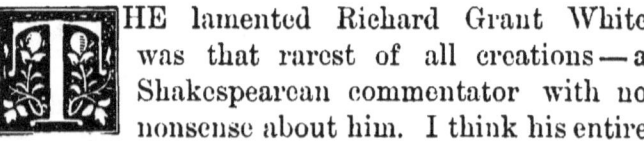HE lamented Richard Grant White was that rarest of all creations — a Shakespearean commentator with no nonsense about him. I think his entire character and career, his whole individuality — the exact, stiff justice and manliness of the man — cannot be better expressed, summed up and covered than in one little note furnished by him to that most perplexing of all the "cruces Shakespeareanæ"— the lines in Hamlet, about that 'dram of eale." The note occurs in his edition of Shakespeare, published in 1865, and is briefly and tersely as follows:

"I leave this grossly corrupted passage unchanged, because none of the attempts to restore it seem to me even worth recording; and I am unable to better them."

That seems to me to include the whole nature of the man. He was as incapable of sham work himself as he was intolerant of it in others. To guess or surmise without data or warrant,— to cover space with words which represented no information to be imparted, to assume comment where he could bring no help,— was simply impossible to his rugged, brusque honesty. His predecessors had speculated on that passage until their speculations could easily be collected into big volumes. He had here an opportunity for a show of profundity which would certainly have been quoted and followed (for whatever one commentator says the next one echoes and discusses). But Mr. White was never afraid to say that he "didn't know"; and his contempt for any sort of pretense was fine and Italian. I am aware that this contempt for sham led him into bitternesses which lessened his friendships and made him enemies far and near. Nay, more, his very consciousness of honesty — the fact that he had never made a comment without first testing his reading, and long revolving it — made him fierce in denunciation, not only of the prig or virtuoso, but often of the scholar as good as himself, who differed with him. That he himself suffered in heart from these enmities, I think I know. And so, in some sort, he was a martyr to his passion for exactitude. But I shall never cease to admire his rugged love of truth, and to hope we may have more like him yet. I doubt if it ever occurred to Mr. White that any moral maxim made it incumbent upon him to hate a literary untruth. With him an untruth did not exactly rise to the dignity of being hated. He simply despised it, and, if he could, ignored it. But to ignore falsehood is not always possible.

It was this greatest characteristic of Mr. White's mind and method which led him, in 1859, when a volume (and there have been dozens of them since) whose purpose was to demonstrate that William Shakespeare was at one time an attorney, or an attorney's clerk, was put into his hands, to use all his powers of sarcasm to indicate what he thought of it. There had been a tradition (preserved by Aubrey) that young William had been apprenticed to a butcher; another (traced to Beeston, one of Shakespeare's fellows in Lord Strange's company of actors), to the effect that he had once been a schoolmaster — and traditions, however unreliable after the growth of generations, are not apt to be cut, at their very sources, out of whole cloth. But of Shakespeare as an attorney, or an attorney's apprentice, there was no tradition anywhere among the plenitude of them unearthed by the microscopic search of two centuries. So Mr. White, who had not the slightest respect for theories, quoad theories, or for mere tours de force, was prepared to give no very gentle handling to this one. But, this being early in his Shakespearean career, before his pen had been galled by question, he treated the fad more gayly than was his wont later on in that career. He began his review of this particular volume as follows:

[1] At the close of a lovely summer's day, two horsemen might have been seen slowly pacing through the main street of Stratford-on-Avon. Attracting no little attention from the group of loiterers around the market cross, they

[1] The "Atlantic Monthly," July, 1859, p. 84.

passed the White Lion Inn, and, turning into Henley street, soon drew their bridles before a goodly cottage, built of heavy timbers, and standing with one of its peaked gables to the street; on the door was a shingle, upon which was painted,

---

Willͫ Shakspere.
Attornei at Lawe and Solicitor
in Chancere.

One of the travelers — a grave man whose head was sprinkled with the snows of fifty winters — dismounted, and, approaching the door, knocked at it with the steel hilt of his sword. He received no answer, but presently the lattice opened above his head, and a sharp voice sharply asked:

"Who knocks?"

"'Tis I, good wife!" replied the horseman, "Where is thy husband? I would see him!"

"Oh master John à Combe, is it you? I knew you not, neither know I where that unthrift William is these two days. It was but three nights gone that he went with Will Squele and Dick Burbage, one of the player-folk, to take a deer out of Sir Thomas Lucy's park; and, as Will's ill luck would have it, they were taken as well as the deer, and there was great ado. But Will — that's my Will — and Dick Burbage brake from the keepers in Sir Thomas's very hall and got off; and that's the last that has been heard of them; and here I be, a lone woman with these three children and — Be quiet, Hamnet! would ye pour my supper all upon the hat of the worshipful Master John à Combe?"

"What! deer stealing?" exclaimed John à Combe: "Is it thus that he apes the follies of his betters? I had more hope of the lad, for he hath a good heart and a quick engine; and I trusted that ere now he had drawn the lease of my Wilmecote farm to Master Tinley here. But deer stealing! — like a lord's son or a knight's, at the very least! Could not the rifling of a rabbit-warren serve his turn? Deer stealing! I fear me he will come to naught!"

For my part I doubt if William Shakespeare could have been much of a "solicitor in chancere," whatever his practice as an attorney at law and draughtsman, since he makes Falstaff, a mere layman, talk down and discomfort a chief-justice, and try to borrow a thousand pounds of him into the bargain,— a thing we lawyers know to be impossible! But Mr. White, while modestly claiming originality for the incident of the two horsemen — and for one of them alighting — in the above sketch, is bound to admit that there is one thing under the sun that is not new, "and that is the representation of Shakespeare as a lawyer. Mr. White had only before him the works of Lord Campbell and Mr. Rushton. Had he taken up the subject again in 1885 (the year in which occurred his lamented death), he could have examined many further works all pressing the same representation. All these works prove the lawyer in Shakespeare by lists of legalisms and technical terms of the attorney's and the counsellor's craft, which, to a greater or less degree, their compilers find in the plays. But in 1884, Mr. Cushman K. Davis, ex-Governor of Minnesota, an eminent lawyer and ripe and thoughtful student of Shakespeare, put the question for the first time beyond this view, and presented scholars with a volume [1] which demonstrated that the very innermost and essential structure of these plays is legal; that their author was, so to speak, saturated with legal processes, especially familiar with the practice of courts; that his nature, like the dyer's hand, was subdued to what it worked in; that even his wit

[1] The Law in Shakespeare. St. Paul: 1884.

and humor travels in legal grooves; that legal language once adopted is exhausted; that legal terms are everywhere preferred as standards of comparison by a writer whose resources in every other treasury of speech were vast beyond computation " with things which nothing but his own despotic imagination could have brought into relevancy"; and who certainly, therefore, did not need to leave the lay tongue to search in technical speech for words wherein to express himself. Moreover, that not only is this legal groove traversed and retraversed unconsciously and unintentionally, but the author, on revising his own manuscript for a new edition, added explanations of statements that none but a lawyer would have perceived to have needed explanation at all : recast sentences not legal over into legal form, and everywhere kept his glowing rhetoric within the very letter and spirit of Tudor forms and precedents.

Coleridge has remarked " that a young author's first works almost always bespeaks his recent pursuits." He might have said with equal correctness that no author's works can ever entirely hide his former pursuits, betrayed by the prejudices, affections, antipathies or affectations of his style. But Mr. Davis goes further. And says, " Shakespeare had a lawyer's conservatism. He respected the established order of things. He chisels the republican Brutus in cold and marble beauty, but paints with beams of sunlight the greatness, bravery, and generosity of imperial Cæsar. Coriolanus is the impersonation of patrician contempt for popular rights. Shakespeare passes unnoticed the causes which led to Cade's insurrection because he cares not for them—causes so just that honorable terms were exacted by the insurgents. His portrait of Joan of Arc, the virgin mother of French nationality, who raised it to glory because the people believed in her, is a great offense. There is nowhere a hint of sympathy with personal rights as against the sovereign, nor with parliament, then first assuming its protective attitude toward the English people, nor with the few judges who, like Coke, showed a glorious obstinacy in their resistance to the prerogative. In all his works there is not one direct word for liberty of speech, thought, religion,—those rights which in his age were the very seeds of time, into which his eye, of all men's, could best look to see which grain would grow and which would not."

Moreover, this same author, even when his wit ran at hap-hazard into puns, directed these puns into legal lines. " Cade makes a bestial pun, suggested by tenancy in capite, and by an infernal privilege of stupration, which is one of the recondite curiosities of the law. Dromio asserts that there is no time for a bald man to recover his hair. This having been written, the law phrase suggested itself, and he was asked whether he might not do it by fine and recovery, and this suggested the efficiency of that proceeding to bar heirs; and this started the conceit that thus the lost hair of another man would be recovered. Again, in the love-making, a 'quest of thoughts, all tenants to the heart, is impaneled to decide the question of title to the visage of the beloved one between the heart and the eye, where the defendant denies the plea, and the verdict is a moiety to each. The word employed becomes suggestive of other words, or of a legal principle, and these are at once used so fully that their powers are exhausted. In one scene the lover, wishing a kiss, prays for a grant of pasture on his mistress's lips. This suggests the law of common of pasture, and she replies that her lips are no common. This suggests the distinction between tenancy in common and tenancy in severalty, the lips being several, and she adds, "though several they be."

In other words, the legalism is structural; could not be uprooted without taking the thought, blood, rhetoric and continuity of the whole text along with it. It comes "from the mouth of every personage; from the queen; from the child; from the Merry Wives of Windsor; from the Egyptian fervor of Cleopatra; from the love-sick Paphian goddess; from violated Lucrece ; from Lear, Hamlet and Othello; from Shakespeare himself, soliloquizing in his sonnets; from Dogberry and Prospero; from riotous Falstaff and melancholy Jacques. Shakespeare utters it at all times as standard coin, no matter when or in what mint stamped. These emblems of his industry are woven into his style like the bees into the imperial purple of Napoleon's coronation robes."

What was the necessity? Ben Jonson was proud of borrowing technical and classical words; but he only made his work dreary and stilted. Besides, the author of the Shakespeare plays needed borrow of nobody. The answer is that he borrowed not anything of anybody, but spoke the speech he was bred to. But Mr. Davis goes yet further, and shows how the writer of these plays deliberately remodeled things not legally expressed, until they satisfied that legal mind of his, and were so dressed in judicial garb that any queen's counsel might use them for a brief. For example, the first quarto of "Hamlet" was printed in 1603. In it were the lines:

> "Who by a seale compact, well ratified by law
> And heraldric, did forfeit with his life all those
> His lands which he stood seized of by the conqueror,
> Against the which a moiety competent
> Was gaged by our king—"

But to state this in legal form there is appended, when "Hamlet" comes to be printed in the folio:

> "—which had returned
> To the inheritance of Fortinbras
> Had he been vanquisher: as by the same covenant
> The carriage of his article designed
> His fell to Hamlet."

Would any playwright or poet have thought necessary, in revising his copy for a second edition, to have added that legal explanation for the benefit of a promiscuous audience at a theater? If this does not show that the writer was a lawyer born and bred, it is hard to believe that such things as lawyers and Shakespearean plays exist.

Again, the quarto reads:

> "I did repel his letters, deny his gifts,
> As you did charge me,—"

Which is changed in the folio to—

> "I did repel his letters, and denied
> His access to me."

The lines —

> "For in that dreame of death, when we awake,
> And, borne before our everlasting judge,
> From whence no passenger euer returned,
> The undiscovered country, at whose sight
> The happy smile and the accursed damn'd —"

Are remodeled by a lawyer into —

> "The undiscovered country from whose bourne
> No traveller returns —"

"bourne" being a law term.
The lines —
> "Yet you cannot
> Play upon me, besides to be demanded by a spunge —"

Are made to read —

> "Besides, to be demanded of a spunge: what replication
> Should be made by the son of a king?"

Besides, in the folio appear the legal propositions:

> "Now must your conscience my acquittance seal.
> * * * * * *
> It will appear: but tell me
> Why you proceeded not against these feats
> So crimeful and so capital in nature —"

which in the quarto were not deemed, it seems, necessary to the dialogue, as indeed, from anything but a lawyer's point of view, they are not.

But most wonderful of all is the dialogue in the grave-yard scene. In the quarto, the two gravediggers are wondering whether Ophelia, having committed suicide, is to be buried in consecrated ground, instead of at a cross-road with a stake driven through her body; and clumsily allude to the probability that, having been of noble birth, a pretext will be found to avoid the law. Now mark what the old lawyer does with this dialogue. It happens that in the first volume of Plowden's reports there is a case (Hales v. Petit, I., Pl. 253) of which the facts bore a wonderful resemblance to the story of Ophelia. Sir James Hales was a judge of the common pleas, who had prominently concerned himself in opposing the succession of Queen Mary. When Mary ascended the throne he expected decapitation, and was actually imprisoned, but by some influence released. His brain, however, became affected by his vicissitudes, and he finally committed suicide by throwing himself into a watercourse. Suicide was felony, and his estates became escheated to the crown. The crown, in turn, granted to one Petit. But Lady Hales, instructed that the escheat might be attacked, brought ejectment against Petit, the crown tenant. The point was as to whether the forfeiture could be considered as having taken place in the lifetime of Sir James; for if not, the plaintiff took the estate by survivorship. In other words, could Sir James be visited with the penalty for plunging into a stream of water? For that was all he did actually do. The suicide was only the result of his act, and can a man die during his life? Precisely the point in Ophelia's case as to her burial in consecrated ground. If Ophelia only threw herself into the water, she was only a suicide by consequence, non constat that she proposed to die in the aforesaid water. So the case was argued, and the debate of the momentous questions — whether a man who commits suicide dies during his own life, or only begins to die; whether he drowns himself, or only goes into the water; whether going into water is a felony, or only part of a felony, and whether a subject can be attainted and his lands escheated for only part of a felony — is so rich in serious absurdity, and the grave-diggers' dialogue over Ophelia's proposed interment in holy ground so literal a travesty, that the humor of the dialogue — entirely the unconscious humor of the learned counsel in Hales v. Petit — can hardly be anything but proof that, admitting William Shakespeare to have written that grave-yard scene, William Shakespeare was a practicing lawyer; especially since it is to be remembered that Plowden's report was then, as it is to-day, accessible in Norman Latin law jargon and black-letter type, utterly unintelligible to anybody but an expert antiquarian, and utterly uninviting to anybody. Law Norman or law Latin was just as unattractive to laymen in Elizabeth's day as it is to lawyers in ours; if possible, more so. The decision in Hales v. Petit — on account of the standing of the parties-plaintiff — might have been town talk for a day or two; but that the wearying and, to us, ridiculous dialectics of the argument and decision were town talk, seems the suggestion of a very simple or of a very bold ignorance as to town life and manners. Besides, nobody sets the composition of "Hamlet" earlier than Nash's mention of "whole Hamlets" in 1587 or 1589 — and every commentator of standing puts it about ten years later. That the hair-splitting of a handful of counsel would remain town talk for twenty-five or thirty-six years is preposterous to suppose. Reference to the arguments in that case could only have been had from Plowden's report. And, moreover, it was no freshman law student or attorney's clerk who could so travesty them as to preserve every humorous point and omit the wearying dialectics of the blackletter.

But having burlesqued and poked fun at the hair-splitting of our "old Father Antic the Law," our dramatist changes his key, and finds solemn and portentous similitude therein. When Hamlet takes up the lawyer's skull, he asks, "Will his vouchers vouch him no worse of his purchases, and double ones too, than the length and breadth of a pair of indentures?" Here the term "double voucher" is introduced as a text for a homily upon mortality, inexplicable certainly to one not a lawyer to whom the intricacies of that term were passing familiar. "A 'double voucher' was an incident to the alienation of lands by a common recovery. A desired to suffer a common recovery so as to bar entails, remainders, and reversions; and thereby to convey the land in fee-simple to B. To effect this, B brought suit against A for the lands, alleging that A had no legal title, but that he came into possession after one C (a fictitious person) had turned the plaintiff out, whereupon A, the defendant, appeared, and called on D (usually the crier of the court, who was used for that purpose), who by fiction was supposed to have warranted the title to A when the latter bought, to come in and vouch and defend the title which he had so warranted. D thereupon pleaded, defending the title; B then requested leave of the court to imparl or confer with the voucher D, in private, which was done. B returned into court, but D absented himself and made default. Whereupon judgment was given that B recover the lands of A, and A had judgment to recover lands of equal value of D, the man of straw. This recovery was with a single voucher. But D, being a mere man of straw, it was manifest that A had only a nominal recompense for the lands. It was customary to have a recovery, with double voucher, by first conveying an estate of freehold to any indifferent person against whom the suit was brought, who vouched the tenant in tail who wished to carry through the recovery, who in turn vouched the man of straw again. The reason of this double voucher was that if a recovery was had immediately against the tenant in tail (A), it barred only such estate in the lands of which he was then actually seized; but if the recovery was had against another person, and A, the tenant in tail, was vouched, it bound every latent or contingent right which he might have in the premises recovered. Death is therefore the fine and common recovery of all things, and the man himself; and his vouchers, single or double, vouch him nothing then."

The reader who has had patience enough to follow the above will surely find himself in a state of mind equal to admitting no other than a lawyer to have been responsible for one at least of Hamlet's similies. Mr. Davis proceeds: " It thus appears that Shakespeare amplified the statement of the compact with Fortinbras; changed Polonius's term, 'a forced graunt,' to a more formal and elaborate legal expression; inserted the word 'canon' to express a divine law; forced the word 'tender' to an ampler use; called lovers' oaths 'brokers'; caught the idem sonans of the word 'borne' and changed it to 'bourne' as the boundary of that undiscovered country; took the suggestion of the word 'demanded' and asked what 'replication' shall be made; added the request for a 'sealed acquittance' and the demand why 'capital' crimes had not been 'proceeded against'; rewrote the dialogue between the clowns solely to enlarge it and make it more accurate in its legal meaning, and more relevant to the case in Plowden; reconstructed Hamlet's meditations on the lawyer's skull; corrected the inaccurate suggestion of an indictment for an action of battery; struck out the words 'leases and freeholds and tenements'; added to the enumeration of the devices of moneylenders the words 'buyer of land,' 'statutes,' 'recognizances,' 'fines,' 'recoveries,' etc," while in the "Merry Wives of Windsor" (the quarto of which is dated the year before this quarto "Hamlet") the same words, "fine and recovery," are put into the mouths, in the folio, of one of the merrie ladies who certainly made no allusion to them in the quarto.

This Shakespeare then was a lawyer. His name could not have been Bacon, says Mr. Davis, because (and here is a telling blow for the Baconians) "Charles I. was sixteen years of age when Shakespeare died. Bacon dedicated to him his history of Henry VII. Shakespeare, in 'Macbeth,' nobly magnified the house of Stuart by a prophecy of its perpetuity. The works of Shakespeare were the closet companion of Charles, who was reproached for this by Milton at a time when the fierce zealots of rebellion had come to look upon the drama as sinful. Falkland was Charles's councilor, and it is from him that we have, respecting Caliban, the first critical estimate extant of any character in Shakespeare.[1]

"And yet from prince, king, courtier, poet, or scholar, we hear no hint which can give this modern theory the slightest support. . . . Shakespeare dedicated his poems to Southampton. But if Bacon was Shakespeare, it is incredible that within a few years Bacon should have appeared as volunteer counsel against Essex and Southampton, or that he should have undertaken afterward in his 'Declaration of the Treason of Robert, Earl of Essex,' the task of proving the complicity of his friend and patron in that conspiracy.

"It is also remarkable that in this same production, in order to fasten guilt upon the conspirators, Bacon lays especial stress upon the fact 'that the afternoon before the rebellion, Merick, with a great company of others, that afterward were all in the action, had procured to be played before them the play of deposing King Richard II. Neither was it casual, but a play bespoken by Merick; but, when it was told him by one of the players that the play was old, and that they should have loss in playing it, because few would come to it, there were forty shillings extraordinary given to play it, and so thereupon played it was. So earnest was he to entirely satisfy his eyes with the sight of that tragedy, which he thought soon after his lordship

[1] *Ante*, p. 143; note 25, De Quincey's "Shakespeare."

should bring from the stage to the state, but that God turned it upon their own heads.' If Francis Bacon wrote Richard II., it was a piece of matchless effrontery for him to maintain that his own production had been displayed as a counterfeit presentment in aid of a treason in which his friend was engaged. . . . Again, Bacon was actively engaged in the Court of Chancery for many years before he became lord chancellor. It was then that the memorable war of jurisdiction was waged between Ellesmere and Coke — and yet there is not in Shakespeare a single phrase, word, or application of any principle peculiar to the chancery."

But, for all this happy relief from Verulam and the Baconian spook, the fact remains that the common law lawyer (ignorant as he was of the chancery), who was so familiar with Plowden's Reports that he could travesty Hales v. Petit, and even find sentiment in Double Voucher, blunders most egregiously over a very simple piece of draughting. "The Merchant of Venice" opens with a legal error. The bond proposed by Shylock and executed before an officer by Antonio was not "a single bond," technically speaking. If it had been, the play would have stopped right there, and there would have been no necessity for either court scene or Miss Portia's periods, or her harsh and inequitable handling of poor Shylock, who would have simply taken his principal and gone, as he offered to do when he discovered the entire court packed against him, and "the learned Bellario"— instead of a second Daniel — a Jeffreys, Scroggs, and an unreasonable young woman all rolled into one. To me the use of the term is only another

bit of evidence that no lawyer or lawyer's clerk
ever revised the play, or had an opportunity to
remove the bad law and manifest inequity of
Portia's eloquent performances. If, by making
Shylock use the word "single" in its simpler sense,
the writer intended to make the Jew express his
confidence either that Antonio would repay the
borrowed money without a surety, or that "the
strict law of Venice" was powerful enough to
restore him at least his principal,— a confidence, I
need not add, in both cases badly misplaced,— then
I think this inference is still more cumulative.

Certainly Mr. Davis will find it difficult to believe
that a man once a lawyer is not a man always a
lawyer. If one single man wrote these plays, in
which we find both deliberate and indeliberate
legal drift, how about glaring and outrageous
misstatements of horn-book legal propositions?
In the trial scene, Portia is as punctilious as a
Pennsylvania tipstaff to get the docket entries
regular. But how could an English lawyer have
made Portia's every single ruling the exact
reverse of what the English law of Shylock's case
was and is? The "law of Venice" was the old
Roman law — the Code; and, however modified by
the Venetian statutes, was not modified as to the
eternal principles of jurisprudence. And, moreover, it is these eternal principles of unwritten
law, and no alleged or actual statute of Venice,
that Portia herself claims to apply to Shylock's
case. It is not until she comes to disposing of his
estates, which she has illegally and illogically
escheated, that she cites (IV., i., 348) anything
"enacted by the laws of Venice" (that is, a statute).

To demonstrate wherein — as it strikes me — this entire trial scene shows, not a knowledge but a most consummate ignorance of all or any legal procedure, I have imagined Portia's decision in the case of Shylock v. Antonio as having been twice appealed from, and that the following appears in a volume of the Reports of the imaginary appellate court.

SHYLOCK'S APPEAL

(affirming Shylock v. Antonio: 75 Italian R., p. 104)

In the HIGH COURT OF APPEAL OF THE KINGDOM OF UNITED ITALY.

January 9th, 1887.

ANTONIO, *respondent (defendant below)* v.
SHYLOCK, *appellant (plaintiff below).*

1. ACTION, REFORMATION OF — Where merits are shown, the court will not dismiss an action because wrongly brought, but will reform it to a case disclosed, and proceed to judgment thereon.
2. AMICUS CURIÆ — An "amicus curiæ," or Friend of the Court, or his delegate, may be called in by the court, and the facts as disclosed by the evidence taken — or a submitted state of facts agreed upon by counsel — laid before him, and his decision will be the judgment of the court (75 I. R., 104).
3. CRIMES — Crimes cannot be presumed; nor have courts power to impute a wrongful intention, and to proceed to punish that intention when not accompanied by any overt act.
4. CONTEMPT OF COURT — *(obiter,* Bonfati, C. J.) — A court has certainly power to waive a contempt, and if the court itself take no notice thereof, it is certainly to be inferred that it does so waive the contempt.
5. EQUITY OF REDEMPTION. FORECLOSED PREMISES — A mortgagee cannot bar the mortgagor of his equity of re-

demption by claiming performance of the penalty in lieu of satisfaction of the mortgage out of the mortgaged premises (affirming, 75 I. R., 104).
6. GRANT, see MAXIMS OF EQUITY.
7. INTENTION, see CRIMES.
8. MAXIMS OF EQUITY — That Equity abhors a penalty — considers that done which ought to be done — and grants with a thing whatever is necessary or convenient to reduce the thing granted to possession, are maxims of equity from time immemorial, and axiomatic in courts of justice (affirming, 75 I. R., 104).
9. MORTGAGE — An action for foreclosure of a mortgage is an equitable action, and will follow equitable precedents in preference to those of law.
10. PUBLIC POLICY — Every sound public policy encourages settlements between the litigants themselves, and courts will not refuse to suspend proceedings before them at any stage of the trial, in order to afford an opportunity for compromise or settlement. Especially is this Italian policy.
11. RELIGION — A man's religion — providing that in the practice of its rites and ceremonies there be nothing contrary to the public peace, safety, or policy, or injurious to one's neighbors, or that works perpesture or nuisance — is as much that man's possession as any other thing, estate, easement, right or chattel, choate or inchoate, that is his. Nor can a deprivation of one's religion or religious liberty ever be, or compose, or form part of, the sentence of a court.
12. SENTENCE, see RELIGION.
13. TENDER — A tender in no case discharges a debt, but only interest and costs accruing subsequently to the tender made (affirming 75 I. R., 104).
SAME — The sum tendered must be exact. Nor will a general offer of "three times the sum," or other words of like import, made in open court, constitute a tender (Ibid.)
SAME — The party making a tender must at the same time offer in court a sum equal to the interest and costs already accrued on the principal thing.

ERROR FROM THE STRICT COURT OF VENICE.

The material facts are stated in the opinion:

BONFATI, C. J.:

This case was argued before Venice, in the person of the Duke, and the opinion delivered by Portia, delegate of Amicus Curiæ, called in by the Duke. The facts were taken in open court, and submitted to an Amicus Curiæ (Bellario), who sent his delegate (Portia) to deliver his opinion and decision upon them in open court. This is a regular, though not a usual practice. There is no report of the first day's session before Venice; and no transcript of the evidence put in on that day is brought here. These proceedings, therefore, are presumed to be regular. The decision, as pronounced by Portia, and the extraordinary scenes attendant upon such pronouncement, the interruptions by the defendant and his friends, harangues by the plaintiff, and sarcastic comments upon the bearing of the latter by the former, are reported with unusual verisimilitude in Shakespeare's Reports (Rolfe's Friendly Edition, vol. VII.) We pass these many and obvious contempts of court, remarking only what appears to us to have been the extraordinary complaisance of the court. Doubtless it is as within the power of a court to tolerate as to punish contempts. But undoubtedly, in behalf of good manners, such scenes as accompanied the delivery of the opinion of the court below ought not to be largely imitated in our nisi prius tribunals.

The plaintiff below loaned the defendant three thousand ducats, taking a written instrument conditioned in a penalty, that if the principal sum were not forthcoming in three months, plaintiff should cut a pound of flesh from the body of defendant in the vicinity of the latter's heart. This instrument was not impeached below, but the case (as reported by Rolfe, *ante)* came before us a year ago on appeal from the first judgment rendered by Portia as delegate Amicus Curiæ, and we then overruled and reversed every single proposition laid down by that young person as contrary to every known principle of law, and monstrous to the very horn-book maxims of jurisprudence. We held on that occasion (75 I. R., 104):

I. That plaintiff below was badly advised in bringing action for the penalty of the instrument. But, nevertheless, it appearing from the evidence that plaintiff had substantial merits, as set forth in his complaint, the court should have reformed his action, making it an action for the recovery of the money loaned. Where merits are shown, a court will not dismiss an action because wrongly brought, or for an improper demand of judgment, but will reform it to the cause of action disclosed, and proceed to judgment thereon. There being no forfeiture here of any of plaintiff's rights by reason of his error, and no prejudice to the defendant being worked thereby, we directed a new trial as aforesaid.

II. The delegate Amicus Curiæ Portia erred in holding:

1. That, not having paid the principal sum of 3000 ducats within or at the expiration of the three months, plaintiff was entitled to a foreclosure for the penalty. Granted that the instrument could stand, the action for its foreclosure was then an equitable action, and equitable maxims would govern. There is no older maxim than that equity abhors a penalty; and defendant would certainly have been entitled to his equity of redemption here.

2. That the plaintiff could elect between the principal sum and the penalty. It follows from the foregoing that, whatever the penalty, he can recover only principal, interest, and costs.
3. That having elected for the penalty, plaintiff could cut therefor; but, in the cutting, was not entitled to a hair's weight of flesh more or less than an exact pound, or a single drop of blood. It is an eternal principle of jurisprudence that, when the law gives anything, it also gives that without which the thing could not be enjoyed or reduced to possession. If I grant a close to Titius to which the only approach lies over my farm, or all the barley that shall be stored in my barn, I cannot withhold from Titius a right of way over my farm to his close, or the right to enter my barn and take the barley granted him. Had plaintiff the right to cut for his penalty, he certainly would have had a title to draw as much blood as it was absolutely necessary to draw in cutting out that pound; and such portions of flesh over and above a pound as it would be absolutely necessary to cut out, providing that cutting out was done by an expert and not by a bungler. The single gleam of reason we have been able to discover in Miss Portia's performances lies in her caution to the plaintiff that he provide surgeons to superintend the foreclosure she warrants him in proceeding to work upon the defendant's person.
4. Could the preceding decisions be surpassed in silliness, we think that the proposition that, plaintiff having refused a tender of "three times the sum," plaintiff must be nonsuited, would clearly surpass them. Since the days of Father Moses, a tender has never quite discharged or destroyed a debt. The utmost it can do is to discharge all or any interest and costs that would have accrued subsequent to the tender. Neither is a grandiloquent offer by a by-stander, friend, or claquer of one party to the other of "three times the sum," a tender in any known or legal sense of the word. However, it would have doubtless been in the power of the court below to have suspended proceedings at this juncture, that any reasonable offer of compromise or settlement should be heard, when the by-stander could have (through the proper channels) reduced his inclination to compromise the case to a formal

and regular offer. Courts of justice always look favorably upon settlements. "It is public policy that there should be as little litigation as possible, " is a very fundamental maxim of every known jurisprudence. But especially has it been the spirit of Italian jurisprudence since when the memory of man runneth not. One of the oldest institutions of our law is that of the Concertiatori. Any judge of a court of Cassation or of Assize has the power, on the request of both parties, and at any stage of a civil trial proceeding before him, to call in these concertiatori or arbitrators to compromise, if they can, the matter, without proceeding to judgment. I believe this custom peculiar to our own country, and unknown elsewhere. Certainly our new Constitution of 1863 very carefully preserves it. The early rulings in the former case below by Miss Portia gave some countenance to the belief that she was called in as one of these concertiatori, and we only wish that her acts could allow us so to have interpreted her presence. But the principle in pursuance of which these concertiatori have become engrafted upon our law (namely, that compromises between litigants are always favored) must obtain in the present case.

Plaintiff, therefore, was entitled to a tender if defendant had seen fit to make it. Nor can he be prejudiced either by the informality in which (if made in good faith) it was made, or by his own refusal to accept it.

Such being our decision, we sent the case back with every ruling reversed, and ordered a new trial on the merits. A new trial was had with the court constituted as before; the same delegate Amicus Curiæ delivering the judgment. With submission to the rulings above quoted, Portia gave judgment at once for the plaintiff in the sum of 3000 ducats, with interest and costs, but coupled it with the following:

"Tarry, Jew:
The law hath yet another hold on you.
It is enacted in the laws of Venice
If it be prov'd against an alien

That, by direct or indirect attempts,
He seek the life of any citizen;
The party 'gainst the which he doth contrive
Shall seize one-half his goods; the other half
Comes to the privy coffer of the State,
And the offender's life lies in the mercy
Of the Duke only; 'gainst all other voice:
In which predicament, I say thou stand'st."

Of Portia's prior judgment we endeavored to speak decorously. But the present branch it is difficult to characterize consonantly with a due sense of the dignity and decorum of this high court. To say that Portia is as reckless and shameless in her construction of statutes as she was densely ignorant and puerile in her comprehension of the common law, is, perhaps, too mild a statement. Certainly there is a Venetian statute to the effect that an alien conspirator against the life of a citizen shall be (upon proper apprehension and indictment thereunder, and trial and conviction had) sentenced to death and confiscation of his goods, a moiety to the state and a moiety to his proposed victim. But penal statutes cannot be applied ex parte and ab initio by a civil court sitting in a civil suit — on its own motion and at its own discretion. The usual processes of charge, arrest, indictment, arraignment, trial, with opporportunity for defense, can hardly be dispensed with entirely, even by a delegate Amicus Curiæ of the feminine gender. The effrontery of the present dispenser of justice — her civil rulings being reversed as fast as uttered — recouping herself, as it were, for the disgrace, at one fell swoop, by citing a penal statute and pronouncing a litigant guilty thereunder,— nay, in the same breath sentencing him to death in the pleasure of the State,— is certainly not paralleled in the history of Europe, whatever in other grand divisions of the globe may have been attempted. That Portia did not at once proceed to execute her judgment, and decapitate the plaintiff with an axe, is perhaps to be wondered at. Certainly the function of headsman is the only function she has not usurped. She has made the charge, arraigned the prisoner, presided at his trial, testified against him, found him guilty on her own testimony, and pronounced his sentence, all in ten lines. She has been informer, arraigner, witness, judge, and jury. Why should not this invaluable young person be executioner as well? This court is certainly not in the habit of indulging in anecdote by way of analogy. But we cannot fail to be reminded of a precedent occurring in an interior county of the State of New York, and related to us by a late lamented chief-justice of that State, of which the facts are substantially as follows:

A stranger in a small country town, having tarried several days without apparent motive or employment, was carried before a local justice of the peace and charged with vagrancy under certain statutes defining that charge. A young lawyer, quite as innocent of employment as the accused, eager for matter, volunteered for the defense. Noticing that the alleged "vagrant" was perfectly well dressed, he said to the justice: "Your Honor, I observe that the defendant wears very good clothes, and I think there is, or at any rate ought to be, a decision of the Court of Errors and Appeals that a man who wears good clothes cannot properly be called a 'vagrant.'"

An impression had evidently been made upon his Honor, and the young lawyer sat down. Nothing more was offered for the defense, and the justice summed up in these words: "I am of opinion that the defendant wears good clothes, and that a man who wears good clothes cannot properly be called a vagrant. But as the defendant hasn't proved to the satisfaction of the court where he got them clothes, I'll bind him over for larceny."

The action of our delegate Amicus Curiae Portia (being ordered by this court to find in the plaintiff Shylock's favor for the full amount of the defendant's debt, with interests and costs), coupling with her judgment to that effect a judgment against the plaintiff for meditated murder, reminds this court of nothing else than the binding over for larceny of a well-dressed man accused of vagrancy. Even if the plaintiff had seriously intended to murder the defendant — a fact which (without such an assault as would enable a jury, or perhaps, even a Portia to presume it) could be known only to an omnipotent searcher of hearts — it would be interesting to inquire from whence our interesting delegate Amicus Curiae, Portia, supposed herself invested with a jurisdiction over the thoughts of mankind.[1]

---

[1] Had the learned judge been inclined to further indulge in anecdote, he might perhaps have been reminded of another, also hailing from the State of New York, about a certain Teuton who punished his boy for saying "d——n it." "But I didn't say 'd——n it,' fader," said the boy. "Never mind, mine sohn," said the father, "you thinks 'd——n it' all the same, and I flogs you for that."

This, happily for judicial nerves, is the summit of illegality. But we think the sublimity of impudence is yet to come. Having in crescendo pronounced sentence of death, Portia now begins in diminuendo to arrogate to herself the pardoning power, and to assume that the condemned man would prefer life — minus worldly goods and the religion of his race — to death. She therefore, upon her own application, proceeds to commute the death sentence to a judgment (1), that plaintiff make a deed of gift of his property, real and personal, to his daughter; and (2), that he himself presently "become a Christian." No court nor state has power to compel a party to alienate by deed his property without consideration. Still less does the power anywhere obtain to confiscate a man's religion. We are of opinion that nothing would be more desirable than that the plaintiff below should become a Christian. Socially, it would be a most happy consummation, for he is of that patient and long enduring race of which — as he himself says — sufferance is the badge. But it does not seem to have occurred to the extraordinary young jurist who invokes mercy (which is a kind of irregular equity) for the Christian but forgets it for the Jew, that the faith of a man's fathers may possibly be as dear to him as life itself, and that it will be ample time for Shylock to become Christian when he himself covets the preferment. Suffice it to say, however, that plaintiff's religion, no more than his worldly goods, have ever come under the jurisdiction of the delegate Amicus Curiae who poses below, or within reach of her decree. A man's religion, provided that in the actual practice of the rites and ceremonies thereof there be nothing contrary to the public peace, or that injures his neighbors, or works perpesture or nuisance, is as much his possession as any other estate, thing, easement, right or chattel, choate or inchoate that is his; nor can a deprivation of one's religion or religious liberty ever be or compose a sentence or parcel of a sentence of a court of justice even after a conviction for crime. Had plaintiff below been legally sentenced to death, and the Duke seen fit to pardon him, this court could not have inquired into the motives or considerations moving the Duke to extend his pardon (and had one of the inducements been a change on plaintiff's part of the religion of his fathers, no record would have been made for this court to review). But not even the Duke of Venice, nor his delegated authority, has yet acquired power to compel an apostasy in open court. If, in the history of the jurisprudence of this planet it has come to pass that it is left to this court to declare that a human being (even though he be a despised Jew) has a right to the accumulations of his own labor, thrift, and economy, and that if he has loaned 3000 ducats, or any other sum, he has the right to expect the assistance and not the hindrance of courts in recovering it if it be withheld: I say, if it is left to this court, and at this stage of the world's history to so declare, this court, at least, will not be found unequal to the emergency.

All the proceedings in the court below are hereby ordered to be, and they are, peremptorily set aside, except the judgment directed by this court in the former appeal; and it is further

ORDERED: That so much of the judgment of the court below as decrees an escheat and penalties against plaintiff be set aside.

ORDERED: That the court below enter judgment absolute for plaintiff in the sum of 3000 ducats, with interest, costs of both trials and appeals, together with an extra allowance on the entire recovery, of five per cent.
All CONCUR.

MARTINI (concurring): Since the brazen offer of 3000 ducats to the delegate Amicus Curiae as the price of her partisan efforts is not called to our judicial notice, we are unable to punish the acceptance of the reward of champerty and malfeasance here. But the court below is directed to hear and grant a motion to disbar the said Portia permanently, and to direct payment by her into court of the 3000 ducats aforesaid, if received by her. Had Bellario or even Portia been merely a referee or master in chancery, to whom the case was referred, the payment alluded to by the associate-justice above might not be irregular. If so, the Duke's speech, "Antonio, gratify this gentleman" (that is, pay him for his services), is properly explained, as I understand the custom of a referee's fees being paid by the prevailing party to be one so old that the memory of man runneth not to the contrary.

But would it not have been as impossible for the pen that reconstructed Hamlet's soliloquy so that even death itself should move in metaphor not repugnant to equity, and wrote into the text a clearer exposition of the Danish entail, to have put into the mouth of the learned Bellario's deputy such burlesques as Portia delivered in the name of law, as for a mathematician to have declared the angles of his triangles equal to three right angles, or for an astronomer to move his comets in concentric circles? A Shakespeare, who had once been apprenticed to an attorney, could not have put rulings—which might have been, if I apprehend rightly, so emphatically reversed—into Portia's mouth. Certainly Lord Bacon, who fought the fight for Chancery against Sir James Coke (who preferred going to prison rather than admit that equity could stay proceedings at common law) could not have done it, unless indeed he, Bacon, had thought to burlesque common law. But in that case, by every rule, he would have put his burlesque into the mouth of a burlesque character, just as the travesty on Hales *v*. Petit was assigned to the grave-digger.

I have pointed out this utter perversion of legal rules at Portia's hands not for the sake of interfering with the eulogies of that young lady as a sort of fountain and virgin mother of justice, but to suggest that perhaps, after all, the solution is simple enough. Perhaps we will come nearer the truth if we take William Shakespeare to have been a dramatist—a practical stagewright—rather than a philosopher or a chancery lawyer; one who sought for dramatic, rather than for didactic or moral or psychological effects. The learned and worthy gentlemen who claim that

William Shakespeare never took up his pen save to teach some great ethical or eschatological lesson to his race and generation,—that his brain teemed, not with plans for running the "Globe" at a profit so as to be able to buy butchers' meat for his children, coats-of-arms and farms at Stratford, but for teaching his countrymen new systems of politics or philosophy—perhaps these gentlemen may be in error. Perhaps, after all, even old Aubrey, when he declared that Shakespeare "did gather humors of men daily" for his comedies, was nearer telling the truth. Perhaps Richard Grant White was not altogether at fault when he declared that "Shakespeare did his work with no other purpose whatever—moral, philosophic, artistic, literary,—than to make an attractive play which would bring him money * * * his first object was money—to get on in life: wrote what he wrote merely to fill the theater and his own pockets. * * * if his public had preferred it, would have written thirty-seven plays like 'Titus Andronicus,' just as readily as he wrote 'As You Like It,' 'Lear,' 'Hamlet,' and 'Othello.'"[1] With true dramatic art, the playwright who mounted that massive trial scene shows us only the final and crucial situation. The mere routine, the taking of the testimony and hearing of the merits, is supposed to have taken place when the curtain lifts and shows us the court, litigants, spectators and attendants, waiting for judgment to be pronounced. Had that scene been molded on the line laid down in the above imagined de-

[1] Studies in Shakespeare, pp. 20, 209. Boston: Houghton, Mifflin & Co. 1886.

cision the theater would have been empty long before the divine Portia had come to her climax. And the dramatist—not the lawyer—who wrote that play, knew it as well as we know it now.

It is a matter of regret, I think, that the most competent gentlemen and the ripest lawyer who has ever touched this Shakespeare problem should have omitted notice of the "Northumberland Manuscript" (so called). It seems to me an entirely unsolved problem, and one that especially calls for juristical treatment. Doubtless it had often occurred to the skeptic that, if the names Bacon and Shakespeare had actually the large correlation assumed for them in the Baconian scheme, it would not be unreasonable or unnatural to expect that somewhere among Elizabethan manuscripts the two might be found written by the same pen upon the same paper. And it would appear that such an expectation had been realized. For Mrs. Potts' celebrated "Promus" is not the only memorandum left behind him by Francis Bacon which, without violence of presumption, may be called one of his scrap-books. This so-called "Northumberland Manuscript," edited by Mr. Spedding in his well-known volume, "A Conference of Pleasure," although found in an imperfect state, unquestionably did belong to Francis Bacon; and unquestionably did—as Mr. Spedding has so irresistibly proved—contain not only material which Bacon afterward used in the composition of speeches to be recited by others upon dramatic occasions, but three or four entire plays since supposed to be his own. Unlike the "Promus," this manuscript consists not of random notes, but of matter written out in full form by Bacon's amanuensis. And, in an interval of employment, this amanuensis, in trying his pen or scribbling listlessly upon the cover of the scrap-book, did actually scrawl, not only the name Francis Bacon, but the name William Shakespeare—the latter at least eight times. To his mind, at least, the names suggested each other, not as matter of abstruse speculation, but it would seem as matter of course. But the clerkly hand went further, and listlessly scribbled not only the names Shakespeare and Bacon, but the names "Richard the Second," "Richard the Third," the long dog-Latin word "honorificabilitudinatibus" (which occurs in "Love's Labour's Lost," v. i., 39), and the line, "Revealing day through every cranny peeps," which (except that the word "spies" is substituted for "creeps") is a line of the Shakespeare poem "Lucrece." Mr. Spedding, to whom ordinarily the slightest scrap of Baconian autograph was priceless text for comment, seems to make no note of these facts, and to utterly abstain from comment. And yet these words occur on a sheet known to have been in Bacon's possession, and upon which not only the names of his own writings but his own name, "Mr. Francis Bacon," is repeatedly scribbled. Such tangible, actual, physical evidence of something unimpeachable, contemporary—I repeat, it seems to me that some lawyer, in refuge from the crowding barrens of conjecture, guess-work and surmise—ought to look into.

And not only the lawyer, but the physician, the surgeon, the alienist and pathologist are still maintaining their right to their day in court over these mysterious plays and poems, developing each for himself, nevertheless, the same pregnant enigma of contradiction. William Shakespeare was certainly not a lawyer either by profession or practice. But, were these plays originally framed as at present before us, the legal and medical allusion can be used effectively by the editorial theorist. Had there been—these gentlemen will submit—a plot selected from some old romance, fable, or historical episode, just as the Shakespeare plots are selected; a dialogue borrowed, scissored or composed by one or two or more collaborateurs; the whole cut, amplified, amended at first reading to the actors; then copied into lengths for each performer, and any localism or "gag" which the individual experience of each showed to be popular noted in the margins of these by the particular actor himself — all this might have gotten in. And when, therefore, the play came to be printed — as the Shakespeare plays were all printed — from the acting copies, it is a bold man, they think, who would claim them to be in any sense monographs, and not the product of contributory literal and editorial work. In no event, it seems to me, is there necessity of remitting Shakespeare from his present pinnacle in the affections of his race.

But who can peep and botanize here? The very motes that people these sunbeams are pregnant. All that is his is but by the way, put into the mouths of journey actors, of giggling boys who played women's parts; the utterance of some mimic character moving to carry out his part of a play before a rabble sitting in the straw of an Elizabethan pit. And yet the plummet of philosopher, poet, and of the special student— in all their laborious nights and days, have sunk, and perhaps shall sink, no deeper. In one passage a profoundness of expert learning, in another, a density of technical ignorance; in one (for example) a formula for the circulation of the blood, and in another a man killed by the infusion of poison poured into his ear, and a tetter covering his body as the accompaniment of death:[1] an impossibility which finds no excuse in physiological science. But — while the paradox in the case of legal matter remains unatoned for — as regards the physician's art it is immensely compensated for. Everywhere quackery was the order of the Elizabethan day, and everywhere it is mercilessly satirized, and the apothecaries, mountebanks, jugglers and "water doctors" held up to the ridicule of the audience. It is hard for us to imagine a day when people were advised to wash their faces only once a week, and to wipe them only on scarlet cloth in order to keep healthy; when pills made from the ground-up skull of a man who had been hung on a gibbet, a draught of spring water that had stood in the skull of a murdered man, the powder of a mummy, the blood of "dragons," the entrails of wild animals, were prescribed for certain disorders; when tumors were ordered stroked with the hand of a dead man; when, to cure a child of the rickets, it was passed head downward between the sections of a young tree split open for the purpose, and then tied together again (the child's recovery to parallel that of the knitting together and healing of the tree); when love philters were prescribed

[1] Among the scores of these books I mention only the latest: "Medical Thoughts of Shakespeare." B. Rush Field, Easton. 1885.

and sold everywhere, and when the king "touched" for scrofula. And yet it was in these days, and such as these, when every quack had his bagful of charms and philters for mental disorders, that Macbeth's physician is made to decline to prescribe for a mind diseased. " Therein the patient must minister to himself," says the good doctor. " More needs he the divine than the physician; good God, forgive us all!" And Lear's physician, instead of hanging a witch's tooth or a toad's wizen around the neck of the poor old king, as we might have expected, prescribes only rest and perfect quiet. That the purpose was to ridicule the charlatans is, I think, inferable from the fact — except only in the case of Cerimon and as above — that the passages evincing profound learning as to medicine or surgery are put into the mouths of laymen, never into the mouths of the professionals. Who can wonder that, brought up here as by a term and fine, our vision met and baffled midway by this majestic mountain of Shakespeare, some of us should give vent to our pent-up longings in theories and "crazes"!

Is not the solution of the mystery, after all, to be found in dramatic necessity? Portia's law is bad, because bad law is more dramatic than good law. Had her decision been sound in equity, Antonio and Bassanio would have been worsted and Shylock have departed with his pound of flesh, while the audience remained behind to tear down the theater and break the actors' heads. Is it not that Shakespeare, whatever he was, was no esthete, no self-singer, no egoist or retailer of his own moods and humors, but rather the dramatist, not only of his own day but of his own far-off future? He framed his Hamlet not only for Burbadge, but for Garrick, for Kean, for Booth, for Irving, for Wilson Barrett. He created Macbeth's queen, Imogen, Desdemona, Rosalind, not only for the boys who simpered and smirked in women's parts, but for Siddons, Cushman, Nielson, Faucit, Anderson. Read him as we will,— with any theory, hobby, crotchet, with any conception of Hamlet or Iago the tragedian may prefer,— Shakespeare is still Shakespeare, and dominates the stage. Find in the plays whatever we will,— law, medicine, the Aristotelian or Baconian philosophies (nay, even the cipher which Mr. Donnelly believes to lurk there), mimic their diction, sift their prosodies as we may,— we can neither replace nor destroy their dramatic fiber and purity. Says Charles Reade: "The Irelands palmed upon literary critics a manuscript play by Shakespeare; it was read, discussed: an antiquarian or so said No! most of the critics said Yes! and fell on their knees before the manuscript. It was put on the stage: coal-heavers and apprentices set literary criticisms right in ten minutes. Why? The stuffed fish thrown down on a bank might pass for a live fish; but put it in the water. No! The stage is Shakespeare's home. . . . . Yet this Shakespeare found in his day actors who, though since eclipsed, could speak his greatest lines up to his intention and more to his mind than he could himself; this is proved by his taking the second-rate parts in his own plays: the only manager in creation that ever did this or ever will."

VII

The Growth and Vicissitudes of a Shakespearean Play

HEN we read a poem by Tennyson, Coleridge, or Longfellow in a peculiar or unusual metre,— in hexameter or anapœsts, — we assume that the metre happened to be the poet's choice. It simply never occurs to us to speculate or to devise learned treatises concerning the poet's reason for preferring that particular form of verse to another when composing that particular poem. But with Shakespeare all this is changed. It seems we are to assign his different prosodiacal forms to different historical or calendar periods of his life not only, but to write his biography from these variations. Possibly we are to imagine William Shakespeare himself never sitting down to prepare a drama for his boards without consulting his almanac, in order to ascertain the metre in which it was proper for him to write it. Certainly it would perplex an average intellect to conceive a conclusion how-

ever hermetic, oracular, far fetched, overstrained or finical as to poor Shakespeare's habits, methods, motives, models, experiences and duties of composition, which has not been formulated by the esthetic, inductive and creative critics, though doubtless the womb of time is yet full of them. At a late meeting of the New Shakespeare Society of London, I understand that penetrative body to have ascertained definitely that Mr. Shakespeare wrote "The Tempest," to "illustrate Enchantment as an engine of Personal Providence." Pending the necessary, and no doubt imminent, work in twenty-five volumes octavo which shall elucidate this discovery, I am disposed to admit it to the chronological catalogue; for doubtless Mr. Shakespeare will be found to have been investigating "personal providences" at that period of his management of the Globe Theater. But I cannot forbear remarking that all this sort of absolute certainty is far less amazing than amusing when we remember that William Shakespeare himself not only never saw the 1623 text of his own plays, but (according to Heminges and Condell) never authorized the quarto texts upon which it was founded. That Heminges and Condell should impeach their own record by the statement that all their own predecessor "copy" was stolen and surreptitious, might indeed add the weight of what lawyers call a "declaration against interest" to their statement, were it not that there is much corroborative evidence to the same effect, though it is hard to believe that if these quartos were stolen at all, William Shakespeare did not himself wink at the theft. Shakespeare might well have been robbed once of his literary property (in days when there was no author's protection except an author's shrewdness in making his bargain before his production got into print) or, by an oversight, he might have even allowed the piracy to be repeated a second time. But that he should be robbed against his will, punctually, regularly and periodically for eleven years, and to the extent of some thirty or forty plays and editions of plays — each one a distinct and damaging piracy — rather passes one's powers of credulity. William Shakespeare was no fool in business matters; and there is the familiar proverb as to the man who twice suffers when forewarned. But here indeed are these quartos, printed in black and broken types, — roman, italic, punctuation and abbreviation marks, words intelligible and unintelligible, all thrown carelessly together, — and, whether stolen or authorized, authentic or spurious, it is behind them that we must dig, if we dig at all, to find the man, the dramatist and poet we are after. For the present, however, let us leave questions of origin, and content ourselves with demonstration of the vicissitudes which this priceless text outlived from its first appearance in the print of these quartos for twenty-one years more or less, to the collected form of 1623, from whence it has substantially come down to us in the general (save here and there by the industry or crotchet of the particular editor) untouched. And first, as to the examples of deeper insight into men and affairs, scientific and philosophical excursusses, and amplification of classical allusion which we find in the folios and not in the quartos.

The dissolution of the learned houses in England,— by which lands were ravished from the clerical and student, and bestowed upon the military and political, classes,— and the scattering of hundreds of scholars to search for whatever "lease of quick revenue" came first at hand, were still very recent in the perspective of years when William Shakespeare arrived in London. Manuscripts produced by these scholars had long since began to look for market; and when—in default of any periodical publications, magazines, or newspapers—managers of the then newly licensed theatrical companies came to be the nearest purchasers and purveyors of literature to the masses of the people — perhaps some of them found a sale at the stage-door. If, in certain of these manuscripts there were forecasts of such propositions as the circulation of the blood, the attraction of the center of the earth for falling bodies, the building of continents by oceanic action — possibly the actual allusions to those theories — which are familiar facts in the folios, but which we cannot discover in the quartos, can be accounted for without violence to probability or history. A manager like William Shakespeare would have been quick to see the dramatic in such an idea as that from a man's heart went forth to every member a compelling fluid, or that the simplest and most silent forces of nature were working always for betterment of the race; and to have availed himself of it for telling declamation. And mayhap there were bits of antique lore and classic allusion in these manuscripts, which also found their way into the plays; and sometimes went in at the wrong places, making the mass of anachronism which affronts the fine sense of critic and scholiast to-day. Without the university training of Marlowe or Jonson, Shakespeare must take his classics, as best he could, at second hand. He could not correct, or even know if they were wrong.

But these excursuses in the Shakespeare plays were evidently not inserted by the stage editor to draw crowded houses — nor material which we submit to our hermeneutics to-day, for the general who drank beer and fouled the straw in the Elizabethan barns called play-houses. To suppose that Elizabethan audiences went to their theaters to listen to philosophical and classical discussions, or to doubt that they would have hooted the metaphysicians off the boards, and tossed the learned Thebans in blankets, is to mis-read the history of the English stage. Whether retained because understood or because not understood is immaterial, since retained this recondite and hermetical matter was. Our next speculation, then, would seem to aptly be — since audiences must be attracted and the general appetite regarded— Was there no growth in the popular as well as in the classical, the humane as well as the didactic, vein? I think that there was, not only, but that,— slim as are our personal items as to William Shakespeare's methods, habits, and personality,— we happen to have a record of it, and that the dramatist was always tirelessly at work vitalizing all he borrowed, with his own genius. Of all that has been written of this man's personality,— of all the libraries of his real and alleged personal history,— we have only one little touch of the pen which shows him thus at work; but, small as it is,— standing alone without elaboration or comment,— it cannot be questioned or improved. "He did gather" says Aubrey, " humours of men daily, wherever they came . . . The humour of the constable [Dogberry or Elbow?] he happened to take at Grendon in Bucks, which is the road from London to Stratford, and there was living that constable about 1642." And in other ways did the newly organized theaters, with their companies, take the place now filled by the daily newspapers. Not only did actors become the willing mouthpieces of whatever was put into their hands in writing; but, in traveling from place to place, dealers in the latest on dits—news, scandal, or gossip; "the abstracts and brief chronicles of their time." Their acquaintance and good opinion were worth cultivating, and " after your death you had better have a bad epitaph than their ill report while you lived," as Hamlet reminded Polonius.

Under such circumstances, it was natural and unavoidable that the written play in the hands of these actors should constantly augment itself by interpolations and localisms. This latitude and license was not only tolerated, but playwrights even essayed to guide it by selecting the exact point in their manuscripts at which it should be indulged in. In the plays of this period we come continually upon such stage directions as "Here they two talke and rayle what they list": " All speak "; Here they all talke," etc. How can it be doubted that the actor found it immensely to his advantage to feel his audience beforehand, by ascertaining the matter of which — when the " business" allowed him — he should "talke and rayle" as he listed? Nor does it seem to me "considering too curiously," to surmise that Shakespeare endeavored to check this license in his own behalf when he made Hamlet direct that "Those that play your clowns speak no more than is set down for them," because conscious that his plays were freighted with much more than ordinarily valuable matter. How, indeed, could he have failed to know what he himself had admitted into them? Matter which it were shame for the clowns to dilute with their horse-play, "for there be of them that will themselves laugh, to set on some quantity of barren spectators to laugh too; though, in the meantime, some necessary question of the play be then to be considered." When the thumbed playbooks (gathered, as they were — each actor's part as far as it went) reached Heminges and Condell's printers, and were used (in default of any unblotted Shakespearean manuscripts) for First Folio "copy"— without editing or even proof-reading — of course any memoranda of this interpolated matter, any "abstract or brief chronicle," the individual actor had found timely and so noted on the margin, stood very little chance of being discriminated against by the compositors. Indeed, these compositors appear to have been allowed to set up pretty much as they pleased, and each to have paged his own work indifferently to the pagination of his fellows; or, if they happened to be short of "copy," they sometimes deliberately left a gap at hap-hazard. Nor was there any proof-reader any where to reconcile these slipshod and despotic journeymen. We see where, for example, they left a space of twenty-nine pages between "Romeo and Juliet" and "Julius Cæsar," in which to print the "Timon of Athens." But all the copy they could find of the "Timon" only made eighteen pages; and so by huge "head-pieces" and "tail-pieces," and a "Table of the Actor's Names" in coarse capitals, they eked out the signatures; and, by omitting the whole of the next signature, carried the pagination over from "98" to "109." The copy for "Troilus and Cressida" seems not to have been received until the volume was in the binder's hands (which is remarkable, too, for that play has been in print for fourteen years), for the play is not mentioned in the table of contents, but is tucked in without paging, except that the first five pages are numbered 78, 79, 80, 81, 82; whereas the paging of the volume had already reached 232. "Troilus and Cressida," thus printed, fills two signatures lacking one page, and so somebody at hand wrote a "prologue" in rhyme — setting out the argument, to save the blank page. And, were further evidence necessary, the careless proof-reading supplies it. In these acting copies of a particular actor's part, the name of the actor assuming that part would be written in the margin, opposite to or instead of the name of the character he was to personate, precisely as is done to-day by the theater copyist in distributing "lines" to the company. It happened that, in setting up the types for this first edition from these fragmentary actors' copies, the printers would often accidentally "follow copy" too closely, and set up these real names of the actors instead of the names of the characters. These were overlooked in the proof; and there still may be read: "Jacke Wilson" for " Balthazar" ("Much Ado About Nothing, II. iii. 37); "Andrew" and "Cowley" for "Dogberry"; "Kempe" for "Verges" (Id. IV. ii. 25), etc. And so in the "Merry Wives of Windsor," although Pistol has disappeared from the stage (along with the landlord, Nym, and Bardolph) for the transformation scene at "Herne's Oak," the stage business in the folio prints invariably "Pist" as a direction to the speeches of the Puck or Hobgoblin; — an error easily accounted for if we suppose this part doubled with that of Pistol — as it easily might have been in the old play. So "Broome" for "Brooke" in that play may not be a misprint, but the real name of an actor. These errors, to be sure, sometimes give us such interesting bits of insight into Shakespeare's green-room that we cannot but be very thankful for the blunderings of the printers. It seems, for example, that there were three actors of minor parts in the company: Sinclo, Humphrey (perhaps the Humphrey Jeaffes mentioned by Henslowe), and Gabriel by name (possibly Gabriel Harvey, an actor also mentioned by Henslowe), whose lines found their way into the hands of the first folio printers, and so down to us. Sinclo, it seems, took the part of one of the players in the Induction to the "Taming of the Shrew" (Induct. 89), and of one of the game-keepers in 3 Henry VI. (III. i. 1). Humphrey played the other game-keeper (the stage direction in the folio 3 Henry VI. (III. i. 1, being, "Enter Sinklo and Humphrey with crosse bowes in their hands," and Gabriel the "Messenger" (I. iii. 48) in the same play. And that this messenger was supposed to enter, as if out of breath with his haste in bringing the news with which he is intrusted, we are assured by finding in this same careless folio, at his second entrance (II. i. 42), printed: not "Gabriel" or "Messenger," but the words, " Enter one blowing." Thus we can gather something, not only of the actors, but of the stage business from the misprint of our First Folio. This player, Sincklo (or Sinklo, sometimes written Sink), took the part of the first of the three beadles who arrest Doll Tearsheet at 2 Henry IV. (V. iv. 21), where the stage direction is in the quarto: " Enter Sinklo and three or four officers." And that he was a spare, lean man, rather than short and fat (as beadles ought to be), we know from the unspeakable Doll's threat, " Thou thin man in a censer, I will have thee soundly swinged," etc. That material errors like these could have remained unnoticed and uncorrected for twenty-three years is therefore not only an illustration of the extreme carelessness in everything except the mechanical part of their employment of the early printers, but of the hurried preparation of the actors' copies from which these printers set up. And it is probably to this habit of preparing plays for the night's presentation hurriedly, and without stopping to assign names to characters (since there were no playbills, it could really make no difference so the parts were effectively cast), that we doubtless owe the name Curtiss, given to one of Petruchio's servants in the " Taming of the Shrew"; otherwise the introduction of an English name into an Italian play (where even Baptista as a male name is accurately used, showing an unusual familiarity somewhere with Italian nomenclature) might still puzzle us. In this same play we have the first speech in Scene I of Act III. given now to a messenger (or servant) assigned to Nicke (or Nick) in the folio; and, as there is known to have been a Nicholas Tarleton among the actors of that period, he has been conjectured as being the one alluded to as cast for this part.

And that these fragments of old quartos and actors' lines contained notes of changes necessary, convenient, or profitable in the text furnished them, according to the varying circumstances or emergencies of twenty-one years of stage service, there is, it seems to me, constant proof. For example: In the quarto, where Falstaff cuts fellowship with Pistol, he says: "I myself sometime, leaving the fear of God, am fain to shuffle, to filch, and to lurch." When it comes to the folio it is printed, "Leaving the fear of Heaven." Similarly in the quarto of the "Much Ado About Nothing" (1602), Dogberry demands of Conrade and Borachio, "Masters, do you serve God?" and upon being answered affirmatively, tells the sexton to "write down that they hope they serve God; and write God first; for God defend but God should go before such villains" (Act IV., ii. 17). But in 1605, the third year of King James, there was enacted a statute (XIX. Stat. 3 Jac., 1 Cap. 21): "If any person in any stage play interlude, show, May-game or pageant, jestingly and profanely use the name of God, or Christ Jesus, or the Holy Ghost, or the Trinity, he shall forfeit ten shillings, one moiety to the King, the other moiety to him that will sue for the same in any court of record at Westminster." In deference to this statute, the name of Deity in Falstaff's speech is changed to "Heaven," the direction to the sexton is omitted, and Dogberry, after the reverent question, "Masters, do you serve God?" gives no opportunity for response, but (since the remainder of the passage admits of no reconstruction) proceeds immediately with "Masters, it is proved already that you are little better than false knaves, and it will go far to be thought so shortly," etc. — indicating that the book used by the First Folio printers for this play was of date subsequent to 1605. The general effect of this statute was to substitute everywhere in the plays of that period this word "Heaven" for "God" (see Richard II., I. ii. 37, and passim), and I am advised that the word "Heaven" has been preferred generally upon the English stage ever since. Here certainly was evidence of reëditing. Again: France and Spain were the countries with which England was oftenest at war, and which, therefore, it was most popular to disparage. Frenchmen and Spaniards were relied upon to make the groundlings roar, precisely as in our American cities we utilize to-day a plantation negro or a Chinaman for the purpose. But, subsequently to 1604, King James, who wished his son Charles to marry a Spanish princess, became anxious to conciliate Spain in every way, and so particularly unwilling that public offense be given to Spaniards. In the quarto of "Much Ado," therefore, where Dom Pedro says that Benedict must surely be in love, since he dresses "like a Dutchman to-day, a Frenchman to-morrow, or in the shape of two countries at once: as a German from the waist downward, all slops; and a Spaniard from the hips upward, no doublet," the stage censor directed that the last half of the sentence be entirely expunged, making Dom Pedro merely say that Benedict had a fancy for appearing as "a Dutchman to-day, and Frenchman to-morrow" (III. ii. 32). Add to these the occasions where the actors deliberately "cut" a long speech, which are quite too numerous to schedule here. Some of the lines we prize most in "Hamlet," were ruthlessly sacrificed by individual actors (e. g., Hamlet, I. i. 108–126, and II. iv. 37), and so never went into the First Folio at all; and the faith of those who are ready not only to make oath that every dot or comma, syllable, exit, entrance, was Shakespeare's own, and that he had a high eschatological purpose in every one of them, ought to be considerably agitated.

Moreover, that the play of those days grew by volunteer localisms, "gags," and "guys" of the actor, there is a curious piece of non-contemporary testimony. Pope, writing his preface in or about 1725, declared that he had seen a quarto of one of Shakespeare's plays where much of the ribaldry of the lower characters now preserved in the First Folio was "in the margin in a written hand," and another quarto, in which a speech and bit of stage business were carelessly run in together, making the line read: "The Queen is murdered, ring the little bell";[1] (to which the watchful Malone

---

[1] The pagination of the First Folio stands pp. 1 to 38, then 61 to 129, and so on, becoming hopelessly mixed up later on, when it begins at 1 again at the Histories. Some of the head-lines are transposed (as e. g., pp. 37, 38 of "The

added: "There is no such line in Shakespeare"). Pope continues: "In the old edition of 'Romeo and Juliet,' there is no hint of a great number of the mean conceits and ribaldries now to be found there. In others, the low scenes of mobs, plebeians, and clowns are vastly shorter than at present; and I have seen one in particular which seems to have belonged to the play-house, by having the parts divided with lines, and the actors' names in the margin, where several of these passages were added in a written hand, which are since to be found in the folio." And, since Pope's time, critical study has unearthed many more such evidences of accretion.

Two Gentlemen of Verona" read "The Merry Wives of Windsor." In "Hamlet" 100 pages are omitted entirely (156 to 257) though the text is all right. I have never, for my own part, wavered in believing, that to the same carelessness and indifference on the part of these editors, we owe the omission of "Pericles" from the First Folio. I am unaware of any standard of internal evidence by which that play can be left out of the Shakespeare Canon. Much of its higher dialogue is magnificent, and, even in the unreadable brothel scenes, the wit is of Shakespearean tension and quality. Nor with such abundant proof of haste or incompetency, or both, on the part of Messrs. Heminges and Condell, is it possible to take their unsupported word as to a Shakespearean authorship. Six quarto editions of "Pericles" bore Shakespeare's name, and the same modern scholarship which affects to concur in its rejection by Heminges and Condell, admits the employment of hack writers (to an extent of something more than three-sevenths of the entire play as printed) to pad the "Timon of Athens" to a necessary length; laying yet other liberties to their charge which would seem to tally with Disraeli's opinion that the publication was not so much an offering of friendship as a pretext to obtain a proprietary right to the plays.

Of course, to search for these interjected lines would be a thankless task, and the result only matter of opinion. But it may avoid disputes as to construction to suspect their occurrence. As, for example, in such a passage as the following: In "Titus Andronicus" (V. i. 90–100) Aaron is telling Lucius that Demetrius and Chiron have ravished his sister, at which Lucius exclaims, "O barbarous, beastly villains, like thyself!" And Aaron concurs:

> "Indeed, I was their tutor to instruct them;
> That codding spirit had they from their mother,
> As sure a card as ever won the set;
> That bloody mind, I think, they learned of me,
> As true a dog as ever fought at head."

Now, all the editors from Johnson downward annotate this passage in two places. They properly explain that "codding" comes from "cod," a pillow, and that the derivative means, lecherous; while Johnson adorns his page with the ponderous and invaluable statement that the line, "As true a dog as ever fought at head" is an allusion to bull-dogs, whose generosity and courage are always shown by meeting the bull in front and seizing his nose."[1] But no editor — so far as I

[1] The old editors (Theobald and Capell excepted), abound in this sort of perfunctory and personal annotation, thereby swelling their array of notes and consequent appearance of erudition with as slight effort as possible. Warburton especially clogged up his pages with remarks weak, whimpering and silly not only, but which suggested that he was not at pains to even read the text he so glibly "edited." Thus Lorenzo's speech ("Merchant of Venice," V. i. 294):

> "Fair ladies, you drop manna in the way
> Of starved people."

am able to discover — has ever grappled with the exceedingly inconsequent and apparently interpolated line, "As sure a card as ever won the set." Nevertheless, that line is utterly meaningless and incoherent as a part of Aaron's speech. The persons are talking of bloody and ferocious deeds, and no analogue is being used to cards or games; the further line, "I played the cheater for thy father's hand," being quite as unintelligible and quite as impossible to connect with any idea of a game with cards. That Dr. Johnson dodges both these lines seems to me no adequate reason why every modern editor should do the same. It is suggested that some actor may have attempted a pun on the syllable "cod" in "codding," or perhaps mimicked the affected pronunciation of a brother actor, as "cahd," "cahding" (certainly not an unusual dropping of the "r" in our own day). The suggestion may appear as far-fetched as Dr. Johnson's bull-dog. But the line seems to me of a source foreign to that of the rest of Aaron's speech, and some hypothetical explanation thereof in order, if only to attract attention to it. Shakespeare at least rarely introduces his puns, however bad, upon tragic occasions. In later days

Warburton annotates as follows: "Shakespeare is not more exact in anything than in adapting his images with propriety to his speakers, of which he has here given an instance in making the young Jewess talk of manna." Even had the "young Jewess" (Jessica) made the speech, the note would have still failed of very large scholarly value. But the fact is that Lorenzo, and not Jessica, makes the speech. The amazement is that our modern variorum editors have not courage to rid the text of Shakespeare from these barnacles.

the interpolations of intelligent actors have so largely added to the acting value of plays, as to become subjects of legal protection; and it does not appear to me finical to look for the origin of the custom among the origins of the drama itself.[1]

But it seems probable that the greatest embarrassment and interruption to the series of presentations at the Shakespeare theaters would have been the policy of Elizabeth. She had been upon her throne not yet four months when she issued her proclamation of April 7th, 1559 — to be repeated in substance in a second decree, dated May 16th, 1559. This first proclamation is not extant; nothing being known of its character except from the allusion to it in Hollinshed.[2] The second was printed and circulated in the form of a Broadside " imprinted " (so runs the colophon) "at London in Powles Churchyarde by Richard Jugge and John Cawood, Printers to the Quenes Magestie. Cum Priuilegio Regiae Maiestatis." From the copy in the British Museum (there being only one other in existence, the copy in the Bodlean) I am enabled to print it entire:

"BY THE QUENE.

"Forasmuche as the tyme wherein common Interludes in the Englishe tongue are wont vsually to be played is now past vntyll All Hallowtide and that also Some that have ben of

[1] In Keene v. Wheatley, the court held that "such interpolations, speeches, and phrases as Mr. Joseph Jefferson added to the part of Asa Trenchard in ' Our American Cousin,' were the property of Miss Laura Keene, the proprietor of that play and of the theater where Mr. Jefferson acted; he being in her employment."—" The Law of Literature," Vol. ii., p. 327. New York: Appleton Morgan. 1875.

[2] See Collier's "History of the English Stage," I., 168.

late used, are not convenient in any good ordered Christian Common weale to be suffred. The Quenes Maiestie doth straightly forbyd al maner Interludes to be playde either openly or priuately except the same be notified before hande, and licensed within any citie or towne corporate by the Maior or other chief officers of the Same, and within any shyre by suche as shalbe Lieuetenaunts for the Quenes Maiestie in the same shyre, or by two of the Justices of pease inhabyting within that part of the shire where any shalbe played.

"And for instruction to euery of the Saide officers her maiestie doth likewise charge every of them as they will annswere — that they permyt none to be played wherein either matters of religion or of the governance of the Estate of the commonweale shalbe handled, or treated; beyng no meto matters to be wrytten or treated vpon, but by menne of aucthoritie, learning and wisedom, nor to be handled before any audience but of grave and discrete persons: All which partes of this proclamation her maiestie chargeth to be inviolably kepte. And if any shall attempte to the contrary — her maiestie giueth all manner of officers that have authoritie to see common peax Kepte, in commandment to arrest and emprison the parties so offending for the spayce of fourteen dayes or more as cause shall nede — and furder also until good asswrance maybe founde and giuen that they shalbe of good behaviour and no more to offend in the like.

"And furder her Maiestie giueth speciall charge to her nobilitie and gentilmen, as they professe to obey and regard her maiestie, to take good order in thys behalfe with thier servauntes being players that thys her Maiestie's commandment may be dulye Kept and obeyed.

"Yeuen at our Palayce of Westminster, the XVI daye of Maye the first year of our Raygue."[1]

Now what plays had been publicly represented in London prior to 1559, which should have appeared to the young queen so subversive of the

[1] This copy was kindly made for me by Hon. T. W. Snagge, a judge of Her Majesty's Common Pleas, from the original Broadside, and, to insure perfect accuracy, with his own hands. So far as I know to the contrary, this may be its first appearance in print since 1559. I am sure its great curiosity justifies its appearance here at any rate.— A. M.

public tranquillity as to call for pause in the crowding labors of a new reign that two proclamations inside of five weeks should issue? We may never know. Shakespeare was yet to be born and to write his first play when the queen was nearing her earthly term and fine. And the dramatic condition under which his predecessors in the reign of Mary had worked do not seem to have lead to, or to have produced any raison d'être for, the edicts of April 7th and May 16th, 1559. The probabilities are, I think, that we owe them to that iron foresight, so to speak, and invincible determination on the part of the young queen to tighten even the rigid Tudor policy to which she had succeeded, and to leave no detail, even of the people's amusements, uncentralized in herself. This item of her policy may in the lapse of years or failure of cause for enforcement have fallen asleep. But that the queen's attention may have been called to the performance of all Shakespeare's historical plays — (as we know it was to the Richard II.) and induced the peremptory order for "Falstaff in Love," rather than further indulgence in his habit of making himself too free with matters not "mete to be written or treated vpon but by menne of aucthoritie, learning and wisdom, nor to be handled before any audience but of grave and discrete persons" — it seems, under the circumstances, hard not to believe. Certainly, did any English compositions ever fall into purview of statutes forbidding plays "wherein either matters of religion or of the governance of the estate of the commoweal shall be handled or treated," the plays we call Shakespeare's are those compositions!

Now we know that Queen Elizabeth had seen with her own eyes the historical plays in which Sir John Falstaff — né Oldcastle — had been delineated. Why were not the Globe and Blackfriars closed under and by virtue of the proclamation of May 16th, 1559? Among the so-called "Bridgewater Manuscripts" brought forward by Mr. J. P. Collier, in 1835–6 (then at the height of his reputation as a scholar, antiquary and Shakespearean) was a "Certificate of the Blackfriars Players," dated in 1589. It was instantly accepted as either the genuine draft or early copy of such paper, until the general dénouement which proved all Mr. Collier's manuscript, as well as the " Perkins Folio," to be spurious, made with intent to deceive, and which left Mr. Collier himself a ruined man,— with the imputation of forgery never to be lifted,— to die unnoticed, broken and friendless, in his ninety-sixth year. In this certificate "the two Burbadges," Shakespeare, and fifteen others (Shakespeare standing twelfth in a list of sixteen) are made to represent to the Privy Council that they "being all of them sharers in the Blackfriars playhouse have never given cause of displeasure in that they have brought into their plays matters of state and religion unfit to be handled by them or to be presented before lewd spectators, neither hath any complaint in that kind ever been preferred against them or any of them."[1]

The largest probability exists, I think, from the considerations above set forth, that there must

[1] A fac-simile of this forgery is given at p. 248 of Ingleby's "The Shakespeare Controversy." London: Natali & Bond. 1861.

have been some certificate or representations of the sort made; otherwise the Master of the Revels, or the Lord Chamberlain, would have closed the Shakespeare theaters, certainly in Elizabeth's, even if not in her successor, King James's reign. We have seen that a rigid stage censorship had forced Shakespeare to remove the name of Oldcastle from his comic character, and to substitute that of Falstaff therefor. The principle of this stage censorship of plays by the Lord Chamberlain not only seems never to have lain in abeyance, but remains in our American common law policy to-day, and is vested in whatever of record takes the place of Chancery in England (*i. e.*, in the State of New York, the Supreme Court, where it has been twice invoked within the last few years, once in the case of George Jones, alias the "Count Joannes," and once in the case of a Mr. Talmadge, a Brooklyn exhorter). Certainly it was by no means suffered to lapse under King James. "In 1633, Ben Jonson gave his comedy, 'The Tale of a Tub,' to the stage, with a savagely satirical caricature of Inigo Jones, under the pseudonym of 'Vitruvius Hoop.' This part was cut out by authority. The office-book of the Master of the Revels, whose duty it was to license plays, contains an entry to the effect that Vitruvius Hoop's part was 'wholly struck out, and the motion of a tub, by command from my Lord Chamberlain; exceptions being taken against it by Inigo Jones, surveyor of the King's Works, as a personal injury unto him.'"[1] But were the Cobham family

---

[1] An interesting note might be made on stage censorships, and the general impossibility of any one rigid criticism reaching anything but absurdity.

satisfied with Shakespeare's apology and substitution? I have never seen it suggested that perhaps the Cobhams believed the only real reparation they would obtain would be by the preparation of a separate play for the same boards where Falstaff had strutted, which should do the career of their ancestor justice to a populace who forgot easily and read not at all; and so procured such a play to be written. But the fact is, that shortly after this apologetic prologue to 2 Henry IV. (which had been entered in the Stationers' Registers, August 23d, 1600, but which is supposed to have been written in 1598), viz., in 1600, there actually did appear a play called "Sir John Oldcastle." This play is noted in Henslowe's diary (as of October, November, and December, 1599) as the collaborative work of Munday, Drayton, Wilson, and Hathaway. The play was, notwithstanding,

---

M. Emile Labiche relates that one of his plays was objected to during the Empire, because a character in it was called "as vindictive as a Corsican." "It is impossible to allow that to pass," said the censor, "on account of the emperor, who is of Corsican origin." "Well, let us say as vindictive as a Spaniard," M. Labiche replied. "And the empress?" queried the censor. "Let us, then, put it vindictive as an Auvergnat." "But what about M. Rouher?" again asked the puzzled censor. "Put down what you like," rejoined the author, and the censor chose a comparison according to his own whim and fancy. Victor Hugo's "Hernani" was permitted to be played only (to quote the official memoranda) " on condition of expunging the name of Jesu wherever found," and omitting in the scenery representing Saragossa any belfry or church, a prohibition which rendered resemblance somewhat difficult, since there were, in the 16th century, 309 churches, and 617 convents in that town.

So much for the stage censor in France!

printed in quarto by Thomas Pavier, with the statement on its title-page that it was written by William Shakespeare. Internal evidence has long since pronounced this statement unauthorized, and relegated Sir John Oldcastle to the interrogative condition of a "doubtful play." But had it been written by anybody under coercion, it would have doubtless had the same perfunctory flavor; and had Shakespeare been the coerced party, he might well have intrusted it to hack writers, and felt himself discharging his part of the bargain by producing the completed play of "Sir John Oldcastle" on his stage. Had William Shakespeare received simultaneous orders to prepare plays, one showing "Falstaff in Love" and the other Sir John Oldcastle as an epitome of virtue, there would, I think, be small question as to which commission he would have executed himself, and which he would have let out to his subordinates. At any rate, I cannot help believing that the sudden withdrawal of the name of Oldcastle from the Henry plays, and the appearance of a play in the opposite vein to which that name was given, were not entirely unconnected circumstances. In changing the stage business from Oldcastle to Falstaff in the quarto, the scribe sometimes overlooked a speech, and left "Old" standing where he should have substituted "Fal,"[1] and at III., ii. 28, the statement that Falstaff had been "page to Thomas Mowbray, Duke of Norfolk" (which the historical Oldcastle actually was), has been left standing. It is interesting, in this connection, to note that, as an actual fact, the Sir

[1] *E. g.*, Quarto, Griggs Reprint, p. 17, line 4 from bottom.

John Fastolfe, whose name was borrowed for the substitution, was actually the owner of the Boar's Head Tavern, or at least of a tavern bearing that name.[1]

The most curious piece of evidence, however, touching the risks which these plays ran of being forever lost, of how they lay unnoticed for years, or were carelessly acted, from the actors' part-books, presents itself in the case of the "Othello." Shakespeare died in 1616. He probably had ceased any active theatrical work four or five years earlier, when he retired to Stratford-upon-Avon and assumed management of his estates there. In the British Museum is a volume containing the manuscript diary of one Hans Jacob Wurmsser von Venderhagen, who accompanied Louis Frederick, Duke of Wurtemberg Mumpelgard, an ambassador who visited England officially in 1610, and in pages of this for the month of April, in that year, occurs the entry:

"Lundi 30 — S. E. alla en globe, lieu ordinaire où l'on joue les commedies ; y fut representé du More de Venise."

This play, thereafter, was left without a custodian, and is not heard of again until in 1622, when it is "Printed by N. O. for Thomas Walk-

[1] Anstis's "Register of the Garter," p. 142, supplies a list of Fastolf's holdings, including "the 'Boar's Head in Southwark,' now divided into tenements yielding £150 yearly." In the muniment room at Warwick Castle is an early lease of "The Boar's Head, situated not far from the Globe Theater, and belonging to Sir John Fastolf." This property formed part of Sir John's bequest to Magdalen College, Oxford. See chapter VIII., post.

ley." The play must have been printed from a copy prepared before 1605, because, as we have seen, it was in that year that the Act XIX. Stats. 3 Jac. I. 21, was passed, forbidding the use of oaths on the stage; and there is at the very beginning the expression, "Sblood" (God's blood). removed, of course, in the folio. Only a year later appeared the First Folio, including this same "Othello." But a comparison of the two versions makes it hard to believe that they came from the same sources. No very great changes in the text of a play certainly could have taken place in a single year. It is difficult to see what further or stronger proof that the Shakespeare plays existed in many different versions and renditions, even during Shakespeare's life, or immediately after his death, could be desired.

Such being the facts,— I., the existence of never less than than two, and often of many versions of the Shakespeare plays before 1623; II., that Heminges and Condell's editorship began and ended with the preparation of certain prefatory matter; and III., that they have never even supplied a proof-reader (their own statement that they printed from Shakespeare's own unblotted manuscript being shown, by the most superficial comparison of their text with that of the quartos, to be a whole cloth falsehood);—such being the facts, we say, who can hesitate to understand that any reasonable historic doubt as to the Shakespeare special authorship is deserving of respectful treatment, and that from the occurrence of any passage in the First Folio, no absolute certainty as to William Shakespeare's life, habits, or experience

can be dogmatically asserted, and peremptorily
and offensively defended, as against the gentle
lovers of the "gentle" Shakespeare, who will perhaps plead a human tendency to error in lieu of
the creative and absolute certainty of the esthetic
and inductive critic? For my own part, while I
do not believe (for example) that Francis Bacon
wrote the Shakespeare plays, yet I would welcome a theory that Queen Elizabeth, or Essex,
or the Court Fool, or Ratsey's Ghost wrote them
were that the only alternative to believing that
the projector and manager of the Globe Theater
realized a fortune by mounting essays on "man's
relation to the universe," or "Enchantment as an
engine of Personal Providence," or on eschatological and ontological problems generally, for
the pennies of the groundlings and the applause
of the dudes and maids of honor in men's attire
who lolled in at his stage doors.

Neither, in considering the historical environment within which Shakespeare lived and wrote,
ought the ecclesiastical conditions of his time to be
lost sight of.

Many and wordy are the disputes as to whether
the dramatist were Catholic or Protestant. But
they all seem to me apart from the matter. I suppose the fact is that had Shakespeare himself been
asked which he was, he would have hesitated quite
as long as the most circumspect of his Nineteenth
Century commentators. His life was not concerned with church politics, with questions of discipline, or ritual or ecclesiastical differentiations.
He lived in an era when, more than ever before
or since, ecclesiastical, polemical, and theological

points were undiscussed, were in a state of suppression, of neutrality, and of peace; and when English Christianity appears to have for once enjoyed that practical church unity which in these days is only the dream of a possible future.

Elizabeth had come to the throne of a people heartily tired of religious quarrels, persecutions, and martyrdoms. Her first care had been to initiate a neutral and conciliatory policy, and she had never suffered it to relax. She proposed making all her subjects over into supporters and friends of her throne. She allowed no criticisms, bickering reflections — no comments even upon the absurdities of the Puritans — to be aired in public, uttering decrees and recommending statutes, when necessary, to insure the performance of her will. Later on, when this policy had relaxed under her successor, Jonson could lash the Puritans at will in his "Bartholemew Fair." As for the differences between Roman and Anglican, for once in English history they were for the nation as a whole completely at rest. The transfer of the throne from Mary to Elizabeth had operated as a transfer of the supremacy of the church from Roman to Anglican; and, while here and there a politician or a scholar may have looked askance at the result, the people certainly knew no difference. Out of nine thousand four hundred of the parochial clergy, less than two hundred hesitated to acquiesce in the change. The strictest Roman Catholic families recognized the rite of baptism as administered in the Established Church. They could not do otherwise, in fact, since there was no other to recognize — (nearly a century was to elapse before Protestant baptism was declared by Rome to be invalid). The same church edifices were there, the same clergy read the same services and administered the same sacraments. And — whereas now there are hundreds of thousands who neglect the services and sacraments of any church — in those times all the people were church-goers — their priests not only their spiritual but temporal advisers — the regulators of the social intercourse, their business, their festivals, and their sports, and, most of all, the school-masters of the children. Recusants there were, of course; but they had no machinery, no organization, no place of worship, no priests, and no effect upon the masses of the people. So peaceful was the result that the best judgment everywhere counseled acquiescence in the statutes as they stood. De Quadra, in 1562, wrote to the Spanish minister at Rome, "begging him[1] to ask the Pope, in the name of the English Catholics, whether they might be present without sin at the common prayers. The case was a new and not at all an easy one, for the prayer-book contained neither impiety nor false doctrine. The prayers themselves were those of the Catholic Church, altered only so far as to omit the merits and the intercession of the saints; so that, except for the concealment and the injury which might arise from the example, there would be nothing in the compliance itself positively unlawful."

Under such conditions was Shakespeare born and reared. The change was only dawning when he died, and came too late to impress itself upon

[1] Froude's "History of England," vii., 472.

him. The rector of Sapperton has told us very tersely that he (Shakespeare) "died a Papist"; and being a Protestant himself, would have been apt, probably, to claim him for his own fold had he any warrant for so doing. But Shakespeare was nevertheless buried with the Anglican rites. And the Anglican Church to-day (whose records contain the first authentic entry as to his personality — his birth) is sole custodian of his mortal remains. John Shakespeare, the dramatist's father, a survivor of the reign of Mary, was undoubtedly not only a Roman Catholic but one of the few recusants. For though his "confession of faith" has disappeared from the biographies of his distinguished son, it remains of record that he would not come to church; and, somehow, possessed influence enough to manage that the commissioners refused to enforce any penalty for the contumacy, on the ground that he "came not to church for fear of process for debt,"— palpably a makeshift excuse, since process for debt has never been, on English soil, servable on a Sunday. But whatever the religion of William Shakespeare's father, or in whatever faith he himself died, the influences under which he lived and wrote were not polemical. His works show a perfect familiarity with the Bishop's Bible, which he used, just as he used Holingshed's Chronicles,— because the people knew its narratives, miracles, and legends by heart; because he wrote for the people and their pence always, and there was no nearer way. His employment of biblical similes argues nothing as to any predilection for Roman, Anglican or Puritan formularies. I think that we can trace the effect of this tranquillity in things theological everywhere in the plays. The laughter of Rabelais was strained, the satire of Voltaire worked up to cope with periods of sceptered ecclesiasticisms and enforced theologies; in Shakespeare there is no trace of the odium theologicum nor of the no less virulent odium anti-theologicum,— none of the bitterness of religious intolerance or the bickerings of sects and sectaries.

Is it not at our own loss and damage that we jettison all this history, this environment,— these sources, conditions, and situations — dramatic, social, political — for the sake of fanciful theories and finical verse-texts, that have developed nothing but absurdity so far, and are utterly without a promise of future fruitage? The form in which any dramatic literature is earliest cast is seldom that in which it ultimately survives; the practiced actor then as now is always consulted; even the highest talent in dialogue or literary effect must submit to his pruning, cutting, and interpolation for technical purposes. And in the work of a young dramatist, lately risen from factotum and call-boy, veteran professionals may not have considered themselves as unequal to arrangement or suggestion. In days when not only was practicable stage scenery unknown, but no drops, wings or flats employed to separate scenes, a dramatist's drafts were often (as were Shakespeare's) similarly undivided into scenes or even acts, whence a sixteenth century actor as well as a nineteenth century student may have made his own separations and thereby missed or supplied meanings to text as well as to action. It is always helpful to see how the practiced actor regards questions which students, commentators, and editors believe yield only to the lamp and to the deepest transcendental insights; and we have a pleasant word from Mr. Boucicault as to this possible rewriting of parts. " Up comes the actor who is cast as Polonius," says Mr. Boucicault: " 'See here,' he says to Shakespeare, 'you have killed my part entirely. You have given me a lot of moralizing stuff that I'll never be able to do anything with. If you can't give me something to get a laugh with, I won't play the part, that's all.' Shakespeare argues that to make Polonius a comic rôle would destroy the design of the play. But the actor will not yield, and Shakespeare says: 'Well, have it your own way, and speak your own text, but for heaven's sake use mine in the first act.' This is settled upon, and that is how Polonius, who in the first act is a dignified and wise old gentleman, giving Laertes the sagest of advice, becomes a 'wretched, rash, intruding fool' thereafter, until Hamlet wisely kills him off. Oh, I can see it all as plainly as if I had been present, and I can trace out in Shakespearean plays changes similarly brought about." No unlikely scheme, when we find, as we do, that the part of Polonius (Corambis, as Shakespeare called him in the draft of 1603) was certainly made heavier for the 1604, and again for the text from which Heminges and Condell printed. Not a play, scarcely a scene, but shows this augmentation and improvement, but never unless the stage practicability and effectiveness is simultaneously and commensurately augmented and improved; showing beyond the peradventure of a doubt that but one hand did the work, and that hand an accomplished stage setter's as well as a dramatist's.

It seems to me that it is to this progress and improvement in stage experience, rather than to printers' dates or variants in rhythm or unstopped endings, that we should look in building our chronologies. For ordinarily the first success of an author is not his first literary composition, but leads to the printing of earlier work which erstwhile neither gods, men nor columns would hear of at any price. And it may have been so in Shakespeare's case. Whether Shakespeare's plays were written in the order of the quartos, or never written at all, but only sketched for the actors, pirated, and so actually printed before they were written, or whether (in the days when literature came from wherever the Stationers' Company listed, and was doled out to the public with prefaces telling them where to applaud—a prerogative to be reassumed by Pope a century later) his first success led to the printing of his earlier pieces, perhaps we may never know. But, since the human nature which Shakespeare painted in the sixteenth century is found to be so exactly that which surrounds us in the nineteenth,— the same passions, motives, appetites, greeds,—that his is still our paramount literature, we cannot, I think, be very far astray if we judge his contemporaries by our own, and so keep a sort of foothold on our own planet, instead of working the hermetic, the vague, and transcendental when we write his biography. Doubtless the style of a writer changes by lapse of time. But can we be sure how and on what lines? The tendency of matureness and usuetude in one writer may be to draw away from form and to only seek expression; with another, toward an increased nicety of scansion and polish. As to which was Shakespeare's tendency we have plenty of opinions, some founded upon very scant information, others from overmuch study of a single detail; but, however formed, still merely opinion. There is more of room for disagreement about Shakespeare and all his works than about almost anything else in creation. But the gentleman who assumes — because others disagree with him — that they do not possess the same access to sources of information as himself, sometimes labors in error, even though most inapt to recognize or acknowledge it.

If, for example, Tennyson's style were found to change on exactly the lines Mr. Furnivall assigns to Shakespeare, that would be a most important argument in favor of Mr. Furnivall's theory, no doubt. But argument is not evidence — neither presumptive, conclusive, direct, cumulative, or even corroborative; or, if evidence at all, only, at the uttermost, evidence of a tendency in Tennyson which might also have been a tendency in Shakespeare. But, then again, it might not. The chronology of the plays as established by the verse-tests either conforms to the chronology established by the printers' dates and the copyright entries, or it does not. If it does, the verse-tests are superfluous. If it does not, then verse-tests are of no value unless corroborated by external and circumstantial evidence; but external and circumstantial evidence are precisely what Mr. Furnivall and his followers decline to consider as against the conclusions reached by the verse-tests. Again, the chronology indicated by these dates and entries may itself be false. Who can say that an author's first success may not — in Elizabeth's day as in our own — have led to the printing of manuscripts which, before, no publisher could be found to touch, and whether it might not have been so in Shakespeare's case? Our friends must not be impatient if we are unable to accept argument for evidence, however unimpeachable from their own standpoint such argument might be. Rowe, who wrote his few lines of careful preface some one hundred and seventy years before revelation of the Furnivall chronology, was possibly nearer the truth as well as the date of Shakespeare, when he said: "Perhaps we are not to look for his beginnings like those of other authors, among their least perfect writing: art had so little and nature so large a share in what he did that, for aught I know, the performances of his youth, as they were the most vigorous and had the most fire and strength of imagination in them, were the best." Of Mr. Furnivall's "Groups"— the Unfit-Nature-or-Under-Burden-Falling Group ("Julius Cæsar," "Hamlet," "Measure for Measure"): the Sunny-or-Sweet-Time Group ("Twelfth Night," "Much Ado," "As you Like it"): the Lust-or-False-Love Group ("Troilus and Cressida," "Antony and Cleopatra"): the Re-Union-or-Reconciliation-and-Forgiveness Group ("Pericles," "Tempest," "Cymbeline"): the Ingratitude-and-Cursing Group ("Lear," "Timon of Athens," "Coriolanus"),[1] etc.,

[1] Introduction to "Leopold Shakespeare," p. vii.

etc., poor Mr. Rowe, alas! never lived to hear. But, as of our own more fortunate generation, I suggest the same arrangement for the poems. Let Mr. Furnivall now give us the Young-Man-Gored - by- a - Boar- Because - He-Ran - Away - From - His-Mistress Group ("Venus and Adonis"): the Danger-of-Leaving-Your-Wife-to-Entertain-Strangers Group ("Lucrece"): the Nobody-Knows-What- They- are-About-or-Why- They - Were-Written Group (the "Sonnets"), and we shall then have a perfect literary biography of the boundless dramatist!

I have never seen a more capital instance of the inevitable tendency of students to resist any other interpretation than their own of the many-sided Shakespeare, than the reluctance of the critics to accept as "Hamlet" the version of that play recently presented in the city of New York by Mr. Wilson Barrett. Mr. Barrett portrays a young, vigorous and determined prince, with his hand upon his sword, conscious from the first of the King's purpose to remove him from the succession by subterfuge — or, if necessary, by assassination — and alert tirelessly to circumvent it. He recognizes Rosencrantz and Guildenstern instantly as spies and would-be assassins (twice Mr. Barrett makes these two dash at the prince behind his back to knife him, and Hamlet foil them by turning abruptly upon them with a question from the text — questions that become marvelously pregnant when so interpreted). And so, I think, given a Hamlet who proposes to kill his father's murderer, but who, at the same time, is obliged to be alert, lest, in the midst of a court packed with spies and honeycombed with intrigue, his father's murderer, murders him instead, Mr. Barrett effectually disposes of the orthodox indecision, dilatoriness, and shilly-shally of the heir to Denmark. Again, in Mr. Barrett's hands, the sympathy of the audience is removed from Ophelia, who, instead of the cruelly deserted maiden, is the conscious Delilah, willing, without compunction or protest, that her charms be utilized to entrap and ruin her lover. Mr. Barrett's "business" to express this is to arrange that Polonius and the King accidentally rustle the arras behind which they are listening. Up to this time Hamlet has spoken tenderly and regretfully. Now he starts, glares suspiciously at the arras, then at Ophelia, rushes at her, seizes her by the wrists, cries, "Ha, ha! are you honest (III. i. 103)?" as if divining the whole plot. Thereafter, Ophelia, overcome by detection, answers only in monosyllables — as indeed the text is.[1] And I cannot help believing that Mr. Barrett is very near in this to the intention of the dramatist. The audiences for which the playwright prepared this "Hamlet," were the same that rejoiced in "Titus Andronicus" and "The Merry Wives." They wanted robust life, and the action of attack and parry. I doubt if they cared much for fine ethical distinctions or appreciated the niceties of that moral revenge which lies in overlooking injuries and turning the other cheek. Moreover, I am inclined to deny if there

[1] I had the pleasure of witnessing Mr. Barrett's treatment of the text in April, 1887. Previously (the "Catholic World," October, 1886, ante p. 105) I had expressed my own suspicions that such was the sense intended by Shakespeare.

is really anywhere on the stage, or ever has been, a standard Hamlet. Burbadge is credited with having represented (on account of his own adipose) the melancholy Dane as, if not blown up with sighing and grief, at least as fat as Falstaff, thereby justifying (or possibly requiring) the expressions: "He raised a sigh so piteous and profound as seemed to shatter all his bulk"; "Duller than the fat weed"; "It is the breathing time of the day with him"; and the queen's exclamation, "He's fat, and scant of breath," and tender of the napkin to wipe his brows in the fencing scene. Until Betterton's time the Hamlets of the stage had talked angrily to the ghost, making the speech beginning "Angels and ministers of grace defend us!" an arraignment of its purposes in revisiting the moon's glimpses. Betterton, the more strongly to show a plaintive sympathy with that shade, omitted this speech altogether. Garrick divided his first act at Hamlet's resolution to watch with Horatio and Marcellus; made Laertes one of the sympathetic characters; saw the ghost in the chamber scene sitting in a chair, and — rising — upturned it behind him with emphatic effect, and delivered the soliloquies with action. Henderson, after the speech over the two portraits, pitches the uncle's into the wings (Mr. Wilson Barrett stamps his heel upon it). John Philip Kemble was the first to add — to his greetings to Horatio and Marcellus — the courteous "Good-evening, sir," to Bernardo: turned to Horatio at the recital by Marcellus, with "Did you not speak to it?" and played the part in the full court dress of his own date. Stephen Kemble followed, playing the part in an auburn wig, which Fechter resurrected. Charles Young was impetuous rather than ruminative. Kean introduced the business of kissing Ophelia's hand after the "Get thee to a nunnery" speeches. Macready carried a cambric handkerchief always ready to his eye to depict the melancholy Dane, and Junius Brutus Booth is said to have never played the part twice alike, so mighty were his inspirations. Fechter made the fencing scene great by using a double staircase, making the King attempt to escape at Laertes' confession, but be met and dispatched by Hamlet; and we need not pause to re-catalogue the points of Mr. Booth or Mr. Irving. In other words, each actor of the part has distinguished his own abilities and rounded his performance out to them.

My own idea is, that this was the exact case in and about Shakespeare's own days: that Elizabethan audiences welcomed and appreciated the merits of a new point in stage business quite as heartily as do our own. In the recently unearthed " Pilgrimage to Parnassus," acted by the students of St. John's College at Cambridge, prior to December, 1597, there occurs the following:

Enter DROMO, *drawing a clowne in with a rope.*

Clowne. What now? thrust a man into the commonwealthe whether hee will or noe? what the devill should I doe here?

Dromo. Why, what an asse art thou! Dost thou not know a playe cannot be without a clowne? Clownes have bene thrust into plays by head and shoulders ever since Kempe could make a scurvy face; and therefore reason thou shouldst be drawn in with a cart rope.

Clowne. But what must I doe nowe?

Dromo. Why, if thou canst but draw thy mouth awrye, laye thy legg over thy staffe, sawe a peece of cheese asunder with thy dagger, lape up drinke on the earth, I warrant thee theile laughe mightilie.

The travesty on contemporary stage methods here is worthy of the best modern burlesque, and if its point could be appreciated by an audience of the sixteenth century, it is not impossible that there might have been more than one popular way of playing Hamlet. Perhaps Ophelia was the mad person of the piece, and not the prince, who — as indeed he himself hints rather broadly to the conspirators—ought not to be set down as clean crazy; is only mad north northwest; but, when the wind is southerly, knows a hawk from a hand-saw.

VIII

Queen Elizabeth's Share in the "Merry Wives of Windsor"

THE selecting of periods of moods and motives for William Shakespeare from the meters or prosodies in the plays, or assignment to him of occult and opaque philosophies from what may be only printers' slips, while requiring a certain amount of ingenuity at the outset, soon becomes a habitude, and goes of itself. There is nothing in it — at least so it appears to me — higher in quality or degree than that lowest of all low grade Shakespearean criticism which sorts out sentiments from the text to prove their author an angler, butcher, soldier, Sunday-school teacher, teetotaler, and the like. The mastery of human nature and of human passion, which is generally accorded to a Shakespeare, might have been, and possibly was, inclusive of literary facility, not to say ear, enough to have enabled him to write in what prosodiacal form he pleased, independently of the universe or the almanac: while he seems to have been rather too fond of his share of the takings at the door to have emptied his playhouses, proscenium and gallery alike, by mounting abstract ætiologies in place of the sanguinary or burlesque or pasquinado material the people loved.

But, however we may evade it, there is one characteristic of all these Shakespeare plays, quite too constant, incessant, and emphatic to be overlooked. There can be no disguising the fact that Shakespeare never missed an opportunity to testify how he despised the people — slurred, slandered, and lampooned them; denied their very right to lie side by side with men nobly born upon their country's battle-fields. That the lowly has no right the lordly is bound to respect; the scriptural doctrine that to him that hath shall be given, while from him who hath not shall be taken away even that he hath; these are the only propositions upon which every one of Shakespeare's eight hundred personages agree; they speak their own thoughts (not Shakespeare's) as to everything else. But on these fundamentals they all preach in common, and always one way. Except in Adam (in "As You Like It"), Shakespeare never extols or praises virtue in anything less than a lord. But in Adam it is his willingness to give his noble master all his savings and to serve him without pay, that is pronounced commendable. "In all Shakespeare," says Mr. Davis, "there is nowhere a hint of sympathy with personal rights as against the sovereign, nor with parliament, then first assuming its protective attitude toward the English people; nor with the few judges who, like Coke, showed a glorious obstinacy in their resistance to the prerogative. In all his works there is not one word for direct liberty of speech, thought, religion — those rights which in his age were the very seeds of time, into which his eye, of all men's, could best look to see which grain would grow and which would not."

"The doctrine of Coriolanus," says Hazlitt, "is that those who have little shall have less, and those that have much shall take all that the others have left. The people are poor, therefore they ought to be starved; they work hard, therefore they ought to be treated like beasts of burden. They are ignorant, therefore they ought not to be allowed to feel that they want food or clothing or rest, or that they are enslaved or oppressed or miserable. Shakespeare had a leaning to the aristocratic principle, inasmuch as he does not dwell on the truth he tells of the nobles in the same proportion as he does on those he tells of the people." "Lords! lords! lords!" says Mr. Wilkes, "and the people always and everywhere are scabs and hedge-born swains." "You will generally find that when a citizen is mentioned, he is made to do or say something absurd," says Bagehot. Even in the comedies (where no political motive can be construed as preaching that the people are better off in suffering any indignity rather than meddle with the order and sovereignty of class) no opportunity is lost. "Go bring the rabble" ("The Tempest"). "Yet I have much to do to keep [the people] from uncivil outrages" ("Two Gentlemen of Verona"). "What hempen homespuns have we swaggering here?" "A crew of patches, rude mechanicals that work for bread" ("Midsummer Night's Dream"). The sole title the reign of King John has to be remembered in history is that it covers the grant of Magna Charta. Yet Shakespeare, in treating of that reign, never mentions it, but instead, fills his pages with such fulsome lines as:

> "Ha, Majesty, how high thy glory towers
> When the rich blood of kings is set on fire!"
> II., i. 350.

> "Out! dunghill, dar'st thou brave a nobleman?"
> IV., i. 87.

And even in "Richard II.," where opportunity for once served to show even kings unthronable, we have the moral twisted:

> "Not all the water in the rough rude sea
> Can wash the balm off from an anointed King;
> The breath of worldly men cannot depose
> The deputy elected by the Lord." III., ii. 54.

> 'Darest thou, thou little better thing than earth
> Divine his downfall?" III., iv. 77.

In "1 Henry VI.," a courtier, prisoner of war, refuses to be exchanged "for base-born soldiers... who dare not take up arms like gentlemen." And even in the stage directions, the people are brought in with such unnecessary stings as "Enter the Ædile with a rabble of citizens" ("Julius Cæsar"), or, "Enter Cade with all his rabblement" ("2 Henry VI."). It taxes the complaisancy even of a patrician to read the stinging and scathing characterizing, in "Coriolanus," of a people who have only so far forgotten themselves as to ask for bread, as — "your herd," "knaves that smell of sweat," "multiplying spawn," "herd of broils and plagues." "you common cry of curs," "that reek of rotten fens," "their thick breaths rank of gross diet,"—"they'll sit by the fire and presume to know what's done in the capitol"—"these rats," etc. Isabella and Portia plead eloquently for mercy, one for a noble youth and the other for a rich man who was evading the judgment of a court for money borrowed; but where is mercy bespoken for a commoner in all these glowing pages? Had Shakespeare cared for the people, their liberties, their rights and interests, surely he might have put into the mouth of one of his eight or nine hundred characters a statement, hint, or suggestion to that effect. But I cannot find that he ever did.

In "1 Henry VI.," we have the King's order to bring back his "anointed queen" from France, and for his

"expenses and sufficient charge
Among the people gather up a tenth." V., v. 92.

A process which recalls the custom of the miners in California, who, when in need of pocket-money, proceed to levy a tax upon any Chinaman in the vicinity. Nay, most of all, when a character is represented as searching a battle-field "to sort our nobles from our common men," lest "our vulgar drench their peasant limbs in blood of princes" ("Henry V.," IV., vii. 77), one is tempted to ask, with Mr. Wilkes, if the commonest sentiment of humanity would not suggest that, whether noble or obscure, by dying in their country's cause a nation's soldiery had not earned the merit of an equal grave?

All this is bad enough. But Shakespeare went further, and lied, gloriously lied, in order to make the uprising of Cade a treason, and Joan of Arc not "the virgin mother of French nationality" (as Mr. Davis says), but a traitress to her country; great as he is, showing a mendacity utterly unsurpassed in literature, as proportionally great as he is himself. Cade led a respectful deputation, and demanded only reforms which the king himself conceded to be just. "The King sent to ask why the good men of Kent had left their homes." Cade answered that the people were robbed of their goods for the king's use; that mean and corrupt persons, who plundered and oppressed the Commons, filled the high offices at court; that it was noised abroad that the king's lands in France had been aliened; that the king's counsellors were giving him bad advice; that misgovernment banished justice and prosperity from the land; and that the men of Kent were specially ill-treated and overtaxed, etc. The rebellion was against the nobles, not the king. Cade's demands were reasonable, as every English historian admits, and the throne treated with him, and proclaimed a truce upon its kingly honor, during which Cade was treacherously murdered by the king's own party. But Shakespeare could find no terms too contemptuous for one who could question whether men nobly born could give bad advice. Cade is represented by Shakespeare, in a story manufactured out of whole cloth, not only as a rebel and a traitor, but a robber of orchards, and as being lawfully shot by one Alexander Iden, a Kentish gentleman, whose inclosed orchard Cade is attempting to burglarize. And so dies "this monstrous traitor," who not only committed no treason, but was consulted with by the throne as to needed reforms in the general weal. And what woman can forget Shakespeare's treatment of Joan of Arc: with all her self-denying patriotism, enthusiasm and achievements, called by every vile name in Shakespeare's great catalogue, represented as perishing with a lie upon her lips as to her birth, while a brutal English bishop stands by and sneers at her dying agonies, crying —

"Break thou in pieces and consume to ashes,
Thou foul, accursed minister of hell!"
1 Hen. VI., V. iv. 92.

The further lie as to her condition of pregnancy (which, if true, even by English statutes would have entitled her to mercy) is not spared that Shakespeare's plays might draw!

Of course all this is not, strictly speaking, an indictment of Shakespeare himself but rather a necessity of the situation which he found himself occupying. Already the strolling player had become a nuisance, and laws had been framed to suppress him. The proprietor of the Globe Theater loved his perquisites and theatrical concessions too well to imperil them by offending the courtiers who only had the legal right under Elizabeth's statutes to license play-houses; a playright, making plays to be performed in London in a permanent theater, must be careful not to interfere with questions of caste — had no charter at all, except from the protection and patronage of some particular nobleman; indeed, the law said, very explicitly, that without such an ægis he was a vagrant, a rogue by statute with no legal resting-place except a jail.

Under the circumstances, it was unlikely that sentiments expressive of a longing for popular liberty, or subversive of title, birth, and rank should be largely put into the mouths of Shakespeare's actors, or that Shakespeare himself should pose as an agitator screaming from his corner, or scattering philippics against things established, especially since what he wrote was mounted upon the boards of two theaters, under the vigilant eye of a sovereign whose definition of treason was notoriously elastic, and with the Tower and the block unpleasantly near to suggest a wholesome prudence. The dramatists of Elizabeth's day were only too happy to be on the safe side when they mentioned the throne and the ruling classes, and to put all their lofty sentiments into noble mouths; and it is but natural to find Shakespeare surpassing them in that, as in everything else, in degree. It might be offered, too, with great reason, that the common people in Tudor days were very far from being ripe for popular government; that their happiness could only come from the permanence of establishments; that the greatest kindness to them was to teach, as did Göethe almost two centuries later, acquiescence in things as they were, since dissatisfaction could only mean license, anarchy, and ruin; death for the overt act, and — for the survivor — worse than before.

Such reflections as these (were it not adding another to the nineteenth century catalogue of

Shakespeare's motives) might well be offered in his behalf. But even then, one cannot fail to be impressed with the contrast between the great Elizabethan and the Frenchman (who, to his own countrymen, stands in literary splendor nearest to where Shakespeare stands to his), Victor Hugo. The life and fiber of Victor Hugo was his love for his kind. The trilogy of Liberty, Equality, and Fraternity was not carved more deeply upon Napoleon's façades by the Commune of 1870 than it was cut into his very soul. His muse dealt with the stateliest and the loftiest themes, with emperors and kings and the buskin of tragedy, as did Shakespeares's. But never did he miss, in its highest and stateliest, to speak a word for the proletariat and the poor, the masses in the faubourgs of poverty or the beggars at the gates. His ear listened, and never lost the still, sad music of humanity; and the cry of Triboulet,

"Come hither, look on her, I will not hinder;
Tell me she is but swooning!"

is just as poignant as that of Lear's "Cordelia, stay a little!" although Lear was a king, and Triboulet but a jester, who had naught to say when the king amused himself. However he blazoned his pages with courts and palaces, he never denied the right of every man to liberty and to bread, even at the cost of the red flag, the guillotine, or the Commune. In "Les Misérables" he wrote the epic of poverty. He no more hesitated to spare himself in the cause of the masses than Jean Valjean hesitated to lay the white-hot metal upon his bare and quivering arm in the Jondrette garret, and everything but death seemed to have been his reward.

But so it is that Shakespeare is the poet of Humanity rather than of Nature. Milton to the contrary notwithstanding, there are no "native wood-notes wild" in the Shakespearean opera. The music is that of camp and court, of tourney and assemblage, and of crowded city streets. The people, the masses, are only and always his accessories and supernumeraries. It is only when a patrician is to be represented in exile or retirement that we have the pastoral or the rural — Perdita among oafs and shepherdesses, the forest of Arden, Prospero's magic island, or eulogy of any life that is exempt from public haunt. In but one single instance are these rules ever suspended. In but a single drama did Shakespeare assume to bring a nobleman to grief, and to make his untitled characters heroes and heroines. In the comedy of "The Merry Wives of Windsor," for the first time, the personages who have the sympathy of the piece are worthy common people, tradesmen and villagers: a school-master, a publican, a French doctor, and, most wonderful of all, a knight for their butt. Ordinary human beings poking fun at a knight! Certainly, so abrupt and radical a change seems to warrant tradition in asserting that Shakespeare wrote the comedy not of his own will, but under direction of a higher will and edict than his own.

Two statements referred back to this tradition have been generally conceded without examination: first, that Queen Elizabeth ordered William Shakespeare to write a play in fourteen days for the purpose of showing Falstaff (with whom her majesty had already become acquainted in the two

parts of the "Henry IV.") " in love"; and that
"The Merry Wives of Windsor," as printed in 1623,
was the result of that order; and second, that the
1602 quarto is a shorthand transcript of the 1623
version, as surreptitiously captured from the
actors' mouths.

But why should Queen Elizabeth — who was
the most scrupulous of monarchs to keep her
people from prating, or even thinking, of any possible weaknesses of their betters — why should
she of all others order Shakespeare to make fun of
a person of quality ? Unwilling as most of us
are to take for granted, in a field where so much
is claimed and so little verified as the field of
Shakespearean biography, I have come to the
conclusion that this first proposition has not only
the adumbration of a fact behind it, but that
Shakespeare's departure from his habitude, and
selection of only middle-class characters for his
personnel, was the result of his effort to obey the
letter of the queen's order. Another curious result of the reasoning by which such a conclusion
may be arrived at is, that if the play written to
meet the order was hurriedly prepared in fourteen
days (plenty of time for so disjointed and careless a
production as the 1602 quarto, especially to a
dramatist of the facility assigned by Jonson to
Shakespeare), then the comedy, as we possess it in
the 1623 folio, is not a monograph at all, but a
composite, a growth, the result of twenty-one years'
performance of the 1602 play by actors to whom
every freedom of interpolation, local allusion
and "gag" was allowed. What seems to me the
evidence of this order and growth — if evidence it

be — is so remarkable, that, whether it be peculiar to this play, or of possible value in studying the origin of other, or of all the other, Shakespeare plays, I am tempted to schedule it for what it is worth, and for the benefit of whom it may concern.

To begin with: In no other Shakespearean play is there such an absence of action, speech, or allusion introductive or descriptive of the characters to be presented. The audience is supposed, at the outset, to be perfectly well acquainted with them. Dame Quickly is imported from Eastcheap, and made the mother of a somewhat backward schoolboy, in the French doctor's service to be sure, but still for the purpose of ministering to Falstaff's uses. Shallow, the rural justice, turns up again fresh from witnessing Falstaff's disgracing in the parade at Westminster; the precious Bardolph, Nym and Pistol still follow the fat knight's impecunious fortunes, but now only to assist in his final humiliation at the hands of a class he has so often maligned and lampooned, and to abandon him, like everybody else, upon its accomplishment. It mattered very little to Shakespeare — however much esthetic commentators may discuss the tremendous question — whether the scenes now to be depicted in Falstaff's career were to be assigned as before or after the "Henry V.," or the "II. Henry IV." All he troubled himself about was to get the play into shape for earning admittance money. From the "Epilogue spoken by a Dancer" at the end of the "II. Henry IV.," it appears that something had occurred to make the omission of the name of Oldcastle judicious. Whether this something was a protest from the Cobham family, or

an intimation that in applying the name of so
noble and esteemed a character to a lecherous old
reprobate the actors were going a trifle too far
(or, perhaps, since Queen Elizabeth's policy was
to make friends of all religions, Romanist, Anglican and Puritan, to prevent a possible reflection
upon any), we may, of course, only surmise. But
there is no doubt that the epilogue was added, as
it states, to assure the audience that the character
of Falstaff was not meant for a libel on Sir John
Oldcastle, Lord Cobham; "for Oldcastle died a
martyr, and this is not the man." It has been
doubted whether Shakespeare himself wrote this
epilogue, stipulating to continue the story with
Sir John in it, "and make you merry with fair
Katherine of France, where, for anything I know,
Falstaff shall die of a sweat." But he was probably not wont to be far off when such promises
were made. The high theme to which the era of
"Henry V." led him, perhaps precluded the by-play
of the fat knight, so that only so much of the
agreement as promised to kill Falstaff off in a
sweat was redeemed in that play. The present
comedy, then, may be reasonably looked at as a
performance of the remainder, and (I think) also
that it was the royal order rather than the Shakespeare taste which decreed that wives, instead of
purses, were to be filched, and rural rather than
city precincts selected for the cruise, as I shall now
proceed to suggest.

It seems to me that there are some further and
very weighty external reasons why the story of
Queen Elizabeth's, or her lord chamberlain's order
for "Falstaff in Love" is to be examined with very

great care before we discard it completely. If the sounding Shakespeare plays, so over-full of religion, politics, philosophy, and statecraft, had been up to this date presented publicly in London, their reputation must have reached Elizabeth's ears. Now, the Lion Queen did not care to have her subjects instructed too far. She proposed keeping them well in hand. Even her clergymen she was in the habit of interrupting if they happened to touch on matters concerning which she had not been previously consulted. "To your text, Mr. Dean! to your subject!" she shouted, when poor Dean Knowell, preaching before her, ventured to touch upon the employment of images in public worship. And in this policy, in whatever else she wavered, Elizabeth persisted always. Indeed, it is difficult to see how, as they stand in the First Folio, these particular plays could have been performed at all in Elizabeth's day without some very vigorous pruning at their first rehearsals. One of Elizabeth's first decrees concerning the public economy forbade the performing of any play wherein "either matters of religion, or of the government of the commonwealth shall be handled or treated."[1] A royal proclamation was not to be lightly disregarded. But the queen, it seems, was familiar with "Henry IV." and "Henry V." Surely, in those two plays alone, matters of government, if not of religion, enough to have closed the Blackfriars on short notice, had been "handled or treated." The queen and her ministers were only too ready to snuff treason in certain things that went by other's names. The run of comedies at

[1] See text of this decree, ante chapter VII.

other theaters were harmless enough—(an adultery for a plot, and an unsuspecting husband for a butt: this was a comedy; plus a little blood, it was a tragedy). Let the people have their fill of amusement, but let them not meddle with politics. So there are things more likely to have happened than that Elizabeth, through her lord chamberlain, should have intimated to Manager Shakespeare that he had best give them something more in the run and appetite of the day, and lose no time about it (the lord chamberlain, perhaps of his own motion, adding the peremptory fortnight limit). If this be accepted as the situation, it is certain that Shakespeare took in the letter of his instructions perfectly. But, somehow or other, their spirit had been bettered in the performance. The "Merry Wives of Windsor" was in due time underlined, but it was with a would-be adulterer rather than an injured husband for a butt. The salaciousness Elizabeth wanted was all there, as well as the transformation scene, but at the end there is a rebuke to lechery and to lecherous minds not equivocal in its character. "This is enough to be the decay of lust and late walking throughout the realm," says Falstaff, and perhaps there is a reproof to the queen herself— who certainly deserved it — in the line, "Our radiant queen hates sluts and sluttery," that is scathing in its satire.

But why should Shakespeare have treated a virgin queen to a homily upon purity and continence in a play not ordered by her for any such purpose? It does not seem to have occurred to the queen that to be comic, as of old, Falstaff must be here and now, for once, unsuccessful; and for a courtier to be unsuccessful in an assault on plebeian virtue, the untitled must resist the titled, and so the general be higher in honor than them of the court. But Shakespeare saw it, and the departure he must make to contrive it. Finding himself pressed for time, it would not have been unnatural had he (as is alleged) adapted the 1592 play known as the "Jealous Comedy" (belonging to Lord Strange's Company, but not now believed to be extant), or found new incident for old-piece men. If the latter, it was not remarkable that — lacking the leisure to overhaul his books or the unused manuscript handed in at the play-house door — he turned for the first and only time to his own memories of the scenes of his own boyhood and early youth. And why should the name Falstaff have been selected to take the place of Oldcastle? It was Shakespeare's custom in comedy always to borrow any name coming first to mind — French, Saxon, Spanish, Italian, classic, with perfect indifference to the place portrayed — though in tragedy, as rule, he was careful to consult his locality. But here he seems — when ordered to select a name to be mocked by tradesmen — to have chosen one already historical.

John Falstaff, or Fastolffe, was the son of John Fastolfe, a mariner, who, born in 1379, and becoming fatherless, was placed in very early life under the guardianship of John, Duke of Bedford, then Regent of France. He afterward accompanied Thomas, Duke of Clarence, to Ireland. In 1409 he married Millicent, daughter of Sir Robert Tiptoft, relict of Sir Stephen Scope (the record of his allowance to her of £100 per annum pin-money, and of its prompt payment to the date of her death are still extant). Falstaff's name also appears as that of a brave soldier in Normandy, Gascony, Guienne, Anjou, and Maine. He was lieutenant of Harfleur on the capture of that fortress in 1415. He fought at Rouen, Caen, Falaise, and Seez, and was made a Baron of France for successfully storming the castle of Sillé-le-Guillaume. In writing the scenes in I. and II. "King Henry IV.," Shakespeare was perfectly justified in making Sir John Oldcastle one of the reckless and profligate companions of Henry, Prince of Wales, such being the exact historical fact. But Oldcastle, in later life, had reversed the lightness of his youth. Marrying into the Cobham family, he had become a Lord Cobham, commonly known as "the good Lord Cobham," a follower of Wycliffe and an enthusiast, who at his own expense maintained an army of preachers in a crusade against the Established Church, and so suffered an attainder, being thereunder tried and executed for high treason (under the changed conditions of Elizabeth's day pronounced to have been martyrdom). There can be, then, no doubt but that the Cobham family raised a clamor of protest when the "Henry IV." was being acted, at their so eminent a name being held up for caricature, and were powerful enough to obtain an order from the lord chamberlain that it be removed, while the apology of the epilogue was to not only be made as publicly as the play had been performed, but should contain disclaimers that any allusion to a Lord Cobham had been ever intended (which certainly was not the fact).

Among other contemporaries the historian of the Church, Thomas Fuller, seems at first to have welcomed the change. "Stage-poets," he says, "have themselves been very bold with, and others very merry at the memory of Sir John Oldcastle, whom they have fancied a boon companion, a jovial royster, and a coward to boot. The best is, Sir John Falstaff hath relieved the memory of Sir John Oldcastle and of late is substituted buffoon in his place." But when this same Thomas Fuller comes to write his "Worthies of England," he appears quite as much annoyed at the use of Sir John Falstaff as he was of Sir John Oldcastle. "To avouch him [Falstaff] by many arguments valiant is to maintain that the sun is bright, though since, the stage has been overbold with his memory, making him a thrasonical puff, and emblem of mock valor. True it is, Sir John Oldcastle did first bear the brunt, being made the makesport in plays for a coward. Now, as I am glad that Sir John Oldcastle is put out, so am I sorry that Sir John Fastalffe is put in to relieve his memory in this base service, to be the anvil for every dull wit to strike upon. Nor is our comedian excusable by some alteration of his name, writing him Sir John Falstaffe (and making him the property and pleasure of King Henry V. to abuse) seeing the vicinity of sounds intrench on the memory of that worthy knight, and few do heed the inconsiderable difference in spelling. He was made Knight of the Garter by King Henry the VI., and died about the second year of his reign."[1] The question — the historical problem, for us to grapple just here

[2] Tegg's Edition, II. 455.

(and it is certainly a very curious one however it has survived any possible importance) is, Did Shakespeare deliberately reverse history, as he did in the case of Joan of Arc and of Jack Cade, and make Sir John Falstaff a coward, from some personal or inherited spite or from assuming the quarrel of, or at the request and instance of one of his titled patrons; or was there anywhere a record of Sir John Falstaffe's or Fastolffe's cowardice on the field of Patay? Guizot says the battle was short, "the English losing heart";[2] but, though he alludes to Sir John's presence at that affair, makes no mention of his particular responsibility for the result. Similarly, all the other authentic records are silent on the point. But Shakespeare is most emphatic as to the charge of cowardice.

Messenger — If Sir John Fastolfe had not played the coward
He being in the vanward, placed behind
With purpose to relieve and follow them
Cowardly fled, not having struck one stroke,
Hence grew the general wrack and massacre.
(I. Henry VI., I. i. 131.)

France before Rouen. An Alarum: Excursions. Enter Sir John Fastolfe and a Captain.

Captain — Whither away Sir John Fastolfe, in such haste?
Fastolfe — Whither away? to save myself by flight; we are like to have the overthrow again.
Captain — What! will you fly, and leave Lord Talbot?
Fastolfe — Ay, all the Talbots in the world to save my life!
(Id. III., ii. 1.)

Paris. A Hall of State. Enter the King, Gloster, Bishop of Winchester, York, Suffolk, Somerset, Warwick, Talbot, Exeter, the Governor of Paris, and others. Enter Sir John Fastolfe.

[1] History of France, II. 261.

Fastolfe — My gracious sovereign, as I rode from Calais,
　　　To haste unto your coronation
　　　A letter was delivered to my hand,
　　　Writ to your grace from the Duke of Burgundy.

Talbot — Shame to the Duke of Burgundy and thee!
　　　I vow'd base knight, when I did meet thee next
　　　To tear the garter from thy craven's leg.
　　　　　　　　　　　　　[*Plucking it off.*]
　　　. . . Pardon, my princely Henry and the rest.
　　　This dastard, at the battle of Patay
　　　When but in all I was six thousand strong,
　　　And that the French were almost ten to one;
　　　Before we met or that a stroke was given,
　　　Like to a trusty squire did run away.
　　　　　　　　　　　　　(Id. IV. i. 9.)

Now, if Shakespeare had ever heard or known of a record to the effect that Sir John Fastolfe was such a poltroon as that, I can well understand why he held the name in pickle for a coward, and so found it ready when a substitute for Oldcastle was wanted. And it would have been a stroke of policy on his part so to have employed it. For the true English audience loves nothing quite so much as successful military or naval valor. Only to such as Marlborough, Nelson or Wellington do they rear columns, which, like Nelson's in Trafalgar Square, far overtop and look a long way down on the mere bric-à-brac Edwards and Henrys and Georges. Had Sir John Falstaff been an unsuccessful hero even, perhaps the ignominy with which Shakespeare treats him would be intelligible, since even Gordon was left to be disemboweled by savages and his memory to perish when once with all his courage he could not command success. But Sir John appears from the record

to have been a singularly successful warrior. Not
only did he capture the division of the Duke of
Alençon, and take the duke himself a prisoner, at
Agincourt; but at the siege of Orleans, in October,
1428, he was able to provision the besiegers at the
head of a small body of troops, in the face of over-
powering numbers, in a most brilliant coup. From
the fact that the provisions Sir John brought
were mostly salt herrings, and that he made a
barricade of his herring wagons against the
French attack led by "le jeune et beau Dunois,"
Sir John's achievement is still known as the " herring affair." M. Guizot[1] concedes it to have been
an exceedingly brilliant action, and for it Sir John
was made Knight of the Order of the Garter by
Henry VI. So far from his having been a coward at Patay (June 18, 1429), it was the year after
that battle that he was made lieutenant of Caen;
and that the garter was never "torn from his
craven's leg" is sufficiently evinced by the fact
that the records of that order show that Sir John
regularly attended its chapters until his death.
Moreover, in peace as well as war does the real Sir
John Falstaff seem to have been a memorable
man. In 1432 he was English Embassador at
Basle, and was afterward sent by his government
to conclude a peace with France. He retired
honorably from service, built himself a castle at
Caistor about three miles north of Yarmouth in
Norfolk, where there is still an inconsiderable village of the name. In his retirement he seems to
have given some attention to literature, and to
have ordered a translation of the " De Senectute "

[1] History of France, II. 241.

made and printed by Caxton in 1481 at his own expense. He was a liberal benefactor of both Cambridge and Oxford, and endowed a college for seven priests; but the foundation has disappeared in the lapse and waste of years. He died in 1459, and was buried in the priory of Broomholm, now a ruin, on the bleak Norfolk coast.

It cannot be offered in Shakespeare's behalf as against a charge of "cooking" history (as previously in the case of Joan of Arc and Jack Cade), that he was misled by the chronicles of Monstrelet, for Monstrelet explicitly states that the circumstances under which Sir John fled without striking a blow at Patay were reconsidered, and his order of the Garter (of which he was at first deprived) restored to him with honor. So far the learned commentators have not added Monstrelet's Chronicles to the list of books consulted by Shakespeare; and just here I am inclined to think the facts agree with them. I think we must presume a motive somewhere for the dramatist's treatment of Oldcastle and Falstaff, as well as of Joan of Arc and of Jack Cade, and I think the motive is not hard to find. Monstrelet testifies as follows:[1]

"Sir John Fastolfe was bitterly reproached by the Duke of Bedford for having thus fled from the battle — and he was deprived of the Order of the Garter: however, in time, the remonstrances he had made in council previously to the battle were considered as reasonable, and this, with other circumstances and excuses he made, regained him the Order of the Garter. Neverthe-

[1] The Chronicles of Enguerrand de Monstrelet, chapter LXI. of Book II.

less, great quarrels arose between him and Lord Talbot on this business, when the latter was returned from his captivity." It seems to me that the last clause fully explains Shakespeare's willingness to perpetuate as a charge to posterity a temporary and reconsidered disgrace. The Talbots were to be consulted and conciliated as well as the Cobhams, and both were cajoled by a single ingenious stroke of the Shakespearean pen.

Provided then, from whatever motive, with another historic name for his butt, the dramatist was able to very promptly comply both with the order to remove the Cobham patronymic, and with that commanding him to mount forthwith a piece in which " neither matters of religion nor of the government of the commonwealth should be handled or treated." And yet, as Mr. Halliwell-Phillipps well says, it is best never to be too certain of anything in Shakespearean matters. Shakespeare, perhaps, never read Monstrelet: and Hollingshed, a century later, certainly tells the story of Fastolffe's disgrace without mentioning its reversal.[1] But if Shakespeare had the historical Oldcastle in mind when he drew the character of Falstaff, why should he so enlarge upon the fat knight's cowardice? why his repeated soliloquies as to the relative expediency of personal honor and corporeal safety? or why, indeed, such stress upon the purse-taking and elastic interpretations of the laws of meum and tuum? Oldcastle may have been a fanatic, but he certainly was never rated dishonest or a coward; while as to Fastolffe, there were certainly rumors as to both. Indeed, he is

[1] Chronicles, II., 601.

said to have so tampered with the income of his stepson, for whom he was trustee during minority, and thereby so kept himself continually in fear of the law, that he placed his entire landed estates in the hands of trustees for his own use during life, and thereafter for the purposes declared in his Will. It happened that among these trustees (often renewed, sometimes in the general and sometimes as to specified parcels of the realty) were John and William Paston, whence the Paston letters become a sort of chronicle of Fastolffe and his affairs, abounding in correspondence of and about him; and not on the whole to his credit. For example, in letter 98, Fastolffe writes to one Parson Howys: "I pray you sende me word who darre be so hardy to keck agen you in my ryght. And say hem on my half that they shall be quyt as ferre as law and reason wolle. And yff they wolle not dredde, ne obey, that then they shall be quyt by Blackberd or Whyteberd; that ys to say by God or the Devyll." In letter 133, he urges Parson Howys to "labor the jury," adding that, on this, an action may be founded against "Dallyng, the false harlot." He would be, like Berney, "rewarded for his labor if it were secretly done, and Dynne also. Ye wete what I meane, etc." Again, in letter 154 he says: "Labor to the Sheriff for the return of such panels as will speak for me, and not be shamed ... entreat the sheriff as well as you can, by reasonable rewards, rather than fail." Frequent allusion is made to the charge of Fastolffe's malversation with the funds belonging to his stepson. And Margaret Paston speaks of one "Will Lynys, that was with Master Fastolffe and such other as he is with him, who went about the country accusing men of being Scots, and only letting them go on payment of considerable bribes" (which might well have been a hint for Falstaff's thrifty disposal of the cases of Mouldy and Bullcalf). Certainly this bribe-giving and bribe-taking in his model would have justified any length in the humorist. But, had it been from such a model that Shakespeare worked, surely our debt to him were essentially enlarged.

And again: Had Oldcastle been Shakespeare's model for Falstaff, why should the dramatist have inserted those constant dissertations on the virtues of sack? It was certainly unnecessary to the mere delineation of dissipation and purse-taking to assert it the first duty of a parent to teach his child to forswear thin potations and devote himself exclusively to dry sherry! But if Shakespeare had the true Sir John Fastolffe in mind, we can understand the alleged discovery of a Mr. W. J. Fitzpatrick, F. S. A., that when the Earl of Ormond — who held the office of Chief Butler of Ireland in capite from the crown — died in the reign of Henry IV., his son being a minor, the king granted that office and its emoluments (estimated in 1810 at £216,000, and purchased by Parliament from the then earl at that figure) to Sir John Fastolffe and John Radcliffe; the grant being made by Thomas of Lancaster, son of Henry IV., Seneschal of England and Lord Lieutenant of Ireland, by letters patent, running as follows:

"Memorandum Roll. Exchequer. 3 Henry IV. Mem. 19. lre patent p Johe   Thomas de lancastre filius Regis Angl' locum ffastolf & Johe   tenens ipius Regis tre sue hibn

& senescallus Radclef p officio Angl' omibus ad quos psentes lre pvenint saltm capit pincne   Sciatis qd de gra ura spali concessim^s dilcis   Armigbis nris Johi ffastolf & Johi Radclef officiu capital' pincne tre pdce in manibus nris exconcessione carissimi dni & patris nri Regis pdci ratione minoris etatis Jacobi fil' & heredis Jacobi Boteller nup Comitis de Ormonia defuncti qui de ipo pre nro tenuit in capite existentis hend' & ocupand' dem officiu' p se aut p deputatos suos cum prisi vinos q in tam pdcam de tempe in tempus venient & adducent^r una cum feodis & aliis pficuis accomoditatibus quibuscunq ad idem officium ronabilit' spectantibus a primo die Januarii ultimo ptita usq ad plenam etatem hered' pdci nup comitis [   ] aliquo nob' seu pfato patri nro p prisis vinos pdcorus reddendo et si de herede pdco [   ] conting [   ] anteqm ad plenam etatem suam pvenit herede suo infra etatem existente tunc iidem Johes & Johes [   ] dem officiu' usq ad legitimam etatem ejusdem heredis sic infra etatem existentis in forma pdca & sic de herede in heredem quousq aliquis heredum pdcous ad plenam etatem suam pvenit In cujus rei testimon has lras nras fieri fecim' patentes data apud londen xiii; die April anno regni [   ] issimi dni & pris nri pdci septimo."

If Falstaff really did have these Irish experiences, Mr. Fitzpatrick seems to have something almost tangible when he points out that Falstaff figures in the play made from the reign of Henry IV., with Thomas of Lancaster appearing therein as Duke of Clarence: that Fastolffe as well as Oldcastle were of the household of Sir Thomas Mowbray, and that at the date called for by the above grants Mowbray was in exile, and the young prince, afterward Henry V., in Ireland, though but ten years old.

These are days of Shapira and the like forgeries, and I would like to receive this find (which reaches my eye in the "Gentleman's Magazine" for May,

1887, while these pages are going through the press) with considerable caution. But Mr. Fitzpatrick says that he has made a discovery in the Chancery Patent Rolls at least equally interesting, which runs:

"Patent Roll. Chancery. Ireland. 3 Henry IV. No. 217. face. p Johe ffostalf R — Omibus ad quos &c. saltm Sciatis qd de gra nra armigero   spali & p bono & laudabili suicio quod dilcus   armig^r nr Johes ffastolf nob & carissimo fil nro Thome de lancastre senescallo Angl' locu nrm tenenti in tra nra hibn ante hec tempora impendit & impendet in futur' dedim^s & concessim^s eidem Johi quendam equ' in custodia cujusdam Edwardi Berie Camarii Prioris ecclie sce Trinitatis Dublin ut dicit^r existen' tanqm deo dandum nrm eo qd intfecit quendam parvulu nob foristem et etia quendam aliu' equ' qui nup fuit Mathei ludewyche ut deo dandum nrm eo qd intfecit ipm Mathm nob' similit' fori sem In cuj' &c. T. pfato locu tenente apud Kilmaynan vii die Septembr'. p peticoem." [1]

To which favor of the Crown Mr. Fitzpatrick thinks that perhaps Falstaff alludes (and he does constantly allude to horses) when he boasts: "Let us take any man's horses; the laws of England are at my commandment" (II. Henry IV., V. iii. 132).

As to certain of the names associated with Falstaff, it may engage the curious to note Fastolffe's

[1] Which Mr. Fitzpatrick translates: "(The church is that now known as the Cathedral of Christ Church, Dublin). The King, for the good and lawful service which his well beloved Esquire, John Fastolf, has performed towards him and his most dearly beloved son, Thomas of Lancaster, grants to him a certain horse in the custody of one Edward Berry, Prior of the Church of the most Holy Trinity, as a deodand forfeited to the King for the murder of a little boy, and also another horse which belonged to Mathew Ledwich as a deodand forfeited for the murder of the said Mathew."

alleged capture of a notable prisoner at Agincourt,[1] whose ransom enriched his captor (some say, even to the cost of the great castle of Caistor), and Pistol's extortion of two hundred crowns from his French prisoner taken on that same field, for his release; that a courier named Bardolph served in Normandy in 1435; while — as to Poins — Gairdner, in his introduction to his edition of the " Paston Letters," gives a curious account of Sir John Fastolffe sending one of his followers, named Payn, as an envoy to Jack Cade, then in camp at Blackheath. " Some one called out to the captain that he was a man of Sir John Fastolf's, and that the two horses were Sir John's. The captain raised a cry of 'treason!' and sent him through the camp with a herald of the Duke of Exeter before him in the duke's coat-of-arms. At four quarters of the field the herald proclaimed with an 'oyez' that Payn had been sent as a spy upon them by the greatest traitor in England or France, namely, by one Sir John Fastolf, who had diminished all the garrisons of Normandy, Le Mans and Maine, and thereby caused the loss of all the king's inheritance beyond the sea. It was added that Sir John had garrisoned his place with the old soldiers of Normandy, to oppose the commons when they came to Southwark; and as

[1] "At Agincourt it was said," writes Oldys, "that Fastolf, among others, signalized himself most gallantly in taking the Duke of Alençon prisoner, though other historians say that the duke was slain after a desperate encounter with King Henry himself." The fact is, that in a succeeding battle Fastolf did take this duke's son and successor prisoner. Hume's account of Agincourt makes no mention whatever of Fastolf.— "The Gentleman's Magazine," May, 1887. I note that Fluellen, on that field, however, has his own slur upon Falstaff.—Henry V., IV., vii, 47.

the emissary of such a traitor, Payn was informed that he should lose his head." And "Payn" is certainly near enough to "Poins" for romantic purposes. If the I. and II. of "Henry IV." were written to fit Sir John Oldcastle as he was in his youth, why these coincidental resemblances to the history and career of a certain Sir John Fastolffe? We have suggested that the part was enlarged in order to make as extreme a butt as possible of a man who had earlier proved himself distasteful to a powerful nobleman, as he might be. It almost looks as if the few years during which the fat character went by the name of Oldcastle, instead of the adoption of the name of Falstaff, were fortuitous; and the use of the latter, rather than the former, the dramatist's first intention. Nobody can guess what personal motive for lampooning Oldcastle Shakespeare may have cherished, but in ridiculing and scarifying Fastolffe I have already suggested he was sure to get himself on the fashionable side.

But if here were the royal orders, Shakespeare would obey. If a knight were to be shown as the butt of tradespeople, Shakespeare at least knew what particular knight he should prefer to select for the base office; while as for the moral, seeing that it was uncongenial anyhow, it seems to me that he proposed to revenge himself by gibing at the Queen herself and the tastes she thus confessed to. Even without the unmistakable drift of her order, or the previous record of Falstaff, there was certainly precedent and temptation enough for making the catastrophe run the other way. Even the good Bishop Wordsworth (while demonstrating with exuberant wealth of parallelism the author of "Venus and Adonis" and

"Love's Labour's Lost," to have been a pious follower of the precepts of the English Bible) concedes to him "the faults of his time." But how happens it that "the faults of his time" are not traceable here? There was every excuse, historical as well as royal, for making the tradesman's wife yield to the courtier. The Elizabethan chronicles state broadly enough that tradesmen ever relied on the charms of their wives quite as much as upon the merit of their goods, for lordly patronage. Was it because Falstaff, when discarded by a king, was no longer to be justified in those liberties with other people's prerogatives and purses to which he had been so entirely welcome when the yoke-fellow of a prince?

Of course the fat knight, in amorous chase after a pair of petticoats, is no more "in love" than previously with Dame Quickly or Doll Tearsheet. The pen that created Imogen and Desdemona, Perdita and Juliet, if seriously ordered to delineate a libertine controlled and ennobled by the passion that drives out self, would scarcely have failed to recognize a field for its genius. However, if Falstaff was still to titillate the fine humors of Elizabeth, he must be concupiscent always, but this time baffled, foiled and put to rout. And so, for the nonce, in a play for the eyes of a Virgin Queen and within the letter, even at the expense of the spirit of her royal orders, must wifely honor live outside of noble birth, and virtue walk in homespun.

Shakespeare was equal to any work assigned him. He could put into the mouth of Portia the most magnificent eulogy of mercy the world has ever heard, and yet find none of it for a poor Jew who had offered to loan money as a friend, but had been challenged, instead, to loan it as to an enemy in order that he might "exact the penalty" ("Merchant of Venice," I. iii., 130, 136), preferring rather to devote the Jew to death by first assuming that he intended murder, and endowing Portia with an earthly power (that indeed did "show likest heaven's" for once) to sentence him to the gallows for the inmost secrets of his heart! After such an achievement as that, it were a comparatively light matter to transpose such a record as the following: "Sir John Fastolfe, Knight, Knight Banneret and Knight of the Garter, a military officer of high reputation during the wars in France in the reign of the Henrys IV., V., and VI., was so bountiful to this college (Magdalen) from the great affection he entertained for Bishop Waynflete, that his name is commemorated in an anniversary speech, and though the particulars of his bounty are not now remembered, because he enfeoffed the founder in his lifetime, it is yet known that the Boar's Head, in Southwark, now divided into tenements yielding £150 yearly, together with Caldicot Manor, in Suffolk, were part of the lands he bestowed on the college. Lovingland, in that county, is also thought to be another part of his donation."[1]

---

[1] "The History of Oxford: Its Colleges, Halls and Public Buildings." London: R. Ackerman, 1814. i. 243. I understand that until about 1838 (when Parliament seems to have relieved of the condition) masses were supposed to be said at Magdalen for the repose of Sir John's soul.

IX

Have We a Shakespeare Among Us?

 HAVE elsewhere called attention to the fact that whatever "copyright," or right to literary property (of whatever description or by whatever name called) obtained in Shakespeare's lifetime, was not by virtue of any statute, but at common law and so perpetual. It follows, therefore, that could we trace the present heirs or assigns of whoever owned the literary rights existing in the plays in Shakespeare's own lifetime, we would find the present owners of those invaluable and constantly reprinted possessions.

It was not from any lawyer's instinct or hope of finding a party in whose behalf I could institute proceedings for piracy — not only against every living editor, and almost every existing publishing house, but for an accounting and mesne profits against the legal representatives of all the editors and publishers since 1616 — but from curiosity that I asked my friend, Mr. John Wallace Bell, to set on foot an inquiry as to whether we had any Shakespeares in America. Indeed, had I cherished only the sordid motive, I should have instructed him to search rather for assigns of John Heminges and Henry Condell, Jaggard, Blount, Arthur Johnson, R. Boniars, H. Walley and all the others (including, perhaps, the unspeakable and shadowy "T. T.") who chiseled Shakespeare — the engrossed man of affairs and proprietor of two theaters — and his assigns out of so much that equitably ought to have been his and theirs. Mr. Bell was advised to hold his search closely to the name Shakespeare. And it is because I think the results of his search interesting (unsatisfactory as they are in the capital object) that I have asked permission to summarize his results here.

It seems that on the ninth day of February, 1884, there were just thirty persons (males) in the United States named Shakespeare. Of these, all but four are married and the fathers of families, so that the question at the head of this paper can be relied on to be constant, and not one to disappear with a single asking. These thirty group themselves as to vocations as follows:

Blacksmith	1
Carpenter	1
City official (Mayor)	1
Journalist	1
Laborer	5
Liquor-dealer	1
Lawyer	5
Physician	6
Printer	2
Real estate	1

Shoemaker	1
Tailor	3
Watchmaker	1
House and sign painter	1
	30

Besides the five lawyers and six physicians, I found the mayor, the printer, the journalist and the house and sign painter, all very deeply interested in the question of their ancestry; the tailor, the watchmaker and the liquor-dealer curious, and the remainder in that state of mind which would certainly be called indifferent, if not stolid. But it must be reluctantly and regretfully stated that, after considerable correspondence, interviewing, and the assistance of an expert antiquary, not one of the aforesaid was able to furnish any further pedigree than that his "family came originally from England." Of course the ultimate in each case where the pedigree was sought was to reach the greatest of that name, William Shakespeare of Stratford-upon-Avon.

Now, in each of the United States there is, and always has been, provision by which an individual may legally—for the trifling expense of an affidavit and perhaps a clerical and a registry fee — assume any surname he pleases. Hundreds of people, besides, do constantly assume one surname and drop another without any formality, legal or otherwise, being considered necessary ; which elements of uncertainty, added to the very little care taken of pedigrees by the vast majority of our people, practically leave the question to the general operation of the laws of chance, in such a case as this hardly likely to find a computation anywhere.

However, I did not leave the hopeless case quite at this point. I found that in 1885 there were living residents of Warwickshire, some forty-three persons, who could trace their lineage directly to George Shakespeare, a tailor, who was born in 1636 in Stratford-upon-Avon, who married, in 1657, Hester, daughter of Thomas Lydiate of that town, and died there in 1696. This George was the son of Thomas (1605-1661), who was the son of Joan, sister of the great Shakespeare, who married William Hart, a hatter of Stratford, in 1590, during her immortal brother's lifetime, and died in 1646, surviving him thirty years. These forty-three persons were as follows:

George Blewitt, Louisa Blewitt, William Walkins, Charles Watkins, Anne Watkins, George Watkins, Henry Watkins, William Hallen, Frederick Hallen, William Moestrich, George Allerton, Susan Allerton, Louisa Allerton, Diana Grubb, Rose Grubb, Joan Shakespeare, George Shakespeare (born in Australia), William Ashley, Ann Ashley, Henry Ashley, Nelly Ashley, Frederick Ashley, William Ashley, Tabitha Ashley, George Ashley, Edwin Ashley, James Ashley, two children named Powell, two children named Pool, and five children named Bradley, besides three children of the above-named George Ashley, two of the above-named Edwin Ashley (Edwin, Lilian), and two children (Isabel, Maude) of the above-named Rose Grubb, now Rose Watson. It will be observed that of the above the only ones whose surname is Shakespeare are Joan and George. These two are children of Thomas Shakespeare, born in 1803, who married Elizabeth Smith in 1837, and died in 1850. He was the son of William Shakespeare Turner, who was a distant descendant of the sixth generation of the tailor, George Shakespeare, above named. Of all this tailor's descendants of his own generation, this Thomas appears to have been the only one who cared, in any registered act, to perpetuate the memory of his illustrious namesake. On coming of age he dropped the Turner, and named his two daughters (sisters of George) by the Shakespeare family names Joan and Judith, the latter of whom died in infancy.

The above list being taken from the labors of Mr. A. W. Cornelius Hallen, M. A., F. S. A. (Scot.) (himself a descendant of George the tailor), and being taken as authentic, it follows that if any of the individuals enumerated by vocations above can recognize in these lines any names of their known kindred, they may be able to verify a remote descent from some of the poet's kin. At least the surnames given ought reasonably to lead to such a result. Having spoken thus openly of my researches of several months ago, I am not at liberty to be more explicit as to the individuals composing my above list of twenty-nine; but if this meets their eyes they will be at liberty themselves to throw such light upon the quest as they see fit or may be able.

But there is another method by which the name may have been accredited to some progenitor of the American Shakespeares. The Earls of Pembroke and Montgomery (to whom the first collected volume of the works of William Shakespeare was dedicated) were proud to bear on their escutcheon the bar sinister of Gwilim-Dhu, the Welsh chieftain descended from King Arthur's youngest son (Morgan of Glamorgan), prolific first of many an intricate Welsh pedigree. And surely a Shakespeare bar sinister is fully equal in the eyes of this people to those royal bar sinisters which are esteemed always as honorable decorations over the sea. Let us look into the possibilities.

The name Shakespeare first appears in the reign of Edward III. in mid-England as a corruption of the French Jacques-Pierre (John Peter), from which patronymic we may judge pretty safely of the social rank of its earliest wearer. The family founded by this first bearer of the name did not advance much in the scale in the next hundred years, if we may judge from the fact that Henry Wilkoe and Thomas Shepeye, bailiffs of Coventry under Henry IV., accounted into the exchequer for two shillings for the goods and chattels of "Thomas Shakespeare, merc" (apparently the abbreviation of mercerio, mercer or merchant), who, being indicted of felony, had fled the bailiwick. But the name stands better and better thereafter, occuring from this reign onward, in wills, deeds, and other Warwickshire indentures, until, we are assured by the 1599 grant of arms, the great-grandfather of the immortal William was advanced and rewarded "for his faithful and approved service to that most prudent prince, Henry VII., with lands and tenements in that part of Warwickshire where they have continued by some descentes." It is a matter of curious reflection that the man who was to illustrate the name for the whole world by his genius, used his first profits in London to ennoble his family by a grant of arms founded upon these otherwise unchronicled and forgotten "faithful and approved services."

The little cottage at Shottery, so long worshiped of tourists as the courting-ground of great Shakespeare, may have to go into the limbo of exploded myths, according to Mr. Halliwell Phillipps, who (1886) announces that in the register of marriage licenses in the Consistory Court of Worcester, is the record, "1583, Nov. 27, William Shaxpere and Anne Whateley, of Temple Grafton." The absence of any entry of the marriage of the poet to "Anne Hathaway" has heretofore been unanimously explained by commentators by learned tergiversation as to the value of marriage bonds, "troth plight," etc. But now this is all lumber. Everybody knows that, whoever the mother, Shakespeare's first child was the daughter De Quincy calls "the premature little Susannah." Nor is there anything in the career of her father, the author of "Pericles," "Measure for Measure," and "All's Well that Ends Well," to indicate that he sat "like his grandsire cut in alabaster," or may not have had offspring born as well as begotten out of wedlock. Anyhow, "troth plight" had its disadvantages, and nobody can disagree with the good bishop who declared that "the Church of England did wisely, no doubt, in uniting the troth plight and the marriage in one and the same ceremony"; especially since William Shakespeare anticipated Malone and his followers by just one hundred and eighty-four years in considering the two formalities as equivalents. Richard Hathaway, of Shottery (owner of the cottage whose glories now bid fair to fade), in his will, dated September 1, 1581, bequeathed his property to seven children, among other provisions, giving six pounds thirteen shillings (about $250 present value of money) to his daughter Agnes, and as no Anne was mentioned (his other daughters being Catherine and Margaret) Agnes has invariably been supposed a clerical error for Anne. But Shakespeare study is fast being guided by modern students into the paths of common sense, and the convenient presumption that everything not accordant with the glib "biographer" of the greatest Englishman who ever lived, was a "clerical error" is about to be pensioned off forever. At any rate, we do know that the great William lived apart from his wife, and that such visits as he paid to Stratford may almost always be found indicated by an investment, a lawsuit, or an arbitration, whereby the thrifty poet did largely increase the body of wealth he left his children.

Of course, beyond these periodical excursions between London and Stratford, Shakespeare was no traveler. Even had he possessed the requisite leisure, the country was not in a condition to make the exertion necessary to move from portion to portion either profitable or pleasant, but, on the other hand, a labor and a sacrifice. Outside of the very city, highwaymen frequented such roads as there were, while, at a little distance, even these roads ceased. The Continent (being reached by ships) was much more accessible to tourists than portions of England not many miles from

London itself. But, except on military or diplomatic errands, people cared very little to leave their immediate homes. And except among the very rich there was a predjudice against travelers, even for business, who were called, "neer do weels" and vagrants. An Englishman's house was his castle, and he was supposed either to be an outcast or commanding in person. But there was another and insuperable reason why William Shakespeare should not move about. At the time when he first arrived in London the country was full of vagrant actors and companies of strolling players. These, however worthy, were huddled together with travelers for any other business purpose, as "schollers, idlers, common players of interludes, and minstrels wandering abroad, jugglers, tinkers, and petty chapmen" in the statutes of the time, and the local constables ordered to arrest, detain, and summarily punish them. William Shakespeare was one of the earliest to establish a metropolitan play-house which should appeal to public patronage as permanent, and, therefore, respectable. His hold upon his audiences, therefore, lay in the very fact that neither he nor his company did stroll about from place to place; nay, it was their claim and capital that they were removed as far as possible from the "barn-stormers" of that day (one troupe of which was actually stranded at Amsterdam, and another in Germany, during the early years of Shakespeare's London career). The quiet rejoinder to gentlemen who will have Shakespeare to have played his Globe or Blackfriars company in the provinces or on the Continent is, that he was quite too shrewd and far-sighted a manager to do anything of the sort. He did not propose, by any means, to give his rival metropolitan managers a pretext for declaring that his was still a strolling company, and the Globe and Blackfriars theaters mere halting-houses for vagrant players. The practice of playing city stock organizations in the interior during vacation is one easily within the memory of men now living. But, whenever originated, William Shakespeare, one of the first of managers of permanent establishments, could least of all afford—in days when moving companies of actors had reached their lowest level of disrepute, when laws had been enacted to abate them—to return to even a semblance of the custom. Mr. Fleay's statement,[*] therefore, that "Hamlet" was written by Shakespeare while on a professional visit to Scotland with his troupe, must be passed over with the small attention usually bestowed upon commentators and biographers whose private definitions of such words as "evidence," "proof," and "proved" are not accessible to the general reader. One "Master Laurence Fletcher" did take his company from London to Scotland in 1599, as another company had been taken ten years earlier, in 1589; but there is no evidence whatever that Shakespeare went thither with either of them. Mr. Knight devotes an entire chapter of his Biography to the question, "Did Shakespeare visit Scotland?" and endeavors to prove that, though he probably did not do so in 1589 or 1599, he did in the autumn of

[*] "A Chronicle History of William Shakespeare, Player, Poet, and Playmaker," p. 232. New York and London, 1886.

1601; but his elaborate argument seems to Mr. W. J. Rolfe inconclusive, who says that, so far as he knows, it has convinced none of the critics. Under the old vagrant system, English companies strolled to the Continent from Holland, whither they went by sea (as we learn from " The Runaway's Answer" to Dekkar's " Rod For Runaways," which was a broadside at certain who left London to escape the plague of 1626. "We can be bankrupts on this side and gentlemen of a company beyond the sea. We burst at London and are pieced up at Rotterdam"—and some of them ultimately found their way into Germany, giving slim ground for numerous volumes entitled, "Shakespeare in Germany," which are still being printed. Shakespeare, of course, may have been in the present United States, but there is no evidence that he was, although during his lifetime many of his countrymen did find their way hither; and when we are writing history it is just as well, perhaps, to look into probabilities. For the last twenty years Mr. Halliwell Phillipps has searched the town records of England and Wales, and, while he has unearthed traces of the company in whose takings Shakespeare had a share at Faversham, Rye, Bristol, Dover, Marlborough, Shrewsbury, Leicester, Bath, Coventry, Oxford, Barnstaple, Saffron-Walden, Maidstone, Hythe, New Romney,—and Folkestone, at dates not exclusively confined to any particular season of the year, and occurring between the years 1596 and 1613,—he has discovered nothing so far to indicate that the purchaser of the Grant of Arms left his London franchises to be managed by subordinates, while he returned to his earliest stage experiences and re-assumed the vocation of a strolling player.

But, however the then head of the house of Shakespeare found it more congenial to make his home in London, and breath of slander never touched the good name and fame of Mistress Anne, his wife. And she forgave her husband,— if peradventure she had aught to forgive,— and dying "did earnestly desire to be buried in his grave." Her request was as far as possible granted. She was laid at his side, and a brass tablet above her still bears legibly the inscription:

"Here lyeth interred the body of Anne, wife of William Shakespeare, who depted this life the 6 day of avgv: 1623 being of the age of 67 yeares.

"Vbera, tu mater; tu lac, vitamq. dedisti.
Vae mihi pro tanto munere saxa dabo!
Quam mallem, amoueat lapidem bonus Ang'l' ore.
Exeat christi corpus, imago tua.
Sed nil vota valent, venias cito, Christe resurget,
Clausa licet tumulo mater, et astra petet."

I do not think a search among such of the antiquities of mid-English counties as may still be accessible will show reason to dispute the fact that " troth-plight " was not the only custom more honored in the breach than in the observance in the Elizabethan era. Unions patriarchal in their character, and not wanton, were not discountenanced, nor did they entail upon the children who were their fruit the slightest social taint. In many counties these children inherited, after the first-born, equally, and the English laws of primogeniture were founded on the presumption of such unions for obviously unwritten reasons. As to the Davenant paternity, the general desire to acquit Shakespeare of that wise child ought to be respected. General report of the vicinage during the lifetime of all concerned — Davenant's own conviction in the premises — are of very little weight as against a public opinion formed some century after everybody competent to the question is dead and gone. Even a suggestion that the greatest expresser of human passion may himself have had the passions of his kind, would have no weight. Therefore it would not be well, in searching for an American Shakespeare, to concern ourselves with any American Davenants.

X

The Donnelly and Prior Ciphers, and the Furnivall Verse-Tests

REGARD the publication of the Third Folio edition of the Shakespeare plays in 1663–4 as by far the most important step in their circumstantial history subsequent to their appearance during William Shakespeare's own lifetime. As early as 1623 we are confronted with a well-recognized and reasonable doubt as to what plays William Shakespeare really wrote. Thirty-six plays had been printed in quarto during William Shakespeare's lifetime, all of them bearing his name, either in full or in abbreviation. Which were his and which were spurious? John Heminges and Henry Condell, two of Shakespeare's fellows and friends, whom he mentioned in his will and made beneficiaries in testimonial of attachment, undertook to make decision, and deliberately sorted out of these thirty-six just twenty-six, thus putting themselves on

record as deliberately rejecting almost fully one-third of the literary matter which traveled as the dramatist's own composition during his own lifetime. Of seven plays contemporary with this list (to only one of which — on its appearing in a second edition — was Shakespeare's name ever attached) they included all. They added one play which belonged to a rival theatrical company which operated during Shakespeare's lifetime a rival theater ("The Rose," which competed with "The Globe" for the public favor and patronage): one that first appeared five years after Shakespeare's death: in all, ten that were never known before their appearance in the First Folio. The numerical result was the same: thirty-six plays in the lifetime list, and thirty-six in the Heminges and Condell list. But the Heminges and Condell list of thirty-six is not by any means the lifetime list of thirty-six. "William Shakespeare" had been a well-known name in London seven years before. It had been signed to more than one dedication addressed to a noble Lord. Had there been an "Athenæum" or a "Saturday Review" in 1623 we need not doubt that these would have called rather peremptorily on Messrs. Heminges and Condell to give their reasons for discarding substantially one-half of what had passed current as "Will Shakespeare's plays" for so many years. But there was no critical press to ask for an accounting, and moreover this Heminges and Condell list does contain — has always been admitted to contain — the best of the plays included in the lifetime list of Shakespeare. But, since there is no literary statute of limitations it appears that there very soon began to be demurrer to the Heminges and Condell pronouncement as to what was and was not Shakespeare. The Revised List of the Third Folio of 1663-4 was, therefore, a demurrer filed in the only way it could have been filed at all, and which, had it appeared in the nineteenth instead of the seventeenth century, would have made the "Athenæum," or the "Saturday Review," or some other prominent critical London journal, its vehicle; and that those demurrers have continued to be filed from that day to this will also appear upon opening any modern edition of Shakespeare, all of which include the "Pericles,"[1] and many of which include the "Edward Third" and "The Two Noble Kinsmen," while "Titus Andronicus," "Henry VIII," and others, though generally included, are by several modern editors admitted on sufferance only.

What editor thus went to the expense and took the critical responsibility of restoring to the name of Shakespeare seven of the lifetime list of thirty-six plays, which Heminges and Condell had set aside as un-Shakespearean, must unhappily always remain matter of conjecture. When we remember that these were years in London very unfavorable to literary ventures,—England being then recovering from the Rebellion,—we can only infer that some other than mercenary motives induced the publication.

But why should the unknown 1663-4 editor have had any doubts as to the Heminges and Con-

[1] Ante, p. 213, note: I have conjectured that the First Folio editors overlooked the "Pericles" through carelessness rather than rejected it from critical motives. They are certainly entitled to the benefit of the doubt.

dell dictum as to which were and which were not Shakespeare's plays? For one thing, he probably had read the plays he edited (not always, as we shall see further on, considered a necessary preliminary) and had noted certain palpable discrepancies. The vast preponderance of lines in the admitted plays had a trend and gait of their own. Such lines as those in "Macbeth":

> "If the assassination
> Could trammel up the consequence, and catch,
> With his surcease, success; that but this blow
> Might be the be-all and the end-all here.
> But here, upon this bank and shoal of time,
> We'd jump the life to come," etc.—[I. vii. 2.]

were everywhere, stamping the plays as from a mind more ratiocinative, an expression more despotic and at the same time more graceful than the run of Elizabethan dramatists. But, at the same time, there were other lines in the plays which had no one of these qualities,—being rather florid, measured, and ponderously magnificent, such as the passage from "Titus Andronicus":

> "Now climbeth Tamora Olympus' top
> Safe out of fortune's shot, and sits aloft,
> Secure of thunder's crack and lightning flash,
> Advanced above pale envy's threat'ning beams,
> As when the golden sun salutes the morn
> And, having gilt the ocean with his beams,
> Gallops the Zodiac in his glistering coach."
> —[II. i. 1.]

And, yet again, here was a passage in "Lear" which hardly arose to the dignity of a doggerel:

> "I have a journey, sir, shortly to go,
> My master calls me, I must not say no."
> —[V. iii. 322.]

Since Shakespeare was dead, and since such alien passages appeared in plays which his intimate friends Heminges and Condell said he wrote, what was the only obviously safe conclusion? Not, surely, that only the first of the above-cited styles was "Shakespeare"— that the second was Marlowe (whom it certainly does resemble), and that the third was some hack writer striving to fill up a gap in the play—for that would be mere speculation apart from any data. Not that the plays were of composite origin rather than monographs (for the lights by which to infer so much did not exist in 1663-4). The obviously safe conclusion was that possibly the same Shakespeare who had written the Heminges and Condell plays had also written the quarto plays they omitted to put on their list; its safety lying, of course, in the presumptive and circumstantial evidence afforded by the fact that these unlisted plays bore William Shakespeare's name during his own lifetime prominently upon their title pages. These are the considerations, presumably, which led the Third Folio editor to include what we now call "the Doubtful Plays" in that edition, and this is why the Third Folio is an extremely valuable possession, since it shows that within forty-seven years of William Shakespeare's death students began to apply circumstantial and historical evidence to the question as to what plays he did or did not write.

Since Shakespeare, grand as it is, is not Holy Writ, not a Bible or a Koran, I respectfully submit that these questions as to the authorship of Shakespeare are legitimate, are dignified and respectable, and entitled to the respectful consideration of students, whether their motive be instruction or mere curiosity. The Baconian theory, for example, is one arising from the very difficulty that confronted the Third Folio editor in 1663-4, and is full of meat. Its investigation leads to the opening of a wide field of Elizabethan history, and—whatever its results, or the final judgment of the world upon it—its devotees have been scholars and thinkers: earnest, sincere and, above all, courteous in their claims, arguments and statements of fact. As to the practical proposition arising out of this attempt to know what William Shakespeare really wrote, I propose in this paper to examine the constant and irrepressible theory of a "Cipher" in the plays: and, as to the merely curious propositions, the later but equally insistive theory that these plays yield their secret readily to the application of a "Verse-Test."

I. THE "CIPHER." Miss Delia Bacon, who proclaimed the Baconian authorship early in the forties (Mr. J. C. Hart in his "Romance of Yachting," published in New-York in 1845, discusses the question without any claim to its origination; everywhere alluding to it as a perfectly familiar theory, if not, indeed, as an already acknowledged discovery), made no effort whatever to work it out with the elaboration of demonstration it has very recently received. Miss Bacon based her theory simply upon the propositions (1) that Bacon had a philosophy he wished at once to proclaim and to conceal; (2) that he did not desire to be known as a poet or a writer of plays ; and (3) that it was the fashion of his day to write in all sorts of verbal concealments, tricks and ingenuities, and hence was only natural that (his sentiments being dangerous ones to utter) Bacon should have concealed them in cipher and at the same time concealed his authorship of the plays. As to these propositions I have never been able to find that Bacon was unwilling to be known either as a play-writer or a poet. On the contrary he did write in both capacities — procured his plays and poems to be respectively played and printed, and constantly (or at least frequently) calls attention to his authorship of both in his letters to friends and acquaintances. (Mrs. Henry Pott and Judge Holmes, the two most learned and powerful champions of the Baconian theory, not only admit this, but make it their most emphatic argument.) As to whether Bacon had any dangerous propositions to conceal, whether what he did conceal (if anything) would have brought his head to the block if proclaimed upon the house-tops, perhaps we shall know more hereafter. At present it appears that Bacon, so far from being a plotter against the State, was a constant and obsequious courtier and servant of the two monarchs who reigned during his lifetime; an inveterate office-seeker who constantly magnified every slightest act or service he performed into a reason why office should be given him. (Letters of his are extant in which he even urges his desire for public employment and self-asserted unfitness for anything else, as entitling him to a place in the public service.) And for my own part, so far as the cipher is concerned, I am utterly unable to understand why, if Bacon had something of which he desired to be ultimately known as the author, but which he was afraid to

19

stand sponsor for in the age of Elizabeth, he should, after taking the trouble to conceal it by means of a cipher in certain plays, take the further trouble to conceal his authorship of the plays themselves. Why should he hide a diamond in a bottle of hay, and then hide the bottle of hay? Why should he run the risk of his cipher being read — and of the precious deliverance — when revealed — being ascribed to the brain of William Shakespeare? However, I do not propose — being entirely uninstructed thereto — to discuss the merits of Bacon's secret, or his purposes in burying it (granted that he had a cipher and that he did bury it) in the plays. It is only as to its alleged discovery that I have any considerations to offer here.

Miss Bacon's theory (as I am able to abstract it from the curiously involved rhetoric—almost a cipher in itself—in which she wrote) was as follows:

"The proposition is: that this philosophy is, . . . with its veil of allegory and parable, applied to much more important subjects in the disguise of the parable than it is in the open statement . . . that it proceeds in both cases from a reflective, deliberative . . . conscious, designing mind . . . which was compelled to have recourse to translations in some cases for the safe delivery and tradition of its new learning."[1]

I surmise that Mr. Nathaniel Hawthorne may have been unable to make head or tail out of this, or the rest of the book to which he was to write

[1] "The Philosophy of Shakespeare's Plays Unfolded." London and Boston, 1857, p. viii.

an introduction, and so asked Miss Bacon for a written explanation. And that — having received it, and being as much literally in the dark as ever — he did as lawyers do when obliged to plead a statute they can't understand,— namely, quoted the exact words and left it to those who might or could. At any rate, this is what Mr. Hawthorne said: "Applicably to this subject, I quote a paragraph from a manuscript of the author's not intended for present publication: 'It was a time when authors who treated of a scientific politics and of a scientific ethics internally connected with it, naturally preferred this more philosophic, symbolic method of indicating their connection with their writings which would limit the indication to those who could pierce within the veil of a philosophic symbolism. It was the time when the cipher in which one could write omnia per omnia was in such request, . . . when all the latent capacities of the English language were put in requisition, and it was . . . inlined with philosophic secrets that opened down into the bottom of a tomb — that opened into the Tower — that opened on the scaffold and the block. . . . The great secret of the Elizabethan age did not lie where any superficial research could ever discover it. It was not left within the range of any accidental disclosure. It did not lie on the surface of any Elizabethan document, . . . was reserved . . . for a research that should test the mind of the discoverer, . . . presented to the world in the form of an enigma.'"[1]

What this great secret was, Ralph Waldo Emerson, at least, was unable to discover. Mr.

[1] Id. Introduction, pp. x, xi.

Emerson (says Mrs. Dall) wished very much to review Miss Bacon's book. "He held the very highest estimate of the critical ability and wonderful insight which her book displayed. He came to me once to ask if I could suggest any volumes which would assist him to illustrate her purpose. He said he could not have the 'seeing eye,' she found so much and he so little." Miss Bacon's book is in some six hundred compactly printed octavo pages, and to ordinary students is very difficult reading, owing to its constant parentheses and parenthetical paraphrases of the original statement. (Indeed, the extracts given above appear to be garbled only from my effort — in quoting them — to get at the proposition itself.) I cannot pretend, any more than Hawthorne or Emerson, to know what the book is about. I can only blindly conjecture that if it were dangerous to state its contents in Elizabeth's day it must have been because Elizabeth herself, like Hawthorne and Emerson, would have been completely befogged, and — being suspicious of what she could not understand — would have sent the occult authors to "the Tower and to the block." Although Miss Bacon was never actually confined in an insane asylum, there can be no doubt but that the chilling reception of her volume broke her heart or turned her brain, or both, for she died soon after, a victim to her own theory. Nobody seems to have been tempted to further handling of the cipher until, about thirty years later, a Mrs. C. F. Ashmead Windle, an English lady in San Francisco, came upon a copy of Miss Bacon's book and set about interpreting the enigma anew, but on an entirely new tack. Mrs. Windle issued, in

August, 1881, an "Address to the New Shakespeare Society of London: Discovery of Lord Verulam's Undoubted Authorship of the 'Shakspere Works,'"[1] in which she has "the honor of informing" that "distinguished association" that she has "discovered an allegorical undermeaning running through the works called 'Shakespeare's,' disclosing their author to have been undoubtedly your distinguished countryman Francis Bacon, Lord Verulam — already, before this halo to illumine his honors, the proudest name on the English roll of fame. It is about two years and a half since," she continues, " entirely of myself, I made the discovery to which I have alluded, and my life being very retired, I have had no opportunity of communicating with any one versed in these dramas, with a view to making it generally known. Feeling more and more deeply that my revelation is of imperative importance to the memory of the illustrious Bacon, to the English nation and to the whole literary world, I have now determined to communicate directly with your society in regard to its public announcement, as my health being lately delicate, I am liable to quit this world at any time, leaving it unrevealed. To satisfy you that my overture of a discovery so momentous is nothing chimerical or unsustained, I submit respectfully to you herewith my underreading of the play of 'Cymbeline.'"

An examination of this address certainly shows that it ought to have been very clear to sundry of the creative critics. It certainly is unintelligible enough to suit the most mysterious of the guild. It premises that the key to the plays "is con-

[1] San Francisco: Joseph Winterburn & Co., 1881.

tained in the mystery of the Sonnets," which, "once pierced and carried into the reading of the plays, reveals an absolute divineness of ideality underlying their mere outward form, as well as a plaintive autobiographical information of the poet's consciousness, enhancing them above all possible eulogy, save the tacit one of reciprocal apprehension of miracle performed." Thus underread, the characters become as follows:

CYMBELINE.—A cymbal. (Used here to represent Britain in the *expansion* of her fame; that is, in the following sense: Tiberius Cæsar — *cymbalum mundi* vocabat — filled the world with his discussions *(Pliny and Virgil).*
LEONATUS POSTHUMUS.—(British) Lion-born Posthumously.
CLOTEN.—Clothing. (Intending the living, bodily personality as but the *clothing* of the immortal parts transmitted in knowledge and character.)
BELARIUS.—Bel-air or Fine air. (Referring to the lofty atmosphere of study and thought.)
MORGAN.— My organ. } (Otherwise called) (Meaning the Novum *organum*.)
GUIDERIUS.— As a guide. ⎱
(otherwise called) ⎰ The learned philosopher.
POLYDORE.— Many ores. ⎱
ARVIRAGUS.— As with the Art of Manhood. ⎱
(otherwise called) ⎰ The Virtuous
CADWAL.— Strong and harmonious through ⎰ Man.
self-government. ⎰
QUEEN *(Second wife to Cymbeline).*— The existing day or generation of British fame.
IMOGEN.— Image-in. (Imagination depicted.)
IACHIMO.— Slander.
PISANIO.— Fear.
SICILIUS.— The genius invoked in the sonnets. (A form of poem of Sicilian origin and introduced by Dante into Italy.)
TENANTIUS.— Dweller in the Sonnets.
EURIPHILE.— Lover of Discovery.

This medley (which I give with all the capitals, italics, parentheses, and hyphens), being duly tabulated, Mrs. Ashmead Windle proceeds to apply through about forty pages to the following solution of "the Riddle" (Cymbeline, V. iv. 138).

SOLUTION OF THE RIDDLE.

When, at the time that a posthumous fame, born of a (British) lion, shall unconsciously, and without seeking, find itself embraced by the tender "Ariel" of its own BOOK, O RARE ONE! *and when the branches of Bacon's Poetry, Philosophy, and Virtue, lopped from the stately cedar of Britain's renown, have been dead many years, shall afterwards revive, be jointed to the old stock and freshly grow, then shall the misery of his delayed recognition terminate, Britain be fortunate and flourish in peace and plenty.*

This reading of the cipher, luminous as it may all be, does not seem to have been welcomed with any honors by the New Shakespeare Society. Indeed, I cannot find that it received the slightest notice at their hands. Mrs. Windle thereupon issued in the following year a second pamphlet, to a possibly more appreciative dedicatee. This second pamphlet was entitled "Report to the British Museum on Behalf of the Annals of Great Britain and the Reign of Her Majesty Queen Victoria: Discovery and Opening of the Cipher of Francis Bacon, Lord Verulam, alike in his Prose writings and in the 'Shakespeare' Dramas, proving Him the Author of the Dramas. By Mrs. C. F. Ashmead Windle. (Letters Patent of England to be Procured.)"[1]

But whatsoever, from the capacity of the first pamphlet, may have led to a reasonable doubt of

[1] San Francisco: Joseph Winterburn & Co., 1882.

the author's sanity, was here dispelled; the matter here dropped the buskin of high-sounding words and became drivel. Every name of a character in the plays was phonetically "interpreted." Othello was "A tale O," "I tell O," or "What Hell, O," "What will O." Titus Andronicus was "Tie t' us and drown a curse," or "Tie t' us and drum the news." The poor lady's friends interfered and found asylum for her, where I understand she has since died.

In 1884, the Hon. Ignatius Donnelly, Ex-Lieutenant Governor of Minnesota, and lately a representative in Congress from that State, publicly announced, through the columns of the Minneapolis "Tribune," that he had discovered a cipher in the plays of Shakespeare; that he had read it and that it proved Francis Bacon to have been the real author of the plays themselves. All three — Miss Bacon, Mrs. Ashmead Windle, Mr. Donnelly, base their labors on Bacon's description of cipher writing in the Advancement of Learning (iii. p. 403), and particularly on his expression therein of a "quintuple" process of some sort — or, as Bacon himself expresses it: "the highest degree is to write omnia per omnia, which is undoubtedly possible with a proportion quintuple at most of the writing unfolding to the writing unfolded." Both Miss Bacon and Mrs. Windle, it will be observed, based their inner readings on mere mental processes, on the significance of words, hints, and mental introspections. Neither of them — so far as I can discover — believed that a mathematical rule was deducible from the premises which, by revealing a selection of certain words, was to uncover an entirely different literary work. But Mr. Donnelly, while agreeing with his predecessors, I understand to avoid Miss Bacon's effort at philosophic interpretation, on the one hand, and Mrs. Ashmead Windle's prophetic unfolding of a Baconian insight upon the other. I understand him to claim simply a discovery which will make Shakespeare — majestic as it is — merely a shell for the massive illuminatus that is to come forth: that Bacon, not from mere whim or caprice, but from sublime reasons, proposed to hoodwink "the next ages" into supposing William Shakespeare the author of certain plays, until "some one reading the plays should notice the concatenation of 'Francis,' 'Bacon,' 'Nicholas,' 'Bacons,' 'Bacon-fed,' etc., etc. (on page 52 of the Histories), and would dovetail all this into what he himself had said in his Essay on Ciphers in the De Augmentis,"[1] etc., until an entirely new and separate composition — not occult, but intelligible to everybody — should come forth. This story, or composition, I understand, Mr. Donnelly proposes to unravel, not by any mental interpretation whatever, but by simple arithmetic — from the uneven pagination of the First Folio, which reads sometimes consecutively, sometimes with great gaps, two or three times starts at 1, and often — after a space unpaged — begins abruptly at with what is apparently a random number, such as 69, or 79, or 83. From multiples supplied by the figures used in this uneven pagination, applied to the utter unreasonableness — from any possible rhetorical point of view — of the italics, hyphens, and parentheses in

[1] The "North American Review," July, 1887.

the First Folio, Mr. Donnelly then arrives at certain fixed numbers, and these he considers to be the simple arithmetical progression, 1, 2, 3, 4, etc., which — on applying constantly to some indicated word (arrived at by Bacon's rule, I suppose, for as to this I am not posted) — yields, word by word, the narrative of the circumstances under which Bacon wrote the plays, and why he borrowed Shakespeare's name as a pseudonym. This is — as I draw from Mr. Donnelly's own published announcements, and not from any private quarter or communication — the Donnelly Cipher for which so much is promised.

Such being the propositions of the third act of the discovery of the Bacon-Shakespeare cipher — the first two acts already passed, and the curtains having fallen upon them in pathetic silence — nothing more should be attempted, in justice to all parties, for the present, than to notice the mise-en-scène, so to speak, the menstrua proposed to be employed. I have always supposed the imperfect pagination of the First Folio to be the result of carelessness,[1] the work having been done by journeymen or by piece-work, different parts going on simultaneously under different roofs, and each compositor or foreman numbering his pages to suit himself, or setting up from loose sheets of actors' lines, or from the quartos printed during the preceding twenty years, and catching at a page-number from them. The circumstances and indications which lead me so to infer I have already given at length.[2] As to the use of italic

[1] Ante, p. 212, note.
[2] Ante, Chap. VII.

and roman type, indiscriminately, the apparent cause is that which makes the First Folio, from a printer's standpoint, a most slovenly work, namely, the very small fonts of type to be found in the Elizabethan printing-houses. Mr. Wyman says "the material in the printing-offices of 1623 was so limited in extent that very few pages could possibly be in type at once (in a single office). It is not clear from the 'signatures' as to the exact manner in which it was printed, but there is every probability that one page went to press at a time." But, says Mr. Donnelly, "the work is vaster than I imagined. I started with an expectation of finding one or two cipher-words on each page; then I advanced to a dozen or two; then to a score or two; then I thought the cipher-words were one fifth of the text. . . . Now I find that more than half the words are cipher-words, and that many words are made to do double and treble duty."[1] This, then, throws the cipher back to the days of the Quartos, and it must have existed in them. The idea, then, that it was put into the First Folio after Shakespeare's death must be abandoned; and we now have the miracle that the plays performed on Shakespeare's stage were the literary unfoldings of a cipher; that the garbled and stolen shorthand versions of these plays unconsciously carried the cipher intact for twenty and twenty-five years onward to the date of the First Folio compositors, and that even the slovenly carelessness or incapacity of these compositors — (even their setting up whole passages found penciled in the margins — even their omission of words

[1] "Journal of the Bacon Society," No. 3. London, June, 1887.

and lines here and there) did not disarrange the delicate mathematical rule by which to-day, in 1877-78, the cipher can be read with a rapidity of rule and precision of arithmetical count which Mr. Donnelly can liken to nothing but the multiplication-table!

Mr. Donnelly's cipher, as he now announces it, seems to me to effectually dispose of the Baconian Theory, per se, once for all. That theory, as I comprehend it, is: that Bacon, being poor and wanting money, wrote for the stage and sold his manuscripts to the theatres; that being played at those theatres, they became known by the responsible name of the proprietor of those theatres, William Shakespeare. One of the strongest pieces of cumulative evidence adduced by the Baconians, therefore, has been that had Shakespeare been great enough to write the plays, Francis Bacon, one of the most prominent literary men of that exact period, living in the same city at the identical time, would have met him and made some mention of him somewhere in some of his plentiful letters, memoirs, or memoranda; and that Bacon did not mention him because he knew that he — Shakespeare — was a nobody, whose only title to notice was really the plays which he — Bacon — was writing for actual bread and butter. In other words, Bacon had no reason for noticing, but every reason for not noticing, his tool.

But if, as Mr. Donnelly says, one half the words in the Plays, as we now have them, are cipher-words, placed there by Bacon, Bacon must have had a hand not only in writing them, but in printing the first Quarto edition of them. This must have

necessitated intimate negotiations with not only
Shakespeare but the printers (who are no longer
to be called piratical, and their editions of the
Plays "stolen and surreptitious"). All this must
have been going on for twenty years or so in
London, a crowded city, in broad daylight. Messengers and go-betweens must have been employed. Shakespeare was a man of many intimates: so was Bacon. Surely in all the chronicles
of those days, when people were using their pens
in broadsides, squibs, sonnets, letters and diaries,
somebody must have mentioned Bacon and Shakespeare in the same breath in print. The junction
of the two names on the cover of the Northumberland Manuscript[1] proved enough for the Baconian theory. But this cipher theory is proving
entirely too much for its security. For if all
these persons — publishers, printers, messengers,
and go-betweens — knew about the secret, then
there was no secret, and hence no occasion for a
cipher to cover it up. If Bacon wrote the plays for
cipher purposes, then the miracle is — not that anybody wrote such plays in Elizabeth's days (Bacon
or Shakespeare, or anybody else) — but simply that
through twenty-five years of vilely-printed Quartos and carelessly-printed Folio, the cipher has
come down to us in perfectly intelligible mathematical accuracy!

Heretofore, in the absence of this demonstration, the use of these italic types has been tacitly
accepted as referable to the paucity of types, the
small fonts kept in each printing-house, and the
large draft on the resources of each in setting up

[1] Ante, p. 194.

so large a work as the First Folio. Italic types were not supposed, as now, to be used for emphasis, but rather for setting up proper names or foreign words; and when, as above, it became necessary to use them from the Roman type running short, they were resorted to without compunction, as the slightest examination of other printed books of the date will testify. Any apparently senseless use of hyphens and parenthesis marks (often found reversed) is tolerably accounted for, perhaps, by supposing that the compositors may have run short of spaces as well as types. But, on more careful examination, I think a reasonable explanation of their occurrence is apparent, especially since they do not appear to be used, as italic types are used, in the Quartos with the same freedom and licence as in the First Folio. That explanation appears to be (assuming, for the sake of the argument, that there is not a cipher in the plays) to guarantee some such explanation as the following. The "copy" furnished the compositors who set the type of the First Folio was obtained largely from actors, and from those who bought or stole or borrowed from them. Since Heminges and Condell, the editors, were themselves actors, I infer that stealing was not very frequently necessary, since they would naturally have their own lines or access to those of their fellows. I have shown elsewhere[1] that so long ago as Pope's day it was understood that a great deal that found its way into the First Folio as Shakespeare, was really the interpolation of individual actors; that dozens of speeches

[1] Ante, p. 212, and see generally Chapter VII.

can hardly be accounted for except upon such a supposition (the lines from "Lear," "I have a journey," &c., quoted above, appear to me to have very probably been the improvisation of an actor who had forgotten his part just there), and that it is beyond any reasonable question that some matter written on the margins of single plays did get itself printed in the First Folio by accident. Now why should not the actor of that day have made marks upon his "lengths," or lines, to serve as memoranda to guide him in their delivery, as well as to have interjected speeches therein? I have before me, at this writing, the personal acting copies of some of Shakespeare's plays, from which certain well-known actors of our own day have studied, which are thick with pencilled memoranda, sometimes in words (as "gesture," "calm," "fast conversation," "very slow," "whisper," etc., etc.), and sometimes in these very parenthesis-marks and dashes. Why should not the Elizabethan actor have made like memoranda? Take, for example, such passages as these from the First Folio text of the "Merry Wives of Windsor" (line 2492):

"About, about
Search Windsor Castle (Elues) within, and out
Strew good luck (Ouphes) on euery sacred roome."

Is it impossible to suppose that the actor supplied these parentheses in pencil in order to remind himself that when he gave the order to search Windsor Castle he was to turn his face to the Elves, and when ordering good luck to be strewn on the floor of every room, he was to look toward the "Ouphes"? Or, take the passage in Falstaff's speech, when he finds himself, disguised as Hearn the Hunter, first at the rendezvous (line 2441):

" You were also (Iupiter) a swan for the loue of Leda. O omnipotent loue, how nere the God drew to the complexion of a Goose, a fault done first in the forme of a beast (O Loue, a beastly fault), and then another fault in the semblance of a Fowle, think on't (Loue), a fowle-fault. When Gods haue hot backs, what shall poore men do ? For me, I am heere a Windsor Stagge, and the fattest (I thinke) i'th Forest," etc.

Is it not more reasonable to suppose that these parentheses indicated that the actor was to raise his eyes when he addressed Jove, or to make the interjected "I think" a sotto voce, than to imagine the complicated machinery of a Baconian Cipher theory in order to account for their presence?

As to the use of hyphens, they appear to be employed uniformly for compound words (whether generally so reckoned or compounded for the occasion), whenever the compound is composed of nouns (as " Foot-land-Rakers," " Long-staffe-sixpenny-swipers," " Mustachio-purple-hued-maltworms," " Sutton-cop-hill," " Waiting-Gentlewoman," etc.), or adjectives made up of nouns, as " Wasp-tongued," " Trumpet-tongued," etc., and sometimes between other parts of speech, as where Shallow says to Falstaff, " Come-on, Come-on." Capital letters are used, so far as my examination has gone, invariably for the initial letters of nouns, whether proper or common ; whether standing by themselves or united by hyphens into compound nouns, or used with the hyphen to make adjectives (as Trumpet-tongued). In other words, if Mr. Donnelly found the words " Bacon," " St. Albans,"

"Nicholas," etc., at all, he must have found them spelled with initial capitals. As to italics,— beyond the possibility mentioned above of the Roman fonts running short,— the evident purpose of the Folio compositors was to employ them for foreign words, quotations, for the interspersed songs, stage directions, proper names, and names of the dramatis personæ. Take the following passages:

(1.)   " Still Virginaling
Upon his Palme; How now (you wanton calfe)
Art thou my Calfe ?
Yes, if you will (my Lord)."
            —[" The Winter's Tale."]

(2.) "You cast th' euent of Warre (my noble Lord),
And summ'd the accompt of chance, before you said
Let us make head."—[2 "Henry IV."]

(3.) "I, then, all-smarting, with my wounds being cold
(To be so pestered by a Popingay)
Out of my Greefe, and my Impatience
Answered (neglectingly) I know not what;
He should or should not—For he made me mad
To see him shine so brighte and smell so sweete
And talk so like a Waiting-Gentlewoman."
            —[1 " Henry IV."]

(4.) "I doe affect the very ground (which is base) where her shoe (which is baser) guided by her foot (which is basest) doth tread. I shall be forsworn (which is a great argument of falsehood) if I loue."
            —[" Love's Labour's Lost."]

(5.) "The rest are Princes, Barons, Lords, Knights, Squires
And gentlemen of bloud and qualitie
The names of those their nobles that lie dead
Charles Delabreth, High Constable of France,
Iaques of Chatilion, Admirall of France,
The Master of the Crosse-bowes, Lord *Rambrues*
Great Master of France the braue Sir *Guichard Dolphin*,
Iohn, duke of Alanson, *Anthonie* Duke of Brabant,

20

> The brother to the duke of Burgundie,
> And *Edward* Duke of Barr: of lustie Earles
> *Grandpree* and *Roussie, Fauconbridge* and *Foyes,*
> *Beaumont* and *Marle, Vademont* and *Lestrale.*
> Here was a Royall fellowship of death.
> Where is the number of our English dead?
> *Edward* the Duke of Yorke, the Earle of Suffolke
> Sir *Richard* Ketly, *Davy Gam* Esquire:"
> — ["Henry V."]

Now, these five quotations, taken entirely at random — except the (2) (which Mr. Donnelly himself cites, and asks "why is 'my noble Lord' in parenthesis?") and the (5) — seem to illustrate the habitude of the First Folio printers. There is not a case in them of the use of parentheses where the actor of to-day would not change his voice or attitude in reading the words parenthesized. The capitals are used, except in one or two instances, for the nouns (the exceptions representing just about the proportion of carelessness evident everywhere in the Folio), and the hyphens are employed only to make compounds that are legitimately though not scrupulously reckoned as such to-day. As to the liberal use of italics in the catalogue of the dead at Agincourt, it would seem as if, being foreign names, the compositor resorted naturally to his italic case. He intended to move carefully, as the "ands" and "Sirs" in Roman between the names in italics show. But when he came to set up the names of the Englishmen who had fallen, he either did not notice the change or habitude still guided his hand, and he set them up also in italics. As to John and Anthonie and Edward, they were indifferently French or English names, and either treatment allowable. Mr.

Donnelly's method with the Baconian theory is the heroic one. He will either prove it beyond escape or bury it forever deeper than did ever plummet sound. But I confess it seems to me that the use of italics, parentheses, capitals and hyphens in the First Folio is neither occult nor suspicious; but, on the whole, normal, reasonable, and guided by an evidently inflexible system.

In discussing his own processes, Mr. Donnelly, after recounting the fact that an 836th or a 900th word is "found" or " out," adds: "It could not occur by chance one time in a hundred millions."[1] Now, this is not all the casuistry here — anything that occurs at all must necessarily occur once. It is a repetition of occurrences only that shows coincidence. But mere coincidences are not unusual anywhere; and, while Mr. Donnelly is undoubtedly right in arguing that inferences to design may be drawn from a constancy of coincidences, he must first show such a constancy of them here as will predicate something more than merely unusual or improbable groupings, that is to say, some coincidences which, without design, would be absolutely impossible. To illustrate: It would not have happened once in a hundred millions of times that a man named Edison would invent a talking machine called a phonograph, unless it did happen; and I think it would be perfectly safe to say that it would not happen twice in a hundred millions of times. And yet there was and is a phonograph. Any legal treatise on circumstantial evidence will be found to teem with verified accounts of the most won-

[1] "North American Review," June, 1887.

derful coincidences which yet did not prove design or crime, and every counsel in a criminal case reads them to juries to illustrate the danger of imputing guilt to a defendant from the mere fact that appearances against cannot be satisfactorily explained away. There is, for an example, a well-authenticated record of a murder having been committed in a certain town by a man with a wooden leg, who had lost his rightarm— who came from a certain landing on the Mississippi river, by a certain boat; and of a man with a wooden leg, minus a right arm, having embarked at that landing on that identical boat, and having been in the town where the murder was committed, and yet who was not the murderer. And it certainly is not necessary to recall here the number of murdered or mutilated bodies found in rivers, which have been wrongly identified over and over again by their nearest friends before their real identity was discovered. And if, on a trial of fact, juries can be misled as to matters only recent and not uncommon, what shall we say of the problem of a cipher being interwritten three centuries ago in a book not traveling under the cipher-writer's name, or acknowledged by him during his own lifetime, but actually asserted to have been written by somebody else?

And when this cipher is proved to have been put there, what is to be its revealed and translated purpose? Mr. Donnelly draws a pathetic picture of Francis Bacon gagged and muzzled, but with his heart full of a story for the good of his race; of his carefully putting this story down on paper and locking it up in cipher, confident that "the next ages" would find it. But, as far as I can read history, Bacon was never muzzled, but wrote books and made speeches by whole libraries; and, so far as I can draw from Mr. Donnelly's own pages, this story, of which Bacon's heart was full, amounts to nothing when it is told. Is it a tale of pathetic moment, like those in which Shakespeare and his fellow Elizabethan dramatists abounded, and were not sent to the Tower or to the block for narrating? What is it that we are to prepare for? Is it going to move the souls of this generation like the murder of Desdemona, or the suicide of Juliet? and, if it is, is it worth while unraveling merely for that purpose? "This sad old earth must borrow its mirth, but has grief enough of its own" as it is. If Mr. Donnelly is right in asserting that more than half the words in the First Folio text of such plays as he finds the cipher in are cipher words, then that cipher must have been in the Quartos, for no Folio play contains more than double the number of words in the corresponding Quarto play. But if the cipher were put into the Folio and not into the Quartos, then Heminges and Condell and all their compositors — not to mention I. Jaggard, W. Jaggard, Ed. Blount, I. Smithweeke, and W. Aspley — must have been in the secret. And if they were — (in the case of the First Folios as in the case of the Quartos) — there was again no secret at all, and no necessity for a cipher at all. And again, who could have read the proof of the First Folio cipher Plays, which (since Mr. Donnelly can read them by arithmetical rule), instead of being the most careless pieces of printing, are really the most accurate pieces of printing the world has ever seen? It seems to me that no author who has ever read a page of printer's proof-sheet—and who therefore knows how almost impossible it is for him to forget the drift of his own thoughts and perform the mere perfunctory work of typographical correction—but will believe that if Bacon wrote a cipher into the Shakespeare Plays he must have set up the types—either of Quarto or Folio, or (if contained in both) of both—with his own aristocratic hands. Says Thomas Heywood in a letter to his publisher, Okes: "The infinite faults escaped in my book of 'Britain's Troy,' by the negligence of the printer, as the misquotations, mistaking of syllables, misplacing half-lines, coining of strange and never-heard-of words: these being without number, when I would have taken a particular account of the errata, the printer answered me, he would not publish his own disworkmanship, but rather let his own fault lie on the neck of the author," which indicates that author's proof-sheets were unknown conveniences at that date. But, had Bacon himself received one, he could hardly have anticipated by twenty-five years the corrections necessary. How could he, for example, have put into the Quarto of 1 Henry IV. the word "S. Albones" (which Mr. Donnelly says is a cipher word when it occurs in the Folio, and alludes to Bacon's title of Viscount St. Albans), when the cipher was only constructed out of the text he prepared in 1623? The trouble thickens just here, since—as Mr. Adee points out—Bacon was not made Viscount St. Albans until January, 1621, or twenty-three years after the Quarto was first printed in 1598, with that word in it, not only, but almost word for word and line for line as it stands now in the Folio. Did plain Francis Bacon, knowing that he was, a generation thereafter, to be Viscount St. Albans, write his cipher; and then, twenty-five years after, print the play in folio, and put up at the head of the folio pages the mysterious numbers which were to reveal that prophetic cipher? And were these mysterious numbers — with slight intervals — consecutive?

II. "VERSE-TESTS." Nobody who knows anything on the subject, or who thinks at all about it, can doubt for a moment of the certainty of changes, through lapse of time, appearing in the style of any one given writer. But that these changes will be invariably the same in the case of every writer is not only uncertain but — to say the least — very highly improbable. Of course, usuetude itself brings ease, facility and polish. Yet some writers will not rely upon the mere operation of this rule, but deliberately and artificially polish first to perfect, and then, again, to remove the smell of the lamp by which the first process of polishing was accomplished. There happen to be extant the numerous drafts of Gray's Elegy, showing the laborious stages by which he brought to absolute perfection the masterpiece by which his reputation is forever secure. And other notable instances, as of Pope and even earlier versifiers, are abundant enough; while, on the other hand, the advancing tendency — as with Tennyson — is said to be to neglect or subordinate refining processes and to seek only expression and emphasis. Perhaps it was only natural that — in this constant examination of the Shakespeare treasury, and the doubts raised in 1623, emphasized in 1663-4, and perpetuated ever since — the same thirst for certitude which gave birth to the Baconian theory and the search for a cipher should lead to other esoteric suggestion. At any rate, there appeared, something less than twenty years ago, a remarkable contrivance called a "Verse-Test," soon to be elaborated by division into what were called "central pause," "stopped endings," "unstopped endings," "run-on lines," etc., etc., applicable equally to the blank verse and the rhyme of Shakespeare's plays, but — strangely enough — not to any other literary matter. This latter fact alone ought to have rendered the adoption of this verse-test suspicious. But its devotees appear to be, instead, increasing in number. My own humble part in the discussion was confined to a very general doubt expressed — modestly, I hope — as to the exact certainty of any result reached by application of a verse-test to the works of Shakespeare which could not be corroborated by other evidence. Certainly I did not expect to be made its anti-champion, and personally identified as the only disbeliever in the virtue of metrical processes. But Mr. Furnivall, an acknowledged champion of these processes, has lately thought best to remonstrate with me publicly for any disbelief, as follows:

"It is difficult to argue with a man whose mind is built on different lines to one's own. But as there may be some folk in America whose faculties are of the same kind as those of intelligent people in England, I should like to say a few words to them about verse-tests. Supposing a Shakespeare student to have eyes and brains, and a power (which many folk have not) of appreciating the difference between the structure of different lines of verse, we say to him, 'Treat Shakespeare's works as the geologist treats the earth's crust, as the comparative anatomist treats the animal creation, as the natural philosopher treats the world. Look on Shakespeare's plays and poems as the product of a mind working in successive periods; and see whether this mind's productions show any characteristic differences by which you can settle the order of their creation.' Thus instructed, the Shakespeare student sets to work as Lyell did at the earth's crust, as Owen and Huxley did at fossil and modern bones, at birds and fishes, as Newton did at the phenomena of nature. The student compares the structure of the verse in (say) 'Love's Labour's Lost,' 'Julius Cæsar,' and 'The Winter's Tale.' He finds an extraordinary difference between the general character of the lines in these plays. He then turns to the thought and knowledge of life shown in these dramas, and he recognizes a like difference. Assuming that he has brains, he sees at once that 'Love's Labour's Lost' is the earliest, most artificial, weakest, and most ryme and quip-loaded play of the three, that 'The Winter's Tale' is far riper and later in material and mental qualities, and that 'Julius Cæsar' holds a middle place between them. The student then says, 'Metrical tests are evidently the easiest ones by which Shakespeare's works can be classified. I'll count how many ryme-lines there are in each of these three plays, how many run-on and how many stopt lines, how many double-endings and weak-endings, how much doggerel, and so on.' He does this, and, to take only the ryme points, he finds the proportion is:

"'Love's Labour's Lost' 1028 ryme to 579 blank, or 1 ryme to .56 blank.
"'Julius Cæsar' 32 ryme to 2181 blank, or 1 to 68 blank.
"'The Winter's Tale' 0 ryme to 1825 blank, or 1 to infinity.

He finds that weak and light endings hardly appear in the two earlier plays, while they are plentiful in the last, and that the other metrical tests, on the whole, coincide with these results. The student then proceeds to apply these verse-tests to the whole of Shakespeare's plays; and, when he has done so, he puts them all into a trial-order. He next compares this internal metrical evidence with the other internal evidence of power, knowledge of life, change from simile to metaphor, weight of meaning, etc., and he finds, on the whole, that all these tests coincide in result with the metrical ones. He then tries them with the allusions to known events, etc., in the plays; and here again the prior results are confirmed; while the dates of publication are never earlier—though of course often later—than the dates arrived at by the metrical tests. He next tries a case like that of 'Julius Cæsar' with 'Antony and Cleopatra,' which he knows ancient critics used to put close together because they were both Roman, and included Antony. He looks at his number-table of metrical tests, and it shows him at once how ridiculous the juxtaposition in time of the two plays is.

"The student, having thus treated his phenomena, his subjects of study, Shakespeare's works, in a thoroughly scientific way, feels quite comfortable about his results. And when Mr. Morgan tells him 'argument is not evidence,' he answers, 'that depends on the hearer's brain-power, and whether the argument is based on duly observed and recorded facts.' Also, when Mr. Morgan lays down this astounding dictum as the law:

"'The chronology of Shakespeare as established by the verse-tests either conforms to the chronology established by the printer's dates and the copyright entries, or it does not. If it does, the verse-tests are superfluous. If it does not, then verse-tests are of no value unless corroborated by external and circumstantial evidence.' [1]

When, I say, Mr. Morgan seriously utters this astounding nonsense, the student answers: 'Mr. Morgan, I really am not a born fool. You know, as well as I, that for more than half Shakespeare's plays we have neither copyright entries nor printer's dates, save the Folio of 1623, published seven years after Shakespeare's death. You know that for many plays we have neither external nor circumstantial evidence.

[1] Ante, p. 232.

You know that Shakespeare's works, like the Creator's and every great artist's, do carry with and on them the evidence of the succession of their creation, just as Beethoven's symphonies and Raphael's pictures do; and you know that this internal evidence is consistent with the external; you would not insult a geologist or comparative anatomist, or a musical or art critic, by telling him that his faithful observation and study of his Master's works could not get at (or near) the time-order of them, unless printed or "circumstantial" evidence for it were forthcoming. Why then do you treat the careful Shakespeare student as a greater fool than the student of nature? The fact is, you have either never apprehended the nature of metrical and internal evidence in matters poetic, or you are verse-blind, as some folk are color-blind and others insensible to music. Given intelligence and perception in a student, the value of the verse-tests, being certain, must be appreciated by him. But if men will not work at these tests, but insist, instead, on going by "authority," as they are pleased to call it, that is, by setting up one of the English Woodenheads as their idol, and swearing by all he says, then of course verse-tests are worth nothing, because old Sawdust thinks so.'"[1]

Since this is not Miss Delia Bacon, or Mrs. Ashmead Windle, or Mr. Ignatius Donnelly, but Mr. Furnivall who is speaking, let us—especially as this appears to be, on the whole, a frank and comprehensive statement of exactly what a "verse-test" is—devote ourselves to an equally frank (if not equally comprehensive) examination of Mr. Furnivall's argument.

I. Says Mr. Furnivall: "Treat Shakespeare's works as the geologist treats the earth's crust, as the comparative anatomist treats the animal creation, as the natural philosopher treats the world. Look on Shakespeare's plays and poems as the product of a mind working in successive periods.

[1] "The Literary World," Boston, July 9th, 1887.

. . . . Thus instructed, the Shakespeare student sets to work as Lyell did at the earth's crust."

But how if the student decline to be "thus instructed"— to so set to work at the plays and poems of Shakespeare? Why should I? I cannot, for my part, find William Shakespeare anywhere brooding apart in solitary periods of incubation; his brain growing by cosmic laws in what Emerson calls

". . . . tendency through endless ages
Of star-dust and star-pilgrimages,"

and so to be studied as one studies the crust of the earth. I find him, instead, a man of like passions with ourselves, fond of his bout and his bottle, going in and out amid the many-colored life of Elizabeth's London; gathering everywhere, as Aubrey says, " humours of men daily"; taking " the humour of the constable at Grendon-in-Bucks," and of Kit Sly, and Marion Hackett, the fat ale-wife of Wincot, down Stratford way. The records of his jokes and his gallantries survive him, and he died in a frolic. I find him growing rich by mounting plays at his theater which the people cared to see, and as fast as the people demanded them; and living and dying so utterly unsuspicious that he had done anything of which his children might care to hear, that he never even troubled himself to preserve the manuscript of or the literary property in a single one of the plays which had raised him to affluence. Why should I set to work at him "as Lyell did at the earth's crust"?

II. Mr. Furnivall selects three plays,—" Love's Labour's Lost," " Julius Cæsar," and " The Winter's

Tale,"— and asks if I cannot see at once "that
'Love's Labour's Lost' is the earliest, most artificial, weakest, most ryme-and-quip-loaded; that
'The Winter's Tale' is far riper and later, and that
'Julius Cæsar' holds a middle place between?" To
this I answer: Yes and No. I can see that "Love's
Labour's Lost" is the "most artificial, weakest, most
ryme-and-quip-loaded," and that "The Winter's
Tale" is far "riper." But I cannot, from such evidence alone, predicate that "Love's Labour's Lost"
was written first, "Julius Cæsar" next, and "The
Winter's Tale" last. I cannot, I say, simply because I am also able to see that "Love's Labour's
Lost" is a farcical comedy, abounding in burlesque
and travesty, a lampoon on the Euphuists, pedants,
players with words and logic-choppers whom the
dramatist presumably had come in contact with (I
believe somebody has suggested that Holofernes
was a caricature of Francis Bacon); that "Julius
Cæsar" is a pure and stately tragedy; while over
"The Winter's Tale" broods a grewsome atmosphere of sorrow, misunderstanding, injustice and
suffering which only needs a tragic denouement to
be itself pure tragedy. Is it not appropriate and
to be expected that these three should be written
in as many different veins and measures? Does
Mr. Furnivall mean to insist that I am to read
"Love's Labour's Lost," "Julius Cæsar," and "The
Winter's Tale" all together, with perfect indifference as to whether they are tragedy or travesty,
but only when I see a "stopped ending" cry, That
is prior to 1592! and when I come to a "run-on
line" exclaim, See, this is in the neighborhood of
1610!

There is a chapter of Thackeray in which Thomas Newcombe says Adsum! And there are also lines by Thackeray, running:

> " There were three sailors of Bristol City,
> Who took a boat and went to sea;
> But first with beef and captain's biscuit
> And pickled pork they loaded she."

Am I to set down the rhyme to Thackeray's nursery period and the chapter to his last days, because no man who has once gone higher can ever again stoop to six and eight? Mr. Gilbert has written a pathetically beautiful play, " Broken Hearts." He has also written " Pinafore." Am I to shut my eyes to the character of these two as works of art, and cavalierly sort them to different cosmic periods in Mr. Gilbert's career, simply because they scan differently? Or if, perchance, Mr. Thackeray and Mr. Gilbert could write in more than one mood, could not great Shakespeare vary his meter with his theme? Or am I to make an affidavit that, once having composed tragedy, William Shakespeare could never again do light comedy; or that, if he had written " Love's Labour's Lost " after having produced " Julius Cæsar," Holofernes would have spouted in the icy periods of Brutus, and Armado in red-hot sentences like Cassius? Or if " The Winter's Tale " had been written before " Love's Labour's Lost," that Costard would have conversed like Florizel and Perdita like Jaquenetta?

III. Mr. Furnivall gives the following figures:

" Love's Labour's Lost " 1028 ryme to 579 blank, or 1 ryme to .56 blank.

"Julius Cæsar" 32 ryme to 2181 blank, or 1 to .68 blank.

"The Winter's Tale" 0 ryme to 1825 blank, or 1 to infinity.

Accepting these figures, from my standpoint they prove nothing but themselves; while, from Mr. Furnivall's standpoint, they simply prove him out of court by proving entirely too much for his purpose. As well say, Sir Walter Scott wrote "Ivanhoe" and "The Lay of the Last Minstrel": "Ivanhoe" has not a single rhyme; "The Lay of the Last Minstrel" is all rhyme; infinity to zero, or zero to infinity. Ergo, anything you like! Poetry is Poetry, Prose is Prose, and that which is a mixture of both is a mixture of both! Let us be grateful to any ghost who will arise to tell us that! To my old-fashioned way of thinking, Shakespeare wrote "Love's Labour's Lost"— being flippant, light, and comic—in flippant, light, and comic verse; in "Julius Cæsar" he employed rhyme with the greatest possible effect by limiting it to the characters whose mouths it becomes; while — rhyme not being artistically necessary at all in "The Winter's Tale,"— that consummate master of fiction did not look at the year of our Lord to decide for him, but employed rhyme not at all therein.

But were these three plays—"Love's Labour's Lost," "Julius Cæsar," and "The Winter's Tale" —written in that exact relative order? There is every reason to believe that they were. The "Love's Labour's Lost" appeared in quarto in 1598, imprinted at London by W. W. for Cutbert

Burby. And in a curious poem, "Alba, or the Month's Mind of a Melancholy Lover," by "R. T. Gentleman," printed by this same Burby, in this same year, occur the lines —

> "Love's Labour's Lost I once did see, a Play
> Y-cleped so, so called to my paine
> Which I to hear, to my small Ioy did stay," etc.

And Meres, in his valuable list of the Shakespeare Plays, in his "Palladis Tamia"— also of 1598 — also mentions it. We have no quarto of the "Julius Cæsar," but in Weever's "Mirror of Martyrs," printed in London in 1601, are the well-known lines —

> "The many-headed multitude were drawn
> By Brutus' speech that Cæsar was ambitious;
> When eloquent Mark Antonie had shown
> His vertues, who but Brutus then was vicious?"

And a reading of Plutarch's history of Brutus and of Cæsar and Antony, then accessible, fixes the reference to the play, and not to the history. So that, without accepting what seem undoubted references to the play in the "Hamlet," we can at once assign "Julius Cæsar" to a later date than the "Love's Labour's Lost" without counting either its blank verses or its rhymes with Furnivall. And in the Bodleian Library there is a manuscript diary kept by Dr. Simon Forman, in which the diarist notes down at considerable length a skeleton analysis of "the Winter's Talle at the glob 1611 the 15 of maye." In other words, it is from a careful search of contemporary records and documents, — and not from the fact that the play contains 1825 blank verses, — that we put it relatively later than the "Julius Cæsar," which itself succeeded the "Love's Labour's Lost" by a considerable gap of years. In other words, the critical world was reasonably certain as to the relative order of the production of those three plays about two centuries before the verse-test was invented (or could have made itself certain, had the question been raised)!

But we cannot leave Mr. Furnivall just yet. Admitting that "Love's Labour's Lost" was written in 1592 and "The Winter's Tale" in 1610 (these are Mr. Furnivall's own dates, taken from his "Leopold" edition of the plays), we see the vastest difference between them. One is all rhyme and the other without any rhyme at all, says Mr. Furnivall. (One is travesty and the other tragedy, I take the liberty to add.) Why this extreme difference, a difference as great as between black and white? Because, says Mr. Furnivall, they were written eighteen years apart. It seems to me that this cannot be the only reason; because, if Mr. Furnivall will look a little further, he will find other canonical Shakespeare plays, differing quite as antipodally, which were not written eighteen years apart, but at very small intervals of time. For example, the "Hamlet" and "The Merry Wives of Windsor" appeared at about the same time — between 1601 and 1603. They are certainly, judged by any possible literary criticism, quite as dissimilar as the "Love's Labour's Lost" and "The Winter's Tale." Had these two come down to us as by different authors, we might indeed have said that "The Merry Wives of Windsor" showed touches worthy of the author of "Hamlet," but would we have set aside the testimony of their title-pages from internal evidence alone?

Perhaps we might have done so. Perhaps it might have come to be the weight of critical opinion that these two plays were written by one and the same hand. But did critical opinion so come to decide, it would certainly not have omitted to point out the corroboration of the internal evidence of identical authorship by the external evidence, consisting in the fact that the two plays appeared, not eighteen years apart, but within a year, or at the most, within two years of each other. "But," says Mr. Furnivall, "for more than half Shakespeare's plays we have neither copyright entries nor printer's dates." Very well, then, let us accept such evidence as far as it goes, and let us move humbly and pronounce with diffidence as to matters whereto we have nothing but criticism to guide us, remembering always that criticism is, after all, only matter of opinion, and that an opinion is of value only until another and better opinion supersedes it. Let us remember the history of Shakespearean criticism, how many wrecks strew its path, how many hulks have been abandoned. Let us remember the criticism of Dryden, of Voltaire, of Pope, of Rymer and of Dennis; that the criticism of their day is not the criticism of ours; and that this criticism of our day may only be foolishness to the eyes which are to come. And, remembering this, let us avoid sweeping assertions; especially let us be chary of our thunder in the index; or our affidavits as to what were the mental processes of men who died two or three centuries before we were born.

Mr. Furnivall says: "The fact is, you have either never appreciated the nature of metrical and internal evidence in matters poetic, or you are verse-blind, as some folk are color-blind, and others insensible to music."

To be verse-blind is perhaps the greatest of misfortunes. No man can regret that infirmity in myself more than I do. But my pangs are mitigated by the fact that even were I not verse-blind I could still not apply the verse-tests to a Shakespeare composition, because, unhappily, I have no access to one of William Shakespeare's monographs in any degree of reasonable completeness which would assure me of the value of any result at which I might arrive. The quartos of Shakespeare plays are mutilated, stolen, and surreptitious copies, pirated from the play-house by shorthand as the text was delivered from the actors' mouths, or patched up in the printing-houses piecemeal from the actors' "lengths." The First Folio was printed seven years after William Shakespeare had been laid in his grave, and when his once-cunning hand had no revising or restoring opportunity; and — beyond quartos and folio texts — I have no access to anything William Shakespeare wrote. Mr. Furnivall, I suppose, is aware that between the dates of sundry of the quartos and the date of the Folio, these plays held the stage — and of the vicissitudes through which their text came down to 1623. If he be not, I have gone to the trouble of collecting the evidence of these vicissitudes and of placing it where anybody who chooses to take the trouble can read it;[1] and even if Mr. Furnivall declines to accept this evidence as collected by me, he will

[1] Ante, Chapter VII.

not deny that between the quarto and folio dates there were such things as stage-censors in England, and that they hacked away at the texts of the Shakespeare plays upon occasion. He will concede, I suppose, (at least admit the publication of,) King James's statute of 1605, forbidding the use of the name of God, or of Christ Jesus, or of the Holy Ghost in stage plays,[1] and that, in taking these names out of the Shakespeare plays, sometimes the stage-censor chopped out whole passages along with them and sometimes not. (Had William Shakespeare himself taken out the interdicted words, we may be very sure he would have done it less bunglingly — certainly not have sacrificed the sense or wasted whole sentences of appropriate and inoffensive dialogue in the deletion.) Mr. Furnivall will perceive, therefore, that, however unfortunate, it is not my verse-blindness which compels me to decline application of the verse-tests to decide as to how and wherein William Shakespeare's style changed from year to year, and which forces me to assign the alternate employments of blank verse and rhyme, and stopped and unstopped endings, and run-on lines to Shakespeare's fancy at the moment, or possibly to his possession of — what Mr. Furnivall declines to credit me with — an ear for music, or else decline to speculate at all concerning it! Did I apply his verse-tests to the only material to which I can procure access, I would be like a lawyer searching a title with only mutilated documents or unverified records for my data. It would only amount to a stultification, or at the best an amuse-

[1] Ante, pp. 210, 224.

ment; no veritable or valuable results could possibly follow.

To be as brief as possible, therefore, I adhere respectfully to what Mr. Furnivall is pleased to call my "astonishing dictum" and "astonishing nonsense" (viz.: that nothing can be proved by the verse-test process which has not already been proved by other methods), (a), because verse-tests are not a method in literary criticism at all, but a species of inductive criticism applied solely to the works of Shakespeare; because inductive criticism is nonsense, and because, since the works of Shakespeare are literature, they are entitled to be criticised — if at all — by methods which can be tested upon other literary matter as well; and (b) because the verse-tests, like the Donnelly Cipher and the Baconian Parallelism, are not a Result but a Process. And any result whatever, reached by these or any of these, must be valuable or worthless precisely in so far as it can be corroborated or exploded by external, circumstantial, or historical evidence.

IV. Mr. Furnivall concludes by saying, "given intelligence and perception in a student, the value of the verse-tests being certain, must be appreciated by him."

Certainly! "Given intelligence and perception in a student, the value of the" Delia Bacon, or Ashmead-Windle, or Donnelly Ciphers "being certain, must be appreciated by him." In other words, given intelligence and perception in a student, Francis Bacon wrote the plays we call "Shakespeare."

I am not called upon to instruct Mr. Furnivall.

But perhaps I can suggest his error, and the oversight by which he has been precipitated into it. It seems that he has been working at a part rather than at the whole; at episodes of internal evidence in the Shakespeare works, rather than at the whole subject—the man, the book, the history of the English theater, the times and manners of the Elizabethan era. It seems that Mr. Furnivall has not even read "Pericles,"[1] and has not "considered" the "Titus Andronicus."[2] And yet in his "Leopold" edition of Shakespeare, Mr. Furnivall includes both those plays. If Mr. Furnivall will edit plays without considering or even reading them,— and will arrive at conclusions from partial and imperfect examination of the facts upon which he assumes to base them—nobody can wonder that he falls into wild and sweeping statements, or that his results are illicit and vicious. But Mr. Furnivall is not the only sufferer in this regard. So far as I am familiar with them, all the æsthetic critics are sinners here. The trouble is that they all shut their eyes to Shakespeare as a whole, and instead, selecting each for himself only his own favorite passages in the plays and poems, build up thereon the astonishing conclusions and alleged findings of fact, certain of which it has been my purpose in the foregoing pages to point out. But I may be all wrong. Perhaps Francis Bacon put a cipher into the plays to prove to the next ages that he wrote them, and then William Shakespeare went and inserted a "verse-test" to prove that he (William Shakespeare) wrote them. Neither Cipherists nor Verse-Testers allude to

[1] Ante, p. 15. [2] Ante, p. 8.

either the "Sonnets" or the "Epitaphs." And yet the Sonnets are certainly hermetic enough to yield the former unlimited pasture, while the "Epitaphs"—at their vast critical distance from the "Venus and Adonis" and "The Tempest"—would certainly afford Mr. Furnivall an unlimited sweep. Was the "Epitaph on Elias James," for example, the youthful practise of Shakespeare's pen or the feeble strokes of our tired Cæsar laying that pen down forever? Does it elbow the great Poems or "The Winter's Tale?" In either case, I am disposed to think that a development of both the Cipher and the Verse-Test theories will lead to an ultimate exchange of base on the part of their adherents. Those who were driven into Baconianism because unable to accept Shakespearean miracles — now called upon to swallow the greatest miracle of all — in self-defense can only fall back into the orthodox faith; while the already orthodox Shakespeareans — now ordered to discard their common-sense and blindly bolt the Verse-Tests under "instruction" of Mr. Furnivall, and to "look on Shakespeare's plays and poems as the product of a mind working in successive periods,"— will have nothing for it except to gallop, horsefoot and dragoons, into the Baconian camp!

INDEX.

A.

A Lover's Complaint — Who wrote it? 73.
Act of Parliament — Necessary to read Sonnets, 81.
Actors. *(See* THEATERS.)
  Note local hits, 48, 207.
  Must be under nobleman's patronage, 245.
  Cautious as to utterances, 70.
  Audiences maltreated, 70.
  Turn up in Holland, 278, 280.
  In Germany, 278.
  Names printed for characters, 208.
  Custom of doing country in vacation, 279.
  Cut long speeches, 212.
  Company of, stranded in Germany, 278.
  Mouth-pieces of gossip, 205.
  In Scotland with Lawrence Fletcher, 280.
  Retailers of news, 205.
  Permitted to improvise at will, 205.
  Good opinion of, valuable, 205.
  Earthly agents of the devil, 141.
  Shakespeare's company of, at Barnstaple, 281.
  Bath, *id.*
  Bristol, *id.*
  Coventry, *id.*
  Dover, *id.*
  Faversham, *id.*
  Folkestone, *id.*
  Hythe, *id.*
  Leicester, *id.*
  Maidstone, *id.*
  Marlborough, *id.*
  New Romney, *id.*
  Oxford, *id.*
  Rye, County Sussex, *id.*
  Shrewsbury, *id.*
  Saffron — Walden, *id.*
Actresses — When first employed, 150.
Adee, Hon. A. A. — Point as to Cipher, 310
"Adventures of Five Hours," preferred to Shakespeare, 145.
"Alba," etc. — Weever's poem of, 320.
Alençon — Fastolffe captures Duke of, 259–265.
"All for Love" — Burlesque on "Antony and Cleopatra," 150.
Allegorical Treatment — Anything susceptible of, 28.
Allerton — George, Louisa, Susan — descendants of Shakespeare, 273.
Almanac — Shakespeare writes by the, 198.
Amicus Curiæ — Portia as delegate of, 181–188.
Amleth — Translation of, 114.
  Overstudied, 91.
Amleth's Heath, 133.
Amsterdam — Strolling actors stranded in, 278.
Anachronisms — Possible source of, 23, 203.
Analogy in Epilogue to "Henry IV.," 250.
Andrew — Played "Dogberry," 208.
Angelo — Made Beatrice's guardian, 151.
  Made brother to Benedick, 151.

Anglican Church — Popularly same as Roman Catholic, 226.
Antiquarian lore — In Plays, why? 203.
Antonio — His bond not "single," 176.
Antony and Cleopatra — Burlesque of, 150.
Apollyon — Idea of Napoleon as, disappeared, 28.
Apostasy — Courts cannot compel, 189.
Apothecaries — Of Elizabeth's day, 195.
Argument is not evidence, 232.
Arms — Grant of, how obtained, 36, 275.
Army — Queen Elizabeth's. *(See* SOLDIERS.)
Ashbies Estate — Shakespeare's suit to recover, 53.
Ashley — Ann, Edwin, Frederick, George, Henry, James, Nelly, Tabitha, descendants of Shakespeare, 273, 274.
Ashmead Windle, Mrs. C. F. — Her Cipher. *(See* CIPHER, WINDLE, MRS. ASHMEAD.)
Aspley, W. — Charged for printing First Folio, 138.
  Was he confederate to Cipher? 309.
Atomic Theory — In the Plays, 203.
Attorney. *(See* LAWYER, LEGALISMS.)
Aubrey, John — First Shakespearean critic, 132.
  Testimony as to Shakespeare's methods, 203.
Audiences — Preferred action to ethics, 235.
  Could appreciate burlesque, 152, 237.
Author had no legal rights in work, 51, 55.
  Style of an — changes in, 311.
  Was not supplied with proofs, 310.
Authorship — Title-pages not presumptive of 51.
  Of Plays, under theatrical conditions, 48.

B.

Bacon, Francis — His Northumberland MS., 194, 195.
  Quarrel with Coke, 178.
  Volunteer Counsel against Essex, 177.
  Why not Shakespeare, 176.
  Unacquainted with Shakespeare, 301.
  Does not claim the plays, 54.
  Connection conjectured with First Folio, 137.
  Lunacy to mention name of, 22.
  What hand in plays possible, 23.
  No authorship in " Misfortunes of Arthur," 23.
  Did he set up type for First Folio? 300.
  Why should he conceal depository of Cipher? 290.
  A persistent office seeker, 289.
  Not a plotter against the Crown, 289.
  An obsequious courtier, 289.
  Curious begging letters of, 289.
  Was he " Gagged " or " Muzzled"? 309.
  Must have read Cipher in proof, 309.
  Could he have anticipated his rank? 310, 311.
Bacon, Delia. *(See* DELIA BACON.)
Baconian Theorists — Reasonable as compared with Esthetes, 18, 225
Baconian Theory — Strong point of, 16.
  Has historical side, 23.
  When theorists would be crazy, 21.
  Lord Palmerston and the,
  Mr. Furnivall as to, 19.
  Why alluded to, 18.
  Arises legitimately, 288.
  Disposed of by Donnelly cipher, 300.
  Its advocates learned and courteous, 288.
Ballet — Brilliant, devised by Davenant, 151.
" Balthazar " — Played by Jack Wilson, 208.
Baptism — Anglican, recognized by Rome, 226.

INDEX. 331

Baptista — Correctly used as man's name, 207.
Bankruptcy — Davenant avoids, 145.
Bar Sinister — A Shakespeare equals royal, 274.
Barnefield — Poems by, among sonnets, 73.
Barnstaple — Shakespeare's company at, 281.
Bartholomew Fair — A hit at Puritanism, 138.
Basle — Fastolffe, ambassador at, 259.
Bath — Shakespeare's company at, 281.
Beaconsfield — Speeches compared with novels, 5.
Beadle — As played by Sinclo, 207.
  The Stratford, threatens summary proceedings, 84.
Bear Baiting — Denounced by Puritans, 140.
Beatrice — Given a guardian, 151.
Beeston — Fellow-actor with Shakespeare, 164.
  Authority for schoolmaster story, 164.
Begetter — What is a, 77.
Bell, John W. — Prepares statistics, 271.
Benedick — Given a brother, 151.
Benefit of Clergy — Abolished in England, when, 67.
Betterton — Sent by Davenant to France, 149.
  His Hamlet lean and thoughtful, 90, 236.
Bible — King James's, 138.
  Supposed to forbid amusements, 140.
  Shakespeare familiar with Bishop's, 228.
  Wide circulation of, 139.
  Immense effect of, 139, 141.
Birchen Rods — Principal course at Stratford school, 61.
Bishop's Bible. *(See* BIBLE.)
Blackfriars — Certificate of players, 219.
  Some foundation for forgery, 219.
Black-letter — Plowden's report in, 173.
  Unattractive, 173.
Blackness. *(See* MASQUE OF BLACKNESS).
Blewitt — George, Louisa, descendants of Shakespeare, 273.
Blood — Circulation of the, 203.
Blount, Ed. — Charged for printing First Folio, 138.
  Was he confederate to Cipher? 309.
Boar's Head Tavern — Owned by Falstaff, 223.
  Falstaff aliens to Magdalen College, 269, 223 (note).
Bond, Antonio's — Not single, 178.
Books of Songs and Sonnets — Popular publications, 52.
Booth, Edwin — His Hamlet, 90.
Bones, Shakespeare's. *(See* CURSE, GRAVE.)
Boucicault, Dion — We do not write his life from plays, 6
  Manly words of, 27.
  Idea of changes in text, 230.
Bradley — Descendants of Shakespeare named, 274.
Bristol — Shakespeare's company at, 281.
British Museum — Mrs. Windle confides Cipher to, 275.
Britton, John — Testimony as to rural schools, 64.
Brokers — Lovers' oaths called, 176.
Brook, Lord. *(See* GREVILLE, SIR FULKE.)
Broome — Played " Master Brooke," 208.
Broomholme Priory — Fastolffe buried in, 260.
Brothel Scenes — In Pericles, Shakespearean, 213 (note).
Brown, Charles Armitage — Early reader of Sonnets, 81.
  Discovery as to, 81.
  Method with, 36.
Browne, Sir Thomas — Complains of piratical printers, 74.
Brutus and Cassius — Rymer on quarrel of, 157.
Bull-Dogs — Dr. Johnson's learned note about, 214.
Burbadge — Required a fat Hamlet, 90, 236.
Burlesque — In Davenant's time, 151.
  Law, equaled by Sonnets, 30.
Butler of Ireland, Chief *(see* FASTOLFFE).

C.

Cade, Jack — His grievance misstated, 167, 244.
   At Blackheath, 266.
   Fastolffe sends envoy to, 266.
Caen — Fastolffe made lieutenant at, 259.
Caistor — Fastolffe's castle at, 259.
   Built by ransom of Duke D'Alençon, 266.
Campbell, Lord John — Believed Shakespeare an attorney, 87.
Cambridge — Fastolffe benefactor of, 260.
Campo Santo — Of Pisa, the 151.
Caning. (*See* SCHOOLS, SCHOOLMASTERS.)
Canon — The First Folio attacked in 1664, 56.
Canon Law — Followed in Hamlet, 97.
Capitals — Use of, in printing First Folio, 304, 305, 306, 307.
Card — As sure as ever won set, 215.
Carew, Thomas — An associate of Davenant, 134.
   Coadjutor of Ben Johnson, 149.
Careless Proof-reading — Of First Folio, 207.
Casuistry. (*See* CIPHER.)
Catechism — Taught at Stratford school, 61.
Catholic — Was Shakespeare a?, 225.
Cassius. (*See* BRUTUS AND CASSIUS.)
Censorship of the Stage. (*See* STAGE CENSORSHIP.)
Certificate of Blackfriars Players — 219.
Chancery — No allusion to, in Shakespeare, 178.
Change of Scene — Announced by signs, 146.
Chapman — Perhaps he wrote Sonnets, 41.
Charles I. — His love of the plays, 143.
   Milton censures him for, 177.
   Sixteen when Shakespeare died, 176.
Chester, Robert — Did he write "Phœnix and Turtle"?, 73.
Chief Justice — Falstaff browbeats a, 164.
Chorus — Pandarus as, 153.
   In Henry V. appeals to audience, 149.
Christ Jesus — Name not used in plays, 210.
Chronicles of the Time — Actors as, 205.
Chronology — By prosody, endings, etc., 10, 232.
   When superfluous, 232.
   When corroborated, 232.
   Verse test may be false, 232.
Church Union — Practical in Shakespeare's time, 226.
Cicerones — Certain Shakespearean, 33.
Cipher — Were boys taught to, 67.
Cipher in Plays. (*See* DELIA BACON, DONNELLY, HON. I., WINDLE, MRS. C. F. A.)
   Bacon must have read proof of, 309.
   What is to be revealed by the Donnelly?, 308.
   Casuistry employed by the Donnelly, 307.
   Donnelly must exist in quartos, 300.
   Details of the Donnelly, 297, 298.
   Half of First Folio claimed to be, 299.
   Difference between Donnelly and predecessors, 297.
   First announcement of claim for, 288.
   Miss Bacon's idea of, 288, 289.
   Will theory of, make orthodox students?, 327.
   Mr. Donnelly's method mathematical, 296, 300.
Circulation of the Blood — Theory of, 203.
Circumstantial Evidence. (*See* EVIDENCE.)
   Furnivall does not allow, 232.
Classical Learning — In the plays, 203.
   Why not taken out, 21.
   Not inserted to draw houses, 204.
   Inconvenient from business standpoint, 204.
Claudio — Made a sinner, 150.

INDEX 333

Claudius — English succession of, 97.
Clerical Error — Convenience of, in writing biography, 277.
Clergy. *(See* BENEFIT OF CLERGY.)
    Parochial, under Elizabeth, 226, 227.
Cliff, Shakespeare's — Imaginary only, 146.
Clowns — Their parts improvised, 206.
    In pilgrimage to Parnassus, 238.
Cobham Family — Complain about Oldcastle, 220, 250.
Cobham, Lord. *(See* OLDCASTLE.)
Coincidences — Legal rule as to, 307.
Coke — His quarrel with Bacon, 178.
Coleridge, S. T. — His method with the Sonnets, 36.
    Theory of internal evidence, 167.
    Early reader of Sonnets, 81.
Collier Forgeries — Evidence in case of, 3.
Collier, J. P. — His Bridgewater manuscripts, 219.
    Ruined by ambition for discovery, 84.
Comedies — Aubrey's early criticism of, 132.
Comedy of Errors — Meres' assigns to Shakespeare, 50, 80.
    Doubts as to, 80.
Comic Characters — Text perpetuated by the, 18.
Commentators — Idea of what is doubtful, 74.
    Read into more than out of, 1.
    Glib as to sources of plots, 22.
Common People — Shakespeare's opinion of, 240, 248.
    Victor Hugo's, 247.
Companies, Theatrical. *(See* THEATRICAL COMPANIES, 205.)
Comparative Criticism — Is internal evidence, 2.
    Valueless unless reënforced, 3.
    A paradox of, 94.
Condell, Henry. *(See* HEMINGES AND CONDELL.)
Confession of Faith — John Shakespeare's has disappeared, 228.
Conquest of Grenada — John Dryden's, 156.
Contemporaries — Secret information of, 54.
    Question as to belief of, 54.
    Cannot stand cross-examination, 54.
    Were they deceived, 54.
    Did they ever discuss authorship, 54.
    Men like ourselves, 231.
"Copy" — For First Folio, what was, 56.
Copyright — Perpetual, 60.
    In Shakespeare's assigns, 270.
    First for term of years, 60.
    Only in members of Stationers' Company, 51.
Cordelia — A spoiled child, 103.
    Responsible for Lear's agony, 103.
Corsican Vendetta — Satisfied if man killed, 111.
    No time limit to, 111.
Coriolanus — Dennis touches up, 153.
Cotes, Thomas — Prints Sonnets in 1640, 49.
    His edition unreliable, 81.
Court Fool — Theory that he wrote plays welcomed, 225.
Coventry — Shakespeare's company at, 281.
Cowley, Abraham — An associate of Dryden's, 134.
Cowley — Plays "Dogberry," 208.
Creative — Esthetic criticism apt to become, 1.
Cressida — Dryden thinks too fairly used, 152.
Criss-Cross Row — At Stratford school, 61.
Critic — Must be allowed to judge for himself, 2.
    Each writes personally, 8.
    Insists on his own criticism as evidence, 8.
    Read into more than they read out, 3.
Criticism. *(See* CRITIC, CREATIVE, COMPARATIVE.)
    A paradox of esthetic, 94.
    Esthetic, apt to become creative, 1.

Criticism. *(Continued.)*
   Shakespearean, a history of extremes, 2.
   Textual. *(See* TEXTUAL CRITICISM.*)*
   Comparative, where a failure, 3.
Cruel Brother, The — A play by Davenant, 134.
Curtiss — An actor named, 209.
Curse — The, on Shakespeare's grave, 84.
   Not against inspection of bones, 84.
   Prevents investigation, 85.
   How circumventable, 85.
"Cut" — Long speeches by actors, 212.
Cymbeline — Mrs. Windle reads by Cipher, 293, 294.
   Explains riddle in, 295.

D.

Daniel — Portia not a second, 178.
Dante — A proposed author of the Sonnets, 40.
   May have written them, 39.
"Dark Beauty," The — How extracted from Sonnets, 39.
Dancer — Epilogue spoken by a, in "II. Henry, iv.," 250.
   Whose apology did it contain? 250.
Davenant, Sir William — Enters Lincoln College in 1621.
   Associates Inigo Jones with himself, 148.
   Invents and imports scenery, 147.
   Released by agency of Milton, 135.
   Buried in Westminster Abbey, 135.
   Epitaph on, 136.
   Shakespeare's literary executor, 133.
   Becomes a dramatist, 134.
   Writes librettos for Jones, 149.
   His Shakespeare paternity, 282.
   At least Shakespeare's godson, 161.
   Contemporary estimates of, 160, 161.
   Has plenty of enemies, 160.
   Custodian of Shakespeare's fame, 153.
   Begins to live by his pen, 134.
   Taught Dryden to love Shakespeare, 133.
   Practical introducer of opera, 145.
   Brings supplies to Royalists, 135.
   Serves at siege of Gloucester, 135.
   Made Lieutenant-General, 135.
   Page to Sir Fulke Greville, 134.
   Intercedes for Milton, 135.
   Bids farewell to politics, 135.
   Opens Duke of York's Theater, 135.
   Becomes a Catholic, 134.
   Expects decapitation, 135.
   Ineffectual memorial to Parliament, 135.
   Especially hated by Puritans, 134.
   Charged with treason, 134.
   Bailed and escapes, 134.
   Reaches France, 135.
   Becomes poet laureate, 133.
   Courtier of Charles I., 134.
   Courtier of Charles II., 134.
   Rewrites "Tempest" with Dryden, 150.
Davis, Hon. C. K. — His "Law in Shakespeare," 166.
   Goes further than predecessors, 167.
   Suggests a new reading, 102.
   Note on legalisms in Hamlet, 97.
Dawson, S. E. — Letter to, from Tennyson, 32.
De Falbe, Compte — His translation of Amleth, 114.
De Senectute — Fastolffe orders translation of, 259.
De Quadra — His letter to the Pope, 227.

Death — Moves in metaphor, 190.
Decree — Queen Elizabeth's, concerning plays, 216.
Debt — Arrest for, none on Sunday, 228.
Deity — Name of, excised from plays, 210.
Dekkar — His use of "begetter," 77.
His "Rod for Runaways," 280.
Delegate Americus Curiæ. *(See* PORTIA.*)*
Delia Bacon. *(See* CIPHER.*)*
Never in insane asylum, 19 (note).
Her Cipher, 288.
Hawthorn could not comprehend, 290, 292.
Explanation of, 290, 291.
Emerson could not comprehend, 294.
Denham, Sir John — Estimate of Shakespeare, 158.
Denmark — No flavor of, in Hamlet, 97.
Dennis, John — Criticises the plays, 153.
Touches up Coriolanus, 153.
Disagreement — Writes over "Merry Wives," 153.
Plentiful margin for, 282.
Descriptive Action — None in "Merry Wives," 250.
Desdemona — Rymer's opinion of, 154.
Devonshire Bust, The — Discovery of, 158, 159.
Estimate of, 160.
Duke of, pays 300 guineas for bust, 159.
Dialects — Not critically studied, 21.
Specimens of all, in the plays, 20.
Dialectics — Of Hales v. Petit, 174.
Not town talk, 174.
Dialogues — Shakespeare may have borrowed, 22.
Disguised Duke, The — Is everybody's friend, 151
Disraeli, Isaac — His speculations as to plays, 213 (note).
Dogberry — Played by Andrew and Cowley, 208.
Where Shakespeare found him, 205.
Doll Tearsheet — Arrested by Sinklo as beadle, 209.
Donnelly, Hon. I. — Believes in Cipher, 197, 296.
Dorinda — A sister to Miranda, 150. *(See* CIPHER IN PLAYS.*)*
Double Voucher — What is a, 174.
Portentous simile found in, 174.
Doubtful Play — Is "Sir John Oldcastle," 222.
Limit as to, 74.
Dover — Shakespeare's company at, 281.
Dowden — Concerning Shakespeare's moods, 47.
His methods of criticism, 47.
"**Dram of Eale**" — R. G. White's opinion of, 162.
Drama — Voltaire's opinion of, in England, 157.
Corruption of the, 141.
Dramatic Element — In certain theories, 203.
Dramatic Poet — No existence in closet, 26.
Dromo — Clown in "Pilgrimage to Parnassus," 237.
Drop Curtain — Davenant invents present style of, 147.
Dryden refines Shakespeare, 152, 153.
Rewrites "Troilus and Cressida," etc., 143, 152.
Sets the literary fashion, 153.
His "Conquest of Grenada," 156.
Rewrites "Tempest," with Davenant, 133, 150.
His "Defense of the Epilogue," 156.
Ducats — Portia ordered to restore, 191.
Duchess of Richmond — Davenant in service of, 134.
Duke of York's Theater — Managed by Davenant, 135.

E.

Ecclesiastical Conditions — Of Shakespeare's time, 225.
Editing — Surreptitious, of plays, 54.

Editors — Province of Shakespearean, 91.
Of Third Folio unknown, 287.
Considerations moving, 287.
Very glib as to sources of plots, 22.
Edward III. — Mr. Furnivall's opinion of, 12.
Elbow — Where Shakespeare found him, 205.
Elizabeth, Queen. (*See* QUEEN ELIZABETH).
Emerson, R. W. (*See* DELIA BACON.)
Endings — Stopped, unstopped, etc, 10.
England — King of, requested to kill Amleth, 120.
Little about, in comedies, 7.
English analogies in Hamlet, 96.
Epilogue — Use of, in travesty, 152.
Epitaph — On Sir Wm. Davenant, 136.
On Elias James, 327.
Epitaphs — Not verse-tested, 327.
Equipment — Shakespeare's scholastic, 61. (*See* PORTIA.)
Errors — Grave legal, in "Merchant of Venice," 178.
Escheat — Of Shylock's property illegal, 179.
Essex, Earl of — Bacon's declaration against, 177.
Marriage with Frances Howard celebrated, 149.
Esthetic Critics. (*See* CRITICS, CRITICISM.)
Make Shakespeare write by almanac, 200.
Generally, 7, 25.
Halliwell Phillipp's estimate of, 16.
Tendency to become creative, 1.
Championed by new Shakespeare Society, 6.
Recently claimed to be evidence, 5.
Originally known as eulogium or panegyric, 5.
Estimated value of, 11.
Evelyn, John — Prefers Hudibras to Shakespeare, 145.
Entries in diary of, 144.
Evidence — No one kind conclusive against another, 4.
Historical. (*See* EXTERNAL, *infra.*)
Esthetic criticism now claimed to be, 5.
Esthetic as to Shakespeare's birthplace, 7.
External is circumstantial, 2.
All kinds must be collected, 4.
Presumptive. (*See* PRESUMPTIVE.)
New Shakespeare Society's idea of, 7.
Applicable to literary matter, what? 2.
External and internal, agree, where, 17.
That Shakespeare had lost child, 8.
Argument is not, 232.

F.

Faerie Queen — George Eliot as to, 29.
Falstaff. (*See* FASTOLFFE, OLDCASTLE.)
Tries to borrow £1000 of a chief justice, 166.
First called Oldcastle, 219.
In love — queen's order for, 218, 222, 267, 268.
Familiar Spirit, A — Found in Sonnets, 39.
Family — Shakespeare's, 59.
Shakespeare restores fortunes of, 59.
Fatal Resentment — Davenant's play, so called, 154.
Fastolffe, Sir John. (*See* FALSTAFF, OLDCASTLE.)
Son of a mariner, 254.
Ward of Duke of Bedford, 254.
Accompanies Clarence to Ireland, 254.
Marries daughter of Sir Robert Tiptoft, 254.
Pin-money of wife of, 255.
Serves in Normandy and Gascony, in Guienne, Anjou, and Maine, 255.
Lieutenant of Harfleur in 1415, 255.
Shakespeare makes out a coward, 257, 258.

Fastolffe, Sir John. *(Continued.)*
  Made a Baron of France, 255.
  Made Knight of the Garter, 256.
  To be comic must be unsuccessful, 253.
  Promise to kill off in a sweat, redeemed, 251.
  " In love," story of, not impossible, 251, 252.
  Matter of policy to lampoon, 258, 261, 267.
  A successful warrior, 259.
  At the siege of Orleans, 259.
  At Agincourt, 259, 265 (note).
  Takes Duke d'Alençon prisoner, 259, 265.
  At battle of the herrings, 259.
  Guizot concedes valor of, 259.
  Not deprived of Order of Garter, 259.
  His castle at Caistor, 259, 266.
  A patron of literature, 259.
  At Patay, 260.
  Monstrelet's testimony as to, 260.
  Tampers with his step-son's income, 262.
  Extracts from letters of, 262.
  Mr. Fitzpatrick's discoveries as to, 263, 265.
  Made a Chief Butler of Ireland, 263.
  Horses granted to, 265.
  Sends envoy to Cade at Blackheath, 266.
Faversham — Shakespeare's company at, 281.
Female Parts — First given to women, 150.
Fenge — Son of Gervendel, 114.
Fialler — Commander in Sconen, 132.
Fine and Recovery. *(See* DOUBLE VOUCHER.)
First Folio. *(See* HEMINGES AND CONDELL.)
  Copies found widely distributed, 137.
  Sources of text of, 56, 206.
  No proof-reader for, 206.
  Nothing known as to success of, 137.
  At whose charges printed, 136.
  Appears unheralded, 136.
  Difference between, and quartos, 57.
  One dated 1622, 60.
  Most accurately printed if containing Cipher, 309.
  Revised by Third Folio, 283, 285.
Fitzpatrick, W. J. — Alleged discoveries of, 263, 265.
Fleay, F. G. — Doubts Meres' canon, 80.
  Thinks Shakespeare had a partner, 18.
  His discovery as to Hamlet, 279.
  Takes nearly half plays off canon, 17.
  Where, agrees with Furnivall, 18.
  Confident errors of, 279.
  As to Shakespeare's travels, 279.
Flecknoe, Richard — Attacks Davenant, 160.
Fletcher, John — Dryden criticises, 156.
  Master Lawrence takes actors to Scotland, 280.
Flower, Francis — Co-author of "Misfortunes of Arthur," 25.
Fluellen — Gibes at Falstaff, 266.
Folio, First. *(See* FIRST FOLIO.)
  Second, supposed prepared by Milton, 142.
  Third, readjusts the canon, 56. *(See* THIRD FOLIO.)
Folkestone — Shakespeare's company at, 281.
Forgeries. *(See* COLLIER, IRELAND.)
Forman, Dr. Simon — His diary, 320.
Fortinbras — His estimate of Hamlet, 113.
  Statement as to contract with Hamlet, 175.
  As to succession, 175.
Form and Expression — Difference between, 232.
  Tendency to separate, 232.
  To incline to or separate, 232.

338   INDEX.

Fortune — Shakespeare's large private, 58.
Fourteen Days — Time limit for " Merry Wives," 248.
    Probability of the story, 248.
Fulbecke, William — Co-author of " Misfortunes of Arthur," 23
France — Stage censorship in 221 (note).
    Devoted to classical models, 157.
Frenchmen — Favorite characters in plays, 211.
Frenzy of John Dennis, The — 154.
Fuller, Thomas — Commends removal of Oldcastle's name, 256.
    Objects to use of Falstaff's name, 256.
Furnivall, Dr. F. J.— Does not "consider 'Titus Andronicus,'" 8
    Doubts Meres' canon, 80.
    Idea of Baconian theory, 19.
    His various methods, 25.
    Never read "Pericles," 15, 326.
    Hears that Shakespeare didn't write it, 15.
    His wonderful "groups," 12, 233.
    Additional "groups" suggested for, 233.
    Opinion of "Venus and Adonis," 8.
    Estimate of his own labors, 13.
    Opinion of the " Merry Wives," 13.
        of the " Edward III.," 12.
        of the Sonnets, 11.
    Agrees with Fleay, where, 18.
    Makes statement as to verse-tests, 312, 313.
    Demands " earth crust " treatment, 313.
    Counts rhymes in " Love's Labour's Lost," 313, 319.
        " Julius Cæsar," 313, 319.
        " Winter's Tale," 313, 319.
    His idea of external evidence, 313, 319.
    As to Shakespeare's cosmic energies, 315.
    Proposes to instruct students, 316.
    Overlooks literary differences, 317.
    Allows only time element in criticism, 317.
    Rhyme count his only criticism, 321.
    Forgets to equalize his counts, 322.
    Where discovers "verse-blindness," 323, 324.
    Overlooks historical data, 323.
    His methods not generic, 326.
    Edits plays without reading them, 326.
    Confesses his own illicit processes, 8, 15, 80, 326.
    Makes sweeping statements, 326.
    Does not treat the epitaphs, 327.
Fytton, Mrs.   *(See* DARK BEAUTY.)
    Found in the Sonnets, 39.

G.

Gabriel Harvey — Played a messenger, 208.
Gamekeeper — As played by Sinklo, 208.
    Played by Humphrey Jeaffes, 208.
Garrick Club — Devonshire bust owned by, 158.
Garrick, D.— Instrument of Shakespearean reaction, 158.
    His Hamlet, 88.
    Discarded graveyard scene, 88.
Garter — Order of the, bestowed on Fastolffe, 259, 260.
    Alleged deprivation of, 257.
Gastrell, Rev. F.— Abolishes real estate, 37.
" Gentle" — Meant "of gentle birth," 35.
    Why applied to Shakespeare, 35.
Gentle — Meaning of, in Shakespeare's time, 35.
George Eliot — Comment on the " Faerie Queen," 129.
Germany — Actors stranded in, 278.
    Shakespeare in (volumes so-called), 280.
Ghost — Hamlet seen by outsiders, 98.
    A very impatient, 92.

Ghost. *(Continued.)*
  A, visits poet of sonnets, 39.
Globe Theater — Must have registered plays it purchased, 59.
Golden Age of Poetry — Dryden's opinion of the, 156. *(See* THEATERS.*)*
Good Clothes — Vagrants do not wear, 188.
Gondilbert — Davenant's play of, 134.
Government — Plays not to discuss matters of, 252.
Government, Popular. *(See* POPULAR GOVERNMENT.*)*
Gower, Lord Roland — Suggests outwitting curse, 85.
Grammar — The first English, 61.
Grammar School — Curriculum of the Stratford, 61.
  Scene in, 62.
Grant of Arms. *(See* ARMS.*)*
Grave — The seventeen-foot story, 37 (note).
  Duty of opening, 86.
  Opposition to opening, 84.
  Where is Shakespeare's, 84.
Grave Diggers — Sit on Ophelia's case, 173.
Grenada, The Conquest of. *(See* CONQUEST OF GRENADA.*)*
Grendon, in Bucks — Home of Dogberry or Elbow, 205.
Greville, Sir Fulke — Davenant, the page of, 134.
Griffin — His poems assigned to Shakespeare, 73.
Groups — Mr. Furnivall's, 12, 233. *(See* FURNIVALL.*)*
Grubb, Diana, Rose — Descendants of Shakespeare, 273, 274.
Guizot — His allusion to Fastolffe, 259.
Gwynn, Nell — Her tragedy burlesque, 152.

H.

Hales, Lady — Petitions in ejectment, 172.
  Sir James — his suicide, 172.
  Escheat of his estate, 172.
  v. Petit, case of, 172.
  Probably not town talk, 173.
  Not for twenty-five years, 174.
  Travesty of, in Hamlet, 97.
Hall, Dr. John — Shakespeare's executor, 54.
  Does not probate will, 72.
  Does not claim plays, 54.
Hallam, Henry — Disbelief as to Sonnets, 77.
  Frederick, William, descendants of Shakespeare, 273.
Hallen, A. O.— Cornelius, 274.
Halliwell Phillipps, J. O. — Estimates of money values, 79.
Hamblett — Of Belleforest overstudied, 91.
  As to theft of Shakespeare's name, 74.
Hamlet — A rational gentleman, 92.
  Disgusts age of Charles II., 144.
  Advice as to clowns, 206.
  As to value of actors, 205.
  An English prince, 98.
  The, that Shakespeare wanted, 92.
  Voltaire's opinion of, 156, 157.
  Written on visit to Scotland? 279.
  First quarto of, rewritten, 170, 171.
  And the commentators, 110.
  Mr. Davis's new reading in, 102.
  A courteous gentleman, 108.
  Fortinbras' estimate of, 113.
  Acting, conceptions of, 90.
  Acts like a lawyer, 100.
  Apologizes to Laertes, 109.
  Did Shakespeare make him mad? 94.
  Time elapsing in play of, 93.
  Why present him to Denmark? 131.
  In exultant mood, 101.

Hamlet. *(Continued.)*
    Rewrites play of Gonzago, 101.
    Sword in hand, 106.
    Graveyard scene in, discarded, 90
    Deliberate in movement, 92.
    Disbelieves in ghosts, 99.
    Efforts to kill Claudius, 106.
    Nash's mention of " whole," 173.
    Was he fat? 236.
    Perhaps not originally mad, 238.
    No standard on stage, 236.
    Sword in hand, 235.
    According to Wilson Barrett, 234.
            Betterton, 234.
            Garrick, 234.
            Kemble, 234.
            Stephen Kemble, 234.
            Young, 234.
            Kean, 234.
            J. B. Booth, 234.
            Edwin Booth, 234.
            Henry Irving, 234.
            Fechter, 234.
    And the " Merry Wives," 321.
Hanmer, Sir T.— Doubts Meres' list, 80.
Hariot, Thomas — Supposed to be " T. T.," 45.
Hart, William — Haller of Stratford, 273.
Harvey, Gabriel. *(See* GABRIEL HARVEY.)
Hathaway, Agnes —Not Shakespeare's wife, 276.
    (See WHATELEY, WIFE.)
Hathaway, Richard — His daughter named Agnes, not Anne, 277.
Havendell — Son of Gervendel, 114.
    Becomes a Viking, 114.
Hawthorne, Nathaniel. *(See* DELIA BACON.)
Hazlett, W.— On Shakespeare and Common People, 241.
Headsman — Portia does not act as, 187.
" **Heaven,**" substituted for " God," in plays, 211.
Hector's — Two drunken for a penny, 156.
Heminges, John. *(See* HEMINGES AND CONDELL.)
Heminges and Condell — Misstatements of, 201.
    Their word unreliable, 203 (note).
    Extent of editorial labors, 224.
    Apologize for 1623 folio, 136.
    Hyperbole concerning Shakespeare's penmanship, 57.
    Used the quartos for " copy," 56.
    Originated doubt as to authorship, 56.
    Their canon attacked in 1664, 56.
    Their copy not in Shakespeare's autograph, 56.
    Utterers of stolen goods, 55.
    How they made up canon, 283.
    Select twenty-six plays, 283.
    Rejecting one-third, 283.
    Nobody demanded their authority, 284.
    Overhauled in 1663-4, 284.
Henrietta, Maria — Davenant, attendant on, 134.
Henry V.— Assigned by Meres to canon list, 50.
Henry VIII.— Pepys does not like, 144.
Hernani — Stage censorship of, 221 (note).
Hippolyto — Character in rewritten " Tempest," 150.
Herbert, William. *(See* PEMBROKE, LORD.)
Hermentrude — Queen of Scotland, 128.
Hermetic Verses — Why should Shakespeare write? 40.
Herrings — Fastolffe at battle of the, 259.
Heywood, Thomas — Assists Ben Jonson, 149.
    Complains of piracy, 73.

Heywood, Thomas *(Continued.)*
   Protests against Shakespeare's name, 51.
   Testifies as to printers' methods, 310.
Holland — English actors visit, 280.
Holmes, Nathaniel — And Baconian Theory, 289.
Holofernes — Caricature of Bacon, 24.
Holy Ghost — Name not used in plays, 210.
"Honorificabilitudinatibus" — Occurs in Northumberland MS., 195.
Horatio — No keeper of madmen, 113.
Howard, Frances — Marriage, with Essex, 149.
Horrors — Catalogue of, in Titus Andronicus, 9.
Hudibras — Evelyn prefers, to Shakespeare, 145.
Hudson, N. N. — Doubts Meres' canon, 80.
Hughes, Thomas — Co-author of "Misfortunes of Arthur," 23.
Hugo, Victor — Advocate of popular liberty, 247.
Humanity, Not Nature — Shakespeare's specialty, 248.
Humphrey Jeaffes — Plays a game-keeper, 208.
Hyphens — Employment of, in First Folio, 304, 305, 306, 307.
Hythe — Shakespeare's company at, 281.

I.

Ideal Love Affair — Why not described in Sonnets? 29.
Improvement — Shakespeare's, in stage experience, 231.
Imputing One's Self — To a poet, 32.
Income — Of Shakespeare on retirement, 48.
Index Hunters — Tennyson's opinion of, 32.
Information — As to authorship exhausted, 48.
Ingleby, C. M., Dr. — Thinks grave should be opened, 85.
   Method of outwitting curse, 85.
Internal Evidence. *(See* EVIDENCE.*)* In literary matters, 2, 238.
Interpolations — By actors on the stage, 205.
Invader of his Country, The. *(See* FATAL RESENTMENT.*)*
Ireland — Fastolffe, a Chief Butler of, 263.
Ireland, W. H. — Makes legitimate parody crime, 84.
   Evidence in case of, 2, 3.
Italic Letters — How employed in First Folio, 299, 301, 302, 305, 306, 307.

J.

"Jack-Puddens" — Rymer calls classical characters, 155.
Jack Wilson — Played "Balthazar," 208.
"Jacques Peter" — Earliest form of "Shakespeare," 275.
Jaggard I. — Issues "Passionate Pilgrim," 50.
   W. — Charged for printing First Folio, 136.
   Was he confederate to Cipher? 309.
Jeaffes, Humphrey. *(See* HUMPHREY JEAFFES.*)*
Jews — Portia has no mercy for, 189.
Joan of Arc — Shakespeare treats cruelly, 245.
John Dennis — The frenzy of, 154.
Johnson, Dr. — His idea of Hamlet, 85.
   Note as to bull-dogs, 214.
Jones, Inigo — Associates with Davenant, 148, 149.
   Unacquainted with Shakespeare, 149.
   Writes "Temple of Love," 149.
   In partnership with B. Jonson, 149.
   Jonson burlesques, 220.
   Complains to Lord Chamberlain, 220.
   Great confidence placed in, 149.
   Pembroke sends to Italy, 148.
   Employed to devise masques, 148.
Jonson, Ben — Hits Puritanism in "Bartholomew Fair," 138.
   Burlesques Inigo Jones, 220.
   Partnership with Inigo Jones, 149.
   Dies in 1637, 134.

342   INDEX.

Jonson, Ben (*Continued.*)
    Hyperbole of, as to Shakespeare's penmanship, 57.
Journeymen;Printers — Of First Folio, 206.
Julius Cæsar — Rewritten by Davenant, 152.
    How, should have been done, 155.
    Rhymes in, counted by Furnivall, 313.
    Historical evidences of date, 320.
Just Italian, The — A play of Davenant's, 134.
Jutland — Gervendel, governor of, 114.

K.

Kean, Edmond — His Hamlet, 90.
Keene and Wheatley — Ruling in, as to accessions, 216 (note).
Kempe — Played " Verges," 208.
King James — Orders Spaniards out of plays, 211.
    Version of Bible, 138.
    His statutes as to plays, 210.
King John — Assigned to canon by Meres, 50.
Knight — A butt of villagers, 248.
Knowell, Dean — Queen Elizabeth interrupts, 252.
Koller — King of Norway, 114.

L.

Lambert, John — Sued to recover Ashbies, 53.
    Wilmecote, 53.
Lameness — Of Shakespeare, figurative, 35.
Lancaster, John — Co-author of " Misfortunes of Arthur," 23.
    Thomas of, grant to Fastolffe, 263.
Launce — And comic characters paid running expenses, 20.
Law. (*See* LAWYER, LEGALISM.)
    Bad more dramatic than good, 198.
Law Against Lovers — Recast of " Measure for Measure," 150.
Law Burlesques. (*See* BURLESQUE.)
Lawyer — Was Shakespeare a, 164, 166.
Learned Houses — Dissolution of the, 203.
Leicester — Shakespeare's company at, 281.
Legal Errors. (*See* PORTIA.)
    Proposition as to grave, 86.
    Protection accorded to accretions, 216.
    Representatives. (*See* REPRESENTATIVES.)
Legalism — In Shakespeare, structural, 171.
    Is constant, 171.
    In plays made exact, 172, 176.
    In Hamlet, 97.
Lenox — First Folio in library, 60.
" Les Misérables " — The epic of poverty, 247.
Leyre — Capital of Jutland, 130.
Liberty, Popular. (*See* POPULAR LIBERTY.)
Library — A gainer at expense of stage, 147.
" Light Endings." (*See* FURNIVALL, PROSODY.'
Lifetime List. (*See* PLAYS.)
Lily's Accidence — At Stratford school, 61.
Lintot, B. — Gets bad opinion of Shakespeare, 154.
Literary Biography — How to perfect Shakespeare's, 234
Localisms — Inserted in plays by actors, 205.
Long Speeches — Cut by actors, 212.
Lord Chamberlain — Jones complains to, 220.
    Orders out hit at Jones, 220.
Lothair. (*See* BEACONSFIELD.)
Love — Temple of. (*See* TEMPLE OF LOVE.)
Love Affair — (*See* SONNETS.) Genuine record of a, 29.
Lovely Boy — Found in the Sonnets, 38.
Lover's Complaint — Anonymous verses called, 81.

INDEX.   343

Lovers, Law Against. *(See* LAW AGAINST LOVERS.*)*
Lover's Oaths — Called "brokers," 176.
Love's Labour's Lost — Assigned to canon by Meres, 50.
    Rhymes in, counted by Furnivall, 313.
    Historical evidences of date of, 319.
    No such play now known, 80.
    Won —   "   "   "   50, 79.
Lucrece — Speculated authorship of, 52.
    Dedication to Southampton of, 49.
    Nature depicted in, 5.
Lunacy — To mention Bacon a sign of, 22.
Lunatics — Two made by Baconian theory, 42.
Lydiate, Hester — Marries George Shakespeare, 273.

M.

Macbeth — Difference between Hamlet and, 92.
    Balle in Davenant's, 150.
    Pepys admires Davenant's, 145.
    His physician will not prescribe, 198.
Mackay, Charles — His treatment of Sonnets, 40.
Mackay, W. D. — Opinion of Shakespeare in 1579, 1601, 71.
    Discovers missing play, 69.
Magdalen College — Fastolffe a benefactor of, 223, 269.
    Bull's Head tavern ceded to, 223 (note), 269.
Maidstone — Shakespeare's company at, 281.
"Maine Laws" — Normal effect of, 141.
Manningham, John — Note on "Twelfth Night," 80.
Manuscripts — Conjectured source of, 203.
        Unblotted, 204. *(See* HEMINGES AND CONDELL.*)*
Marlborough — Shakespeare's company at, 281.
Marlowe — His poems assigned to Shakespeare, 73.
    Similarity to his style, 9.
Marriage — Of Essex and Frances Howard, 149.
    (See PATRIARCHAL UNIONS, TROTH-PLIGHT.*)*
Mason, Peter — His account of provincial schools, 66.
Masque — Is "Midsummer Night's Dream" a? 148.
Massey, Gerald — Disposes of Shakespearean authorship, 83.
    Treatment of Sonnets, 28.
Master of the Revels — Deletes burlesque on Jones, 220.
Masque of Blackness — Prepared by I. Jones, 149.
    Costly properties of, 149.
Masses — For soul of Fastolffe at Magdalen, 269 (note).
Measure for Measure — Interwritten with "Much Ado," 150.
Meditated Crimes — Courts have no jurisdiction over, 188.
Merchant of Venice — Assigned to canon by Meres, 50.
    Trial scene in, 193.
    Portia's rulings in. *(See* PORTIA.*)*
Meres, Francis — His testimony hearsay, 83.
    His canon, 80.
    His status as critic, 81.
    Commentators disbelieve him, 80.
    List must stand or fall together, 79.
    What Sonnets did he allude to? 77.
    His "Palladis Tamia," 49.
    Method with Sonnets, 37.
Merrick — Represents Richard II., 177.
Merry Wives of Windsor — Shakespeare's rule suspended in, 248.
    Descriptive action or speech wanting in, 256.
    Dennis works over, 155.
    Relative date of, immaterial, 250.
    Pepys does not like, 147.
    Local allusions in, 15.
    Legalisms inserted in, 176.
    Queen Elizabeth's share in, 239.
    And Hamlet, 323.

Messenger, A — Played by Gabriel Harvey, 208.
Metrical Styles. (*See* FURNIVALL, GROUPS, PERIODS, PROSODY.)
Middleton — His hand in Macbeth, 46.
Midsummer Night's Dream — Is it a masque? 148.
  Pepys thinks insipid, 144.
  Assigned to canon by Meres, 50.
  Familiarity with theatrical usage in, 7.
Milk-women — Rebellion of the, 151.
Milton — Censures Charles I. for reading plays, 75.
  Pamphleteer to Parliament, 142.
  Davenant intercedes for, 135.
  Supposed to edit Second Folio, 142.
Miracle — New statement of the, 299, 301.
Miranda — A sister provided for, 150.
"Mirror of Martyrs" — Weever's, 320.
"Misfortunes of Arthur" — Bacon devises dumb-show for, 23.
  Name of alleged author, 23.
  Resemblance to plays, 23.
  Played before Queen Elizabeth, 23.
Menæchmi — Foundation of "Twelfth Night," 80.
  Not "Comedy of Errors," 80.
Moestrich, William — A descendant of Shakespeare, 273.
Monasteries — Dissolution of the, 203.
Monographs — The plays are not, 48, 196.
Monstrelet — Fastolffe mentioned in chronicles of, 260.
Montgomery, Earl — A dedicatee of First Folio, 136. (*See* PEMBROKE AND MONTGOMERY.)
Mowbray, Thomas — Fastolffe, page to, 222, 264.
  Oldcastle, page to, 222, 264.
Mr. W. H. (*See* W. H., MR.)
  A friend of Thomas Thorpe's, 76.
  Only begetter of the Sonnets, 76.
"Much Ado About Nothing" — Interwritten with "Measure for Measure," 150.
Music. (*See* ORCHESTRA.)

N.

Narrative of Dr. Norris — Pope's, 154.
Nash — Mentions "whole Hamlets," 173.
Nature — Poets should go to, 35.
New Readings — Usually torturings of passages, 27.
New Romney — Shakespeare's company at, 281.
New Shakespeare Society of London. (*See* SOCIETY.)
  A discovery of, 201.
  Labor in a circle, 16.
  Microscopical amenities of, 24.
  Esoteric criticism of, 24.
  Includes not all esthetes, 24.
New York — Stage censorship in, 220.
Nicke — Probably Nicholas Tarleton, 210.
Noblemen — Theaters must be under patronage of, 245.
  Players must be under warrant of, 245.
Non-Theatrical Matter — No stage-right in, 81.
Northumberland Manuscripts, 194.
  Contents of cover of, 194.
  William Shakespeare written on, 195.
  Line from Lucrece written on, 195.
  "Honorificabilitudinatibus" written on, 195.

O.

O'Connor, W. D. — Thinks Raleigh author of Sonnets, 45.
  Surmise as to W. H., 45.
  As to dedicatee of Sonnets, 43.
Oceanic Action — In geology, 203.
Odium Theologicum — No trace of in plays, 229.

INDEX.   345

Oldcastle, Sir John — Shakespeare's doubt as to, 138, 251, 261.
   Fuller protests against use of, 256.
   Companion of Prince of Wales, 255.
   Heads crusade against Established Church, 255.
   Maintains army of preachers, 255.
   His attainder, 255.
   Suffers martyrdom, 255.
   Was not a coward, 261.
   Carelessness in substituting Falstaff for, 222.
   Why Shakespeare may have used, 267.
Opera — Davenant practically introduces, 145.
Ophelia — Argument as to her burial, 172, 193.
   Resemblance to Hales and Petit, 172.
   A commonplace character, 103.
   Not a Lady Macbeth, 106.
   Gives key-note to commentary, 91.
   Betrays Hamlet, 103, 235.
   Suspected by Hamlet, 235.
   Sympathy removed from, 235.
   Is mad character of the play, 238.
Opinions — More plentiful than facts, 232.
Orleans — Fastolffe at siege of, 259
Orleans, Maid of. *(See* JOAN OF ARC.)
Ormond — Earl of, Chief Butler of Ireland, 263.
Othello — Pepys does not admire, 145.
   Curious evidence from play of, 223.
   Allusion to in foreign diary, 223.
   Comparison of two versions of, 224.
   Erasure of name of Deity in, 224.
   Rymer's name for, 154.
   Method of preparing it, 154.
Orchestra — Placed between audience and stage, 150.
Ovid — Translation from, in Sonnets, 81.
   Meres compares Shakespeare to, 50.
Oxford — Fastolffe benefactor of, 260. *(See* MAGDALEN COLLEGE.)
   Shakespeare's company at, 281.

P.

Pagination of First Folio — Defective, 207.
   Analysis of, 212 (note).
   Foundation of Donnelly cipher, 298.
   How may be explained, 298.
Palladis Tamia — A sort of literary critique, 50.
Palladio — Influences style of Inigo Jones, 148.
Palmerston, Lord — Inclines to Baconian theory, 19.
Pandarus — Officiates as chorus, 153.
Parallelisms — Tennyson's opinion of, 32.
Parentheses — Use of, in printing First Folio, 302, 303, 305, 306, 307.
Parliament — Elizabeth's — their confusion of tongues, 62
Partner — Fleay thinks Shakespeare had a, 18.
Passionate Pilgrim — Not copyrighted, 72.
          Nor probated, 72.
   Jaggard prints, 50.
Paston, John and William — Trustees of Fastolffe, 262.
   The letters full of Fastolffe's doings, 262.
Patay — Fastolffe at battle of, 257.
   Alleged cowardice at, 259, 260.
Patriarchal Unions — In early England, 282.
Patrician — Plays written by a, 21, 167.
Pavier, Thomas — Pirates Shakespeare's name, 74.
Payn — Perhaps origin of Poins, 266.
   Envoy to Cade at Blackheath, 266.
Pedagogues, Rural. *(See* SCHOOLS, SCHOOLMASTERS.)

Pembroke, Lord — Not Mr. W. H., 74.
  A dedicatee of First Folio, 136.
  And Montgomery show the plays some favor, 136.
  Wore bar sinister, 274.
Petit — Crown tenant under escheat, 172.
Penroodocke — Co-author of "Misfortunes of Arthur," 23.
Pence — Shakespeare wrote for, 225.
Pepys — Entries in diary of, 144.
  Liked the ballet in Macbeth, 151.
Performances — Held by daylight, 145.
  Davenant changes hours of, 147.
Pericles — And new Shakespeare Society, 14.
  Theory as to omission of, 213 (note).
  Mr. Furnivall never read, 15.
Periods — Mr. Furnivall's, 12.
Personal Equation — In estimating evidence, 2.
Philosophical Lore — In plays, 21.
  Not inserted to draw audiences, 204.
  Might have reverse effect, 204.
Plagiarism — Tennyson's opinion of, 32.
"Phœnix and Turtle" — Assigned to Shakespeare, 73.
Physician — Lear's, prescribes rest, 198.
  Macbeth's, declines to prescribe, 198.
Pilgrimage to Parnassus — The newly discovered, 69.
  Burlesque in, 237.
Piracy — A constant and punctual, 54, 202.
  None, according to Cipher theory, 301.
Pistol — His part doubled with Puck, 208.
Plautus — Meres estimates Shakespeare equal to, 50.
  His Menæchmi imitated in "Twelfth Night," 80.
Platonic Philosophy — Why should Shakespeare rhyme, 38.
Player, A — Part of, taken by Sinklo, 208.
Plays — How to see the Shakespeare, 155.
  Classical matter in. *(See* CLASSICAL MATTER.*)*
  Philosophy in. *(See* PHILOSOPHICAL LORE.*)*
  Augmented by actors at will, 205.
  Did Shakespeare wink at theft of, 201.
  Anachronisms in, 203, 204.
  Pope indicates interpolations in, 212.
  Long speeches in, cut out, 212.
  Expurgated as to Spaniards, 211.
  King James's statutes touching, 210.
  Name of Deity excised from, 210.
  Localisms written in margin of, 207.
  Attract Elizabeth's attention, 218, 219.
  Elizabeth's policy concerning, 216, 218.
  Her first decree touching, 216, 218.
  Accretions in, legally protected, 216.
  Favorites with Charles I.'s ministers, 176.
  Milton censures Charles I. for reading, 177.
  Are they monographs? 196.
  Legalisms in. *(See* LEGALISMS.*)*
  How presumably written, 47.
  Perhaps edited by veterans, 229.
  The present, not verbatim versions, 48.
  Printed from actors' "lengths," 48.
  Dryden's criticism of, 156.
  Composed as others, 47.
  Shakespeare mounts as well as writes, 47.
        Claims no proprietorship in, 54.
  Neither does Bacon, 54.
  No registry of purchase by "Globe" found, 59.
  Shakespeare's executor does not claim, 54.
  Possible reason why not, 58.
  No probate of, 54.

Plays. (*Continued.*)
  Not mentioned in Shakespeare's will, 54.
  No assignment of right in, 54.
  Literary property in them perpetual, 60.
  Sounded in a juridicial key, 87.
  Why known as Shakespeare's, 58.
  Noticed in Evelyn's diary, 144.
       in Pepy's diary, 144.
  Davenant keeps nine on boards, 145.
  Little to do with Puritans, 137.
  Go into abeyance, 141.
  Too pure for stage of Charles I., 142.
  Were they written in order printed? 231.
  The doubtful. (*See* DOUBTFUL PLAYS. THIRD FOLIO.)
  Canon revised in 1663-4, 287.
  Lifetime list of, 284.
  Examples of diversity in, 286.
  Thirty-six in quarto, 283.
Players. (*See* ACTORS.)
Playwrights — Supposed agents of the devil, 141.
Plowden's Reports — Hales v. Petit reported in, 172.
  Was Shakespeare familiar with, 173.
Pocket Handkerchief — The tragedy of the, 154.
Poems, The — Of composite authorship, 49.
Poet — Imputing one's self to, 132.
Poetry — Not a commercial investment, 58.
Poins — Possible origin of. (*See* PAYN.)
Polemics — Not rampant in Shakespeare's time, 225.
Policy — Elizabeth's, concerning plays, 216, 218.
Politics — People must not meddle with, 253.
  Plays must not handle, 253.
Polonius — Reminded of actor's value, 205.
  Changes in part of, 230.
  His terms legalized, 175.
Pool — Descendants of Shakespeare named, 273.
Pope, Alex. — Testifies concerning interpolations, 212, 213.
  His narrative of Dr. Norris, etc., 154.
Popular Liberty — Shakespeare disbelieves in, 240, 248.
Popular Government — Tudor times not ripe for, 246.
Portia — Made a soubrette, 91.
  Worse than Jeffreys or Scroggs, 185, 186.
  Assumes jurisdiction over motives, 185, 186, 190.
  Assumes every function except headsman's, 187.
  Gross misstatements of law, 180, 190.
  Has no mercy for the Jew, 189, 268.
  Her law more dramatic than legal, 192.
  Assumes power "likest heaven's," 269.
  Bacon not responsible for her law, 192.
  Harsh and inequitable rulings of, 178.
  Punctilious as a tipstaff, 179.
Pott, Mrs. Henry — Difficulty with her theory, 48.
  A concession by, 289.
Posterity — Rights of, as against sepulchers, 86.
Powell — Descendants of Shakespeare named, 273.
Practicable Scenery — Very little up to Davenant's time, 146.
  What constituted, 146.
Prescriptions — Superstitious, for various maladies, 197.
Presumptive Evidence — What might be, as to authorship, 81.
Prior, Sir James — Descriptions of Shakespearean craze, 33.
Probate — None whatever of plays, 54.
Proclamation — Elizabeth's, concerning plays, 213.
Proof-reader — None of First Folio, 206, 207.
Proof-sheets — Authors not furnished with, 310.
  First Folio, did Bacon read? 309.
Properties. (*See* PRACTICABLE SCENERY.)

348 INDEX.

Proprietorship of Plays — Bacon does not claim, 54.
  Nor Shakespeare, 54.
Prosody — Shakespeare's life guided by his, 200.
  Arranged by the almanac, 200.
Protestant — Was Shakespeare a ? 225.
Printers. *(See* JOURNEYMAN PRINTERS.*)*
  Follow copy too closely, 207.
Psychological Effects — Did Shakespeare strain after, 192.
Puns — Shakespeare's, often legal, 168.
  One conjectured in Titus Andronicus, 214.
  In serious passages, 215.
Puritans — Their advent in England, 139.
  Little trace of them in plays, 139.
  Shut up Shakespeare's theaters, 140.
  Close the bear pits, 140.
  His rise and opportunity, 140.

Q.

Quackery — Prevalent in Shakespeare's time, 197.
  The plays ridicule, 197.
Quartos and Folios — Differences between, 57.
  Must be searched behind for Shakespeare, 202.
  Used for First Folio "copy," 56.
Queen Elizabeth — Theory that she wrote plays welcomed, 225.
  Order for "Falstaff in Love," 278.
  Her definition of treason elastic, 246.
  Attention called to plays, 218.
  Receives merited rebuke, 253.
  Her policy in theological matters, 251, 252.
  Her proclamation concerning the stage, 216, 252.
  Does not discourage Puritanism, 135.
  Record of Bacon playing before, 22.
  None of Shakespeare playing before, 22.
  Particular as to Henry plays, 219.
  Her decree satisfied, 253, 267.
  Her share in "Merry Wives," 239, 267, 268.
  Desired no theological quarrels, 326.
  Or religious criticisms, 226.
  Her conciliatory policy, 226.
  Her taste in plays, 267, 268.
Question of Authorship — Raised by Heminges and Condell, 56.
  Legitimate, however treated, 287.
Quiney Family — Looking after Shakespeare's money, 82.

R.

"**R. T., Gentleman,**" — Poem by, 320.
Raleigh, Sir Walter — Was he "Mr. W. H."? 45.
  Was he author of Sonnets? 45.
  Mr. O'Connor's theory as to, 45.
  Was he dedicatee of Sonnets? 45.
Ratcliffe, Sir John — Associate Chief Butler of Ireland, 263.
Ratsey's Ghost — Theory as to, welcomed, 225.
Ravenscroft — Rewrites certain plays, 143.
Reade, Charles — Estimates dramatic power of plays, 199.
Readings, New. *(See* NEW READINGS.*)*
Reconsideration — Not a madman's act, 103.
Recovery. *(See* DOUBLE VOUCHER.*)*
Re-editing. *(See* EDITING, EDITORS, FURNIVALL, JOHNSON, DR. WARBURTON.*)*
Report — Imaginary, in Shylock's case, 180.
Representatives — Of Bacon do not claim plays, 54.
  Of Shakespeare do not claim plays, 54.
Return from Parnassus. *(See* PILGRIMAGE TO PARNASSUS.*)*
Revenue — A lease of quick, 203.

Revival — The first Shakespearean, 150.
Richard II. — Name on Northumberland MS., 195.
  Merick pays for performance of, 177.
  Elizabeth's attention called to, 218.
  Assigned to Shakespeare by Meres, 50.
Richard III. — Name on Northumberland MS., 195.
  Assigned to Shakespeare by Meres, 50.
Riddle in " Cymbeline " — As read by Mrs. Windle, 295
Ritson, Dr. — Doubts Meres' list, 80.
Rival Poet, The — How extracted from Sonnets, 38.
" Robert Le Diable " — Ballet scene in, 151.
Robertson — Life not written out of plays, 6.
Rolfe, Dr. W. J. — Disagrees with Knight about travels, 280.
Roman Catholic Church — Popularly same as English, 226.
" Romeo and Juliet " — Assigned to Shakespeare by Meres, 50.
  Pope's description of quarto of, 213.
Rörick — King of Denmark, 114.
Rose Theatre — A rival of the Globe, 284.
Rowe, Nicholas — Comments as to Shakespeare's style, 233.
" Run on Lines." *(See* FURNIVALL, PROSODY, VERSE-TESTS.)
Running Expenses — Of Shakespeare's theaters, how paid, 18.
Rye, Sussex Co. — Shakespeare's company at, 281.
Rymer, Thomas — His short view of tragedy, 156.
  Critique on Shakespeare, 156.

S.

Sacrilege — To mention Bacon, 23.
Saffron-Walden — Shakespeare's company at, 281.
Sapperton, Rector of — As to Shakespeare's religion, 228.
Saxo Grammaticus — Translation of his "Amleth," 114.
Scenery, Practicable. *(See* PRACTICABLE SCENERY.)
  Davenant imports and invents, 147.
  Idea of, conveyed in words, 146.
  None in Shakespeare's day, 146.
School Books — What, in Shakespeare's day, 65.
School-masters — Quality of, at that date, 65.
  Sergeant Ballantyne's, 66.
  Anthony Trollope's, 66.
  Charles Reade's, 66.
  Tradition that Shakespeare was a, 164.
  Peter Mason's description of, 66.
Schools — Condition of, in 1570, 64, 65.
  Provincial, in England, 64.
Sconen — Fialler, commander in, 130.
Scotland — Did Shakespeare ever visit, 280.
Second Best Bed — Wife might take, without will, 59.
Seeland — Viglet collects forces from, 130.
Seneca and Plautus — Shakespeare compared to, 50.
Sermon — Play to be treated as a, 155.
Shaftesbury, Lord — His critique on Shakespeare, 154.
" Shakespeare " — First form of name, 275.
Shakespeare, John — First bearers of name not eminent, 275.
  Was a Roman Catholic, 228.
  His confession of faith disappears, 228.
  Fears imprisonment for debt, 228.
  Joan, 273, 274.
  George, 273, 274.
  The tailor, 273, 274.
  Thomas, 273.
  Thomas, the merchant, 275.
Shakespeare, William — Was not a traveler, 277.
  Devises no masques, 148.
  Error as to Oldcastle, 138.
  Careful of theatrical privileges,
  Represents Cliff in words, 146.

Shakespeare, William. *(Continued.)*
Did not write Danish play, 131.
Did he ever visit Scotland? 280.
Where is grave of? 84.
Speculates in real estate, 87.
Not attorney nor attorney's clerk, 87.
Dryden's critique of, 156.
Cared nothing for the Unities, 157.
His text remodeled to legal precedents, 170.
Had a lawyer's conservatism, 167.
Lived apart from his wife, 277.
Shrewd in money matters, 82.
Did he sell use of his name? 82.
His authorship of Sonnets? 83.
Visits Stratford for investment purposes, 277.
Not ignorant of value of his name, 82.
Could write his own dedications, 82.
His proprietary right in plays, 81.
Name on title-page, presumption which way? 81.
Social inequality with Southampton, 78.
Did he circulate Sonnets? 77.
Familiar with Bishop's Bible, 228.
Was he a subjective poet? 63.
His scholarly equipment, 61.
Not influenced by polemics, 228.
Does not claim plays, 54.
Takes minor parts in his own plays, 199.
Did he write hermetic verse in his youth? 88.
Plays not in handwriting of, 48, 57.
Contrives to fill Elizabeth's order, 254.
His rule for selecting names, 254.
New method pursued in "Merry Wives," 248.
Becomes very wealthy, 20, 48, 58.
Why he may not have claimed plays, 48, 58.
His reasons for writing "The Tempest," 201.
Never saw or authorized 1623 text, 201.
His calendar periods, 200.
Allows periodical robbery, 201, 202.
Unless he acquiesced therein, 201.
Where he found Dogberry or Elbow, 205.
Picks up classics where he could, 204.
What his genius did do, 204.
Knew what plays contained, 206.
Complimented House of Stuart, 176.
Was favorite author of Charles I., 176.
His elders may have revised text, 229.
Wrote for the people's pence, 228.
His opinion of common people, 240, 248.
Why, could not be Bacon, 176, 301.
Familiar with Plowden's reports? 173.
What were his prosodial tendencies? 232, 239.
Restores the family fortunes, 59.
His representatives do not claim plays, 53.
Makes no entries on Stationers' registers, 54.
Pays up family mortgages, 53.
Sues for Wilmecote estates, 53.
Sues John Lambert, 53.
Education of, 52, 53.
Name makes books salable, 52.
Increases in stage experience, 192, 229.
Unacquainted with Inigo Jones, 149.
Wrote hastily for occasion, 25, 47.
His "central ideas," 24.
Too manly to despise calling, 35.
Was he lame? 35.

Shakespeare, William. *(Continued.)*
  Apologizes for Oldcastle, 221.
  Was he Catholic or Protestant? 225.
  Probably unable to tell, 225.
  Ordered to write " Falstaff in Love," 222.
  Cajoles Talbot family, 261.
  Other reasonable doubts as to, 224.
  Did he write by the almanac? 200.
  Believes in Fastolffe's cowardice, 257, 258.
  Was first and always a dramatist, 198, 199.
  Not concerned with church affairs, 225.
  In his day theological matters quiet, 225.
  Did not try for psychological effect, 192.
  His gentleness of birth or manners? 35.
  Chose material at random, 26.
  Did he suppose himself immortal? 36.
  Representatives have still copyright, 276.
  Reads Hollingshed, 261.
  But not uncontradicted, 261.
  Bribes the Herald's College, 35.
  Borrowed dialogues as well as plots, 22.
  His diffident and retiring nature, 7.
  Leads a jolly life, 8, 316.
  Had he lost a child, 8.
  No slander touches wife of, 281.
  Lifetime list of plays of, 284.
  A man of many intimates, 301.
  Did he know Bacon, 303.
  Did he insert verse-tests in plays? 326.
Shakespearean Revival — The first, 152.
Shakespeare Society, New, of London. *(See* NEW SHAKESPEARE.)
Shakespeares — In the United States, 271.
Shrewsbury — Shakespeare's company at, 281.
Shirley, James — Co-worker of Ben Jonson, 151.
Shylock. *(See* PORTIA.)
  Harshly and inequitably handled, 178.
  Misplaced confidence in Antonio, 179.
  And in "strict" court of Venice, 179.
  v. Antonio — imaginary appeal affirmed, 180.
  Had not sympathy of spectators, 198.
  A riot had he been spared, 198.
  Made a low comedian, 91.
Sinklo — Spare and thin, 209.
  Plays the beadle, 209.
  Plays gamekeeper and " player," 208.
Stuart — House of, magnified by Shakespeare, 176.
" Sir John Oldcastle " — The play, when written, 221.
  First assigned to Shakespeare, 74.
Smithweeke, I. — Charged for printing First Folio, 136.
  Was he confederate to Cipher? 309.
Snagge, Hon. T. W. — Reference to, 217 (note).
Society, New — Shakespeare, of London, 6.
  A discovery of, 201.
Soldiers — Elizabeth's, spoke local dialects, 62.
Sonnets — Why circulated among Shakespeare's friends? 77, 78.
  If relating to Southampton, 77, 78.
  Armitage Brown's discovery as to, 28, 81.
  Meres' evidence as to, hearsay, 83.
  Massey disposes of Shakespeare's claim to, 83
  Translation of Ovid's among, 81.
  Cotes edition of unreliable, 81.
  Kept alive by Shakespeare's name, 82.
  Are they a continuous poem? 78.
  Probably not those mentioned by Meres, 77.
  Not dedicated to Southampton, 75.

Sonnets. *(Continued.)*
   Title-page of 1640 edition, 51.
              1609   "   50.
   Shakespeare does not print, 75.
   Not composite in authorship, 49.
   Not autobiographical, 34.
   Or biographical, 34.
   Easily treated hermetically, 34.
   Why not record of ideal courtship, 29.
   Esoteric theories as to, 27.
   Act of Parliament to read, 39.
   Origin of Southampton story as to, of, 44.
   Meaning of, perhaps never known, 43.
   Coleridge's method with, 36.
   Unitary method with, 36.
   G. Massey's treatment of, 28.
   Extreme inequality of, 29, 31.
   Why bound up together, 31.
   Mr. Furnivall's idea of, 11.
   Contain key to Mrs. Windle's Cipher, 294.
Sources — Historical, of plots plentiful, 22.
   Of First Folio text, 206.
Southampton — Social gulf between Shakespeare and, 78.
   His private amours recorded in Sonnets, 78.
   If so, why Shakespeare's, 35, 78.
   Dedication to, not complimentary, 77.
   Poems dedicated to, 49, 67.
   Not remarkable occurrence, 44, 68.
   Not a rich man, 79.
   Would not give away $25,000, 79.
   Records of, silent as to Shakespeare, 79.
   Certainly not " Mr. W. H.," 75.
   Brown-Massey hypothesis as to, 45.
   Untraceable into vicinity of Sonnets, 115.
   Might be "poet" of the Sonnets? 40.
Spaniards — Taken out of plays, 211.
Spedding, J. — His dictum as to style analysis, 2.
   Edits Northumberland MSS., 194.
Speeches — Shakespeare may have borrowed, 22.
St. Albans — Did Bacon anticipate title of? 310.
Stage Business — How managed in "Titus Andronicus," 10.
Stage Censorship — In Shakespeare's time, 220.
   In B. Jonson's time, 220.
   Modern, 220.
   In France, 221 (note).
   In New York, 220.
Stage Door — A market for manuscripts, 203.
Stage Experience — Shakespeare's improvement in, 231.
Stage Right — None in non-theatrical matter, 81.
Stagewright — Shakespeare a practical, 192.
Stationers' Company — Copyright transferable through, 5
Statute. *(See* DECREE.)
   Of King James regulating plays, 210.
Steevens, Geo.— Declines to read Sonnets, 81.
Stopped Endings — Mr. Furnivall's, 10.
   (See FURNIVALL, GROUPS, PROSODY.)
Stratford — No internal evidence of Shakespeare's birth in, 7.
"Students of Shakespeare "— Mr. Boucicault as to, 25.
Style, Literary — Changes with age, 230.
   Shakespeare's and Tennyson's, compared, 232.
Sunday — No arrest for debt on, 226.
Subjectively — Tendency of criticism toward, 6.
Suckling, Sir John — An associate of Davenant, 134.
Suicide — Can a man commit, during lifetime? 173.
   Caused by Baconian controversy, 42.

Supernatural, The—In Shakespeare's time, 93.
  Reversed in Hamlet, 93.
  In medical science, 197.
Surnames— Easily assumed in the United States, 272.
Sutherland, Earl of — Dryden dedicates revision to, 152.
Syllabus — Of imaginary appeal in Shylock's case, 185.

T.

Talbot — Shakespeare cajoles family of, 261.
Tale of a Tub — Jonson lampoons Inigo Jones in, 220.
Taming of the Shrew — Pepys thinks it silly, 145.
Tamora — Apostrophe to, resembles Marlowe, 9.
Tate, Nahum — Rewrites certain plays, 143.
Tempest, The — Rewritten by Davenant and Dryden, 150.
  Esthetic reasons for writing it, 201.
  Chosen by Davenant for opening night, 150.
Temple Grafton — Home of Shakespeare's wife, 276.
Temple of Love — Masque, by Davenant and Jones, 149.
Tennyson, Baron — His idea of Parallelisms, 32.
  Cited as example of style tendency, 232, 311.
  Possible theory as to, 39.
  Reads Pericles to the Mr. Furnivall, 15.
Text — Biographical matter extracted from, 1, 2.
  Meanings supplied to, 230.
Textual Criticism — What is, 4.
  What it can do, 4.
Theatres. (*See* ACTORS.)
  Davenant opens Duke of York, 135.
  Only permitted under noble patronage, 245.
  Supposed agents of the devil, 141.
Theatrical Companies — Filled place of newspapers, 205.
  Knowledge shown in plays, 5.
Theobald, L.— Doubts Meres' canon, 80.
Theologies— Quiescent in Shakespeare's time, 225.
Thorpe, Thomas — Wishes "W. H." a long life, 76.
Third Folio — Great value of, 283.
  Editor of unknown, 285.
  Why he doubted First Folio, 283, 285, 286.
  Revised canon of, 287.
Time Limit — None to kill a king, 117. (*See* VENDETTA, CORSICAN.)
  To writing "Merry Wives," 278.
Timon of Athens — Padded in First Folio, 213 (note).
Title-pages — Not evidence of authorship, 51, 55.
Titus Andronicus — Stage business of, how managed? 9.
  Remarkable passages in, 212.
  Assigned to Shakespeare by Meres, 50, 80.
  Catalogue of horrors in, 9.
  Mr. Furnivall does not "consider," 8, 9.
Townshend, Charles — Coadjutor of Ben Jonson's, 149.
Tradesmen — Custom of Elizabethan, 268.
Traditions — Usually a foundation for, 164.
Trap-Door — Known in Dekkar's time, 146.
Traveler — Why Shakespeare could not afford to be, 278, 279.
Traveling — Prejudice against, 278.
  Local constables not friendly to, 278.
  Geographical difficulties of, 278.
Treason — Elizabeth's elastic definition of, 246.
Trial Scene— Characteristics of Shylock's, 193.
Triboulet — Character in "Le Roi s'amuse," 247.
Trinity — The name not used in plays, 210.
Trinity Church, Stratford — Bones not to be moved from, 86.
Troilus and Cressida — Rewritten by Dryden, 152.
  First Folio, "copy" for, 207.
  Dowden's method with, 7.

INDEX.

Troth-Plight — Mistaken by contracting parties for marriage, 276.
 Shakespeare considers equivalent to marriage, 276.
Trott, Nicholas — Co-author of "Misfortunes of Arthur," 23.
"Truth Found Too Late" — Dryden's version of "Troilus and Cressida," 152.
Tomb, Shakespeare's, 84. (*See* GRAVE.)
Tudor Times — Not ripe for popular government, 246.
Turner, William Shakespeare, 274.
Twelfth Night — Manningham's entry as to, 80.
"Twenty-five Thousand Dollars" — Southampton's alleged gift of, 79.
Two Gentlemen of Verona — Assigned to Shakespeare by Meres, 50.

U.

Udensacre — Locality so-called, 130.
Unblotted Manuscripts, 204. (*See* HEMINGES AND CONDELL.)
Unities, the Dramatic — Shakespeare disregarded, 157.
Unstopped Endings, 10. (*See* FURNIVALL, PROSODY, GROUPS.)
Upton — Doubts Shakespeare authorship of certain plays, 80.
Usage — Shakespeare's knowledge of theatrical, 5.
 Improvement in, 231.

V.

Vagrancy — Anecdote of case of, 187.
Vagrants — Do not wear good clothes, 188.
Venderhagen, Von, 223. (*See* WURTEMBURG-MUMPLEGARD.)
Vendetta, Corsican — Satisfied if man killed, 111.
Venetian Law — Was the civil code, 179.
Venus and Adonis — First heir of Shakespeare, 62.
 Dedication to Southampton, 49.
 Authorship of, discussed in 1597-1601, 69.
 Furnivall's opinion of, 8.
 Well known by contemporaries, 69.
 Title-page not conclusive, 52.
"Verges" Played by Kempe, 208.
Verse-Blindness — Not available as excuse, 323.
Verse-Tests. (*See* CHRONOLOGY, FURNIVALL, F. J., GROUPS, PROSODY.)
 When superfluous, 232.
 Not highest criticism, 239.
 Mr. Furnivall's statement as to, 312, 313.
 Are legitimate efforts to elucidate authorship, 312.
 Will make Baconians, 327.
Vestrymen — Stratford. Opposed to opening grave, 86.
Viglet — Son and successor to Rörick, 130.
Village Schools — In early England, 67.
Viola — Made Beatrice's sister, 151.
Vitruvius Hoop — Burlesque on Inigo Jones, 220.
 Excised by Master of Revels, 220.
Vocations — Of Shakespeare name in United States, 271.
Voltaire, A. de — His criticisms on Shakespeare, 156, 160.

W.

"W. H.," Mr.— Who was he? 44.
 Sir Walter Raleigh, 49.
 Not Pembroke, 76.
 Not Southampton, 76.
Wager — Between Hamlet and Fortinbras, 97.
Waller — An associate of Davenant, 134.
Warburton — Ridiculous annotation of, 214 (note).
Ward, A. W.— His esthetic methods, 7.
 Says Shakespeare was diffident, 7.
Warwickshire Customs — Evidence of, in plays, 7.
 Dialect universal in Stratford, 58.
 Not more common in plays than others, 21. (*See* DIALECT.)

Water Doctors Of Elizabeth's day, 197.
Watkins — Descendants of Shakespeare by name of, 273.
Watson, Rose — A descendant of Shakespeare, 273.
Waynfleete, Bishop — A friend of Fastolffe, 269.
Wednesday — Bad day for plays, 154.
Werder, Karl — His theory of Hamlet, 112.
Westminster Abbey — Davenant buried in, 135.
Wet Nurses — Rebellion of the, 151.
Whateley, Anne — Of Temple Grafton, 276.
 Becomes Shakespeare's wife, 276.
White, Richard Grant — His opinion as to Middleton, 46.
 As to Shakespeare's motive, 193.
 Manly character of, 162, 163.
 Contempt for random guess work, 162, 164.
 Opinion as to Shakespeare's legal knowledge, 164.
 Embittered by adverse criticism, 163.
 Doubts Meres' canon, 80.
Wife — No slander touches Shakespeare's, 281.
 Epitaph on tomb of Shakespeare's, 281. (*See* WHATELEY.)
Wilkes, Geo. — On Shakespeare and the people, 241.
Will — Superfluous mention of second best bed, 59.
Windle, Mrs. C. F. Ashmead. (*See* CIPHER.)
Winter's Tale — Furnivall finds no rhymes in, 313.
 Historical evidence as to date of, 320.
Witches' Curse. (*See* CURSE, GRAVE.)
Wilmecote Estate — Shakespeare sues to recover, 53.
Witnesses, Contemporary. (*See* CONTEMPORARIES, EVIDENCE.)
Women — Female parts given to, 150.
Words — Changed meanings of, 35.
Wordsworth — Bishop and his parallelisms, 267.
Wriothesley, H. (*See* SOUTHAMPTON.)
Wurmsser, Hans Jacob. (*See* WURTEMBURG, MUMPLEGARD.)
Wurtemburg, Mumplegard, Duke of — Ambassador to England, 223.
 Entry in diary of, 223.
Wyman, W. H. — Bibliograyhy of Baconian controversy, 42.

Y.

Yarmouth — Fastolffe builds castle near, 259.
Young Shakespeare. (*See* SHAKESPEARE, WILLIAM.)

www.ingramcontent.com/pod-product-compliance
Lightning Source LLC
Chambersburg PA
CBHW031424230426
43668CB00007B/430